THE FIVE ENTERPRISE DOMAINS

THE NATURAL ORDER OF ENTERPRISE BEHAVIOR AND HOW COHERENT SYSTEMS PRODUCE ENTERPRISE VALUE

CHUCK TEEL CPA

ENTERPRISE SCIENCE

THE FIVE ENTERPRISE DOMAINS

Exclusively licensed to Enterprise Science Inc.

Published by Enterprise Science Inc.
Under the imprint Enterprise Science

For rights inquiries, bulk orders, or speaking engagements, contact: Enterprise Science Inc. permissions@entersci.com.

ISBN (hardcover): 978-1-971628-00-4
ISBN (paperback): 978-1-971628-01-1
ISBN (e-book): 978-1-971628-02-8

Cover design by: Resound Creative Media, LLC
First Edition published 2026.

Library of Congress Control Number: 2026939521

Printed in the United States of America

ENTERPRISE SCIENCE REFERENCE AND LICENSED ACCESS

This book is reference material within the Enterprise Science™ system.

The Five Enterprise Domains™ defines the structural system through which enterprises operate in practice. The material presented here is intended to be used as a reference—returned to as conditions evolve, execution changes, and enterprise behavior develops over time.

Readers who wish to engage the system beyond this book may do so through the Enterprise Science website. Digital resources extending the system into sustained leadership application are available at entersci.com. Enterprise Science materials and related digital resources are proprietary and are made available under license. Access may require account registration, scope definition, and acceptance of applicable terms of use.

Access is provided at https://entersci.com

CONTENTS

PART I

SEEING THE ENTERPRISE AS IT IS

PART III

LEADING THE COHERENT ENTERPRISE

APPENDIX

This book is dedicated to my colleagues and clients who build great enterprises

PREFACE

ENTERPRISES TODAY BEHAVE DIFFERENTLY from those most leaders were schooled and trained to manage. They operate without fixed boundaries, move faster than traditional structures can support, and interact with customers, partners, platforms, and distributed teams in ways that look nothing like the enterprises of the twentieth century. Yet most leadership thinking still assumes the enterprise can be understood through functions, reporting lines, and internal versus external activity. This mismatch creates confusion for leaders who sense that something deeper is shaping performance but lack the language to name it.

From the outset, one fact matters more than scale or sophistication: the Five Enterprise Domains™ apply everywhere. From a child's lemonade stand to the largest multinational enterprise, the same five domains govern how work is coordinated, decisions are made, customers are served, and resources are allocated.

As enterprises scale, more is exposed, more depends on coordination, and the consequences of misfit increase—even though the underlying structure remains the same. What changes is not how the enterprise operates, but how much is at stake when the structure no longer supports the work being carried out.

Wherever people coordinate effort, make decisions under constraint, serve customers, and commit resources, the same patterns appear. The domains are not something enterprises grow into; they are present from the moment an enterprise comes into existence.

This work began with an observation that repeated itself across engagements: The problems leaders named were rarely the problems they were actually facing. Pricing issues, process breakdowns, customer challenges, and financial surprises appeared distinct on the surface, yet they consistently behaved as expressions of a single system acting out of alignment. Once those situations were read structurally rather than categorically, the enterprise stopped appearing erratic and began to appear patterned, even when the organizational forms and leadership arrangements varied widely.

What follows connects enterprise behavior to enterprise value through causation rather than coincidence. It explains how day-to-day operational decisions, structural fit, and cross-domain coherence determine whether enterprise value compounds over time or is consumed by internal resistance.

Over more than two decades—first in senior financial leadership roles and later as a practicing corporate strategist—I worked within midmarket enterprises as they scaled, reorganized, and sought to keep their structure aligned with the work they were asking people to do. Across industries and operating models, the same forces shaped outcomes. Some enterprises advanced with comparatively little effort, while others increased effort quarter after quarter only to lose ground.

The difference came down to coherence—whether the enterprise reinforced itself in motion or opposed itself through its own design.

Once observed, coherence announced itself everywhere. It showed up in how priorities were interpreted, how work moved across teams, how decisions traveled under pressure, how customers responded to what the enterprise delivered, and how financial patterns expressed underlying system conditions long before strategy shifted. When coherence held, the enterprise felt stable even in environments of high demand and rapid change. Weakening coherence produced the opposite—performance issues multiplied in ways conventional explanations could not resolve.

What confounded many leaders was not the presence of problems—they expected those—but the consistency beneath them. Work took longer even as effort increased. Deals were pushed in sales pipelines while internal operating load increased. Financial reports diverged from operating reviews. Teams advanced at different speeds. These symptoms were treated independently because there was no way to see how they were structurally linked. Corrections in one area simply shifted the problem elsewhere, because action was being applied at the wrong level of the system.

The Five Enterprise Domains emerged from watching these patterns repeat until they could no longer be dismissed as coincidence. These domains describe the natural architecture of enterprise behavior: the systems through which purpose is translated into alignment, work is integrated, execution behaves under pressure, value is interpreted by the market, and financial outcomes materialize. They were observed as a recurring reality, not designed as a model to adopt. By naming what leaders already sensed, they gave form to patterns that had previously resisted explanation.

Structure, however, is only part of the picture. Modern enterprises are not confined by walls or charts; they operate in an open field where expectations, signals, and consequences travel freely across enterprise, customer, and market contexts. This is the operating environment itself—permanent, not transitional. Leaders who read this environment structurally can interpret behavior with accuracy. Those who cannot are left with partial explanations that miss the forces shaping results.

The Five Enterprise Domains are a structural system that governs enterprise behavior whether recognized or not—this book makes that system visible. What leaders do with that visibility is implementation—not of the Domains themselves, but of the discipline required to sustain coherence. Through that visibility, leaders stop mistaking symptoms for causes. Compensating for misfit with added effort becomes structurally illegible once the condition producing the misfit is exposed, and escalation ceases to substitute for design. Performance registers through relationships, movement, and fit rather than through activity and function.

The purpose of this book is to make the enterprise readable. It provides language for the forces leaders encounter daily but struggle to articulate: why execution varies, why customer response becomes inconsistent, why processes fail at interfaces rather than within teams, and why financial signals shift ahead of stated priorities. When these patterns become visible, enterprise behavior becomes explainable. When it becomes explainable, it becomes governable—through structural understanding rather than force or oversight.

What follows is not a new theory of leadership, but a description of an order observed repeatedly across enterprises in motion—one that requires learning to see interdependence, interpret signals, and steward coherence across the whole. If this book succeeds, it will alter how you read your enterprise, give form to patterns you already sense, and make misalignment recognizable early, before cost accumulates.

This journey begins with a pattern that appeared repeatedly across enterprises—one organized through five interdependent systems of activity: People + Alignment, Processes + Integration, Execution + Intelligence, Customer + Interaction, and Economics + Metrics. By the end, you will see it too—and once you do, the enterprise will never appear the same. You will recognize why execution varies under consistent leadership, why customer response shifts ahead of any internal change, why financial signals diverge from operating reviews, and why correcting one area produces symptoms in another. These are not mysteries. They are structural conditions, and this book gives them a name.

A NOTE ON METHOD AND EVIDENCE

METHOD AND EVIDENCE BASE

The structural system presented in this book emerged from embedded, day-to-day fieldwork inside more than forty midmarket enterprises over the course of nearly a decade. The fieldwork was conducted through Teel & Company Strategists & CPAs, a corporate strategy and CPA firm that assumes direct day-to-day responsibility for finance, human resources, operations, and administration inside midmarket companies. This mode of engagement placed the author inside the operating reality of each enterprise for sustained periods, participating directly in how work moved, how decisions formed, and how performance emerged across the full scope of enterprise activity.

The enterprises observed span manufacturing, professional services, technology, healthcare services, distribution, construction, real estate, hospitality, retail, financial services, and business-to-business services. They range in annual revenue from approximately USD 10 million to over USD 100 million. Roughly one-third of the enterprises owned and operated subsidiaries in more than one country. The observations were produced through sustained operational participation rather than through external consulting, interviews, surveys, or academic research protocols. This embedded position provided access to how enterprises operated under real conditions—including conditions they do not disclose to external observers, consultants, or researchers.

The evidence base carries known scope boundaries. The sample is concentrated in midmarket enterprises, the observations originate from one practitioner's embedded fieldwork, and the enterprises that engaged Teel & Company represent a self-selected population—they were actively seeking embedded operational support, which may distinguish them from enterprises that did not. The author operated simultaneously as observer, advisor, and operational participant—a position that provides access no external methodology can replicate and introduces interpretive proximity that independent validation should test. The evidence base also carries survivorship characteristics: the enterprises observed longest contributed disproportionately to the pattern recognition that produced this system, while enterprises that disengaged early during the engagement period are underrepresented in the structural observations. No controlled comparisons, randomized designs, or large-sample statistical analyses were conducted.

These boundaries are stated explicitly because the claims derived from this evidence base are significant. The patterns described in this book appeared with sufficient consistency across diverse enterprises to warrant the structural system presented here. Whether that consistency extends to enterprises of significantly different scale or institutional context remains a question that additional observation and independent validation should address.

The standard of evidence in this work is structural consistency across diverse operating conditions. The audience for which this work is written—enterprise leaders and practitioners who operate within the conditions described—will recognize the patterns from direct experience. That recognition is the first and most immediate test of the Five Enterprise Domains System's validity.

NOTES ON SOURCES

Where the language of this system intersects with terms used in other published work, the endnotes identify the intersection, provide a full citation, explain the cited author's concept, and describe how the usage in this book differs. Where a term shares a label with a concept in a different field, the endnote acknowledges the existing usage and clarifies the distinction. The reader should be able to see exactly where this system's language touches existing scholarship and where it departs.

Endnotes are numbered per chapter and appear at the end of each chapter. All citations follow the Chicago Manual of Style, 18th edition, Notes-Bibliography system.

THE PRACTITIONER'S POSITION

The most consequential contributions to understanding how enterprises behave have come from practitioners—people who operated inside real enterprises, observed what occurred, and recorded what they found. Peter Drucker's practice of management was not produced in a laboratory. W. Edwards Deming's system of profound knowledge was not derived from controlled experiments. Jim Collins's research began with publicly available data, but his lasting contribution was the interpretive framework he brought to it from direct engagement with operating enterprises. Clayton Christensen's disruption theory originated from observing what incumbents actually did when confronted with disruptive competition—not from modeling what they should have done.

These practitioners wrote differently because of what they knew. Their evidence was not a sample drawn from a population and tested for statistical significance; it was sustained observation of enterprise behavior, accumulated across years of direct engagement, producing pattern recognition that no external study design could replicate.

This book follows that tradition. The author worked inside more than forty enterprises over the course of nearly a decade—not as a consultant brought in to advise, but as an embedded participant with direct operational accountability in each enterprise. That fieldwork produced not forty data points, but tens of thousands—because each enterprise was observed across hundreds of decisions, interactions, processes, interfaces, and outcomes over sustained periods of engagement. Every observation was tested in real time: The author was simultaneously observing the enterprise, advising its leadership, and participating in its operational execution. Patterns that appeared in one enterprise were tested against the next. Structural interpretations that failed to account for what was actually occurring were discarded. What survived across enterprises, across industries, and across operating conditions is what appears in this book.

The distinction from academic research is worth stating directly. Academic research in management and organizational behavior typically targets sample sizes sufficient for statistical significance—often one thousand or more observations, drawn from surveys, interviews, or secondary data sources. Those observations are necessarily external: The researcher observes from outside the enterprise, using instruments that capture what participants report rather than what the enterprise actually does. The resulting findings are statistically valid but lack operational depth. They describe what correlates with what, but rarely describe why.

Practitioner research inverts these properties. The sample of enterprises is smaller, but the depth of observation within each enterprise is orders of magnitude greater. The observer is embedded inside the operating reality, with access to conditions, behaviors, and consequences that external instruments cannot capture. And the practitioner acts on what is observed, which means the observation is tested against enterprise response in real time, not validated retrospectively through statistical analysis.

Both forms of research produce genuine knowledge of different kinds. Academic research establishes what is generalizable across large populations at low observational depth. Practitioner research establishes what is structurally present within operating enterprises at high observational depth. For the subject matter of this book—how enterprises behave as systems in motion—practitioner research is the more authoritative source, because the phenomena being described are structural, relational, and dynamic in ways that external observation cannot fully capture.

This work does not claim to have produced findings that are statistically generalizable to all enterprises everywhere. It claims to have identified structural patterns that appeared with sufficient consistency across diverse midmarket enterprises to constitute a reliable system for interpreting enterprise behavior. Leaders and practitioners who work inside enterprises will recognize these patterns. That recognition is the practitioner's validation—and for this subject, it is the form of validation that matters most.

Academics, researchers, and independent practitioners are invited to test this system against their own observations and data. The structural claims in this book are stated with sufficient precision to be independently evaluated. Where the system accounts for observed enterprise behavior, it merits adoption. Where it does not, it merits revision. Both outcomes advance the discipline.

THIS WORK AND ITS PREDECESSORS

This book builds on a long tradition of inquiry into how enterprises behave as systems. Readers familiar with that tradition will recognize several lines of influence, and the distinctions between this work and its predecessors are worth stating directly.

Systems thinking entered management practice through the work of W. Edwards Deming, whose System of Profound Knowledge established that enterprise outcomes are produced by system structure rather than by individual effort alone. Peter Senge extended this insight into how enterprises learn, showing how mental models, shared vision, and team learning interact to produce or prevent systemic change. Donella Meadows provided the analytical language —stocks, flows, feedback loops, and leverage points—that remains the foundation of systems dynamics. Stafford Beer's Viable System Model demonstrated that viability requires specific subsystems operating in defined relationships. These contributions are foundational. This work does not replace them.

What this work adds is specific to the enterprise—not to organizations in general, but to enterprises that must create, sustain, and protect economic value through coordinated motion across people, processes, execution, customer relationships, and financial constraint. The Five Enterprise Domains emerged from embedded fieldwork inside operating enterprises, not from theoretical modeling or laboratory observation. They name the specific structural domains through which enterprise behavior is organized and through which coherence is sustained or lost. The domains are not functional categories, value-chain activities, or balanced-scorecard perspectives. They are fields of motion that interact simultaneously, producing the observable patterns this work describes.

Porter's value chain analysis describes a linear sequence of activities; the Five Enterprise Domains describe fields of motion with feedback operating in multiple directions. Kaplan and Norton's Balanced Scorecard treats the domains as measurement perspectives, while the Five Enterprise Domains name structural conditions that produce the phenomena measurement perspectives attempt to capture. McKinsey's 7S framework lacks the directional dependence and structural simultaneity that govern the Five Enterprise Domains under Natural Order. Socio-technical systems theory addresses the joint arrangement of social and technical systems in general; this work applies specifically to enterprise value creation under modern unwalled conditions.

The concept of responsible autonomy, as used in this book, differs from Andrew Friedman's 1977 usage, which described a labor management strategy. Here, it describes an observable condition of enterprise execution that emerges from structural design rather than supervisory philosophy.

The connections between this work and complex adaptive systems theory, lean thinking, and the contributions of Jim Collins and Clayton Christensen are real. Where these traditions describe phenomena that this book also describes, the overlap is acknowledged. The original contributions—the five-domain architecture, the enterprise value function dualities, the enterprise archetype distinction, the coordination taxonomy, and the embedded-practitioner evidence base—build on what these predecessors established.

Readers who wish to engage with the traditions on which this work builds will find the following works useful: Deming's *Out of the Crisis*, Senge's *The Fifth Discipline*, Meadows' *Thinking in Systems*, Beer's *The Heart of Enterprise*, Porter's *Competitive Advantage*, and Kaplan and Norton's *The Balanced Scorecard*.

HOW TO USE THIS BOOK

This book is organized into three parts, each built on what precedes it.

Part 1—*Seeing the Enterprise as It Is*—establishes the structural system through direct observation. It begins with the recurring patterns that prompted this work, introduces the concepts that explain those patterns, and builds the case for a system-level reading of enterprise behavior. By the end of Part 1, the Five Enterprise Domains, their governing properties, and the two enterprise archetypes are in place.

Part 2—*The Five Enterprise Domains*—examines each domain in sequence: People + Alignment, Processes + Integration, Execution + Intelligence, Customer + Interaction, and Economics + Metrics. Each chapter describes a single domain's internal structure, its relationship to the domains surrounding it, and the consequences that follow when correspondence between structure and work weakens. The sequence is not arbitrary. It follows the directional dependence that governs how the enterprise moves—interpretation before structure, structure before motion, motion before recognition, recognition before economic consequence.

Part 3—*Leading the Coherent Enterprise*—addresses the changes that occur once the system is visible. It does not prescribe action. It describes the perceptual shifts required to lead an enterprise as a system rather than as a collection of functions.

Appendices follow. The operational appendices begin with activity blueprints that map business functions across the five domains, establishing the structural grid through which all subsequent instruments operate. A weekly signal scan and observation log records what the leader sees at each intersection. Three progressively deeper diagnostic instruments—a monthly interface review, a quarterly coherence conversation, and a coordination audit—build on the accumulated observation data. Appendix 6 presents ten leadership patterns observed across the enterprises studied: Recurring configurations of leadership behavior and their consequences for enterprise value. Enterprise signal tables identify what to look for within each domain. A glossary collects governing terms and definitions. Digital resources extending these instruments are available at entersci.com.

The Enterprise System Architecture, presented immediately after this section, provides a structural reference point that becomes meaningful as the book explains each element.

A domain chapter may become relevant months after first reading; a distinction between coordination types may clarify a condition the reader had not yet encountered.

THE ENTERPRISE SYSTEM ARCHITECTURE

Natural Order (governing architecture)

- **Enterprise System** (the enterprise operating as a unified whole)
  - **Relational Fields** (environments of continuous interaction)
    - 1. **Enterprise Field**
      - **Five Enterprise Domains**
      - People + Alignment
      - Processes + Integration
      - Execution + Intelligence
      - Customer + Interaction
      - Economics + Metrics
    - 2. Customer Field
    - 3. Market Field
  - **System Properties**
    - Structural Simultaneity
    - Directional Dependence
    - Reverse Causation
    - Performance Topology
  - **Enterprise Archetypes**
    - Physical Asset Enterprises
    - Intangible Asset Enterprises
  - **Enterprise Value Function Dualities** (output of the system in motion)
  - Create / Destroy
  - Amplify / Dilute
  - Protect / Erode
- **Exogenous Forces** (act upon the Enterprise System from outside the relational fields)

PART I

SEEING THE ENTERPRISE AS IT IS

1

THE PATTERN I COULDN'T UNSEE

THE CALL THAT CHANGED EVERYTHING

I was responding to a familiar call: a CEO describing what sounded like a pricing problem and asking for confirmation. I had heard the framing many times before. Pricing issues are rarely about pricing. But in 2017, one such call became the hinge on which everything that followed turned.

The enterprise was an USD 11 million software development services company coming off a period of rapid growth. However, revenue had stopped compounding, deal cycles were being pushed, and margins were quietly compressing quarter by quarter. Leadership had concluded that price resistance in the market was the cause and wanted validation.

As the operating detail came into view, it became clear that the issue was not pricing, but structure. Sales managers were discounting aggressively because there was no shared understanding of margin requirements across different categories of billable work. Pricing decisions were made contract by contract, disconnected from delivery cost profiles and long-term financial thresholds. Customer contracts locked in multiyear rates without mechanisms for inflation or the rising compensation required to retain technical talent. Costs increased, and margins eroded invisibly, embedded inside agreements no one was reexamining.

At the same time, the enterprise had no formal mechanism for linking performance, compensation, and role economics. Raises were granted ad hoc, disconnected from role economics or pricing models. Human resources operated with policies appropriate to a small firm, even as the organizational structure and leadership expectations attempted to scale into something far larger. Each decision made sense in isolation. Taken together, they produced a structural squeeze that no price change, in isolation, could relieve.

Across the enterprise, effort was sincere and misaligned. Sales believed product value was being positioned correctly. Marketing believed messaging was resonating. Operations focused on delivery stability. Finance saw no immediate breach in hourly unit economics. Each function could justify its logic. Yet the enterprise as a whole could not convert activity into predictable results.

What appeared to be a pricing problem was, in fact, a connection failure—a breakdown in how energy moved across the system.

Over the following months, the work did not proceed by fixing categories one at a time, but by reconnecting the structural relationships that had separated across the enterprise. Compensation structures and discounting authority were established, changing how decisions were made during customer contract negotiations. Role-based margin targets were introduced, and delivery cost visibility was extended into sales planning. Reflexive discounting declined, and project allocation shifted accordingly. Customer contracts were revised to include annual price adjustments, protecting target margins without undermining market position.

Gross margins increased from 38 percent to 43 percent within twelve months. Revenue continued to grow, and profitability grew with it. More importantly, leadership gained a different understanding of how their enterprise behaved.

At the time, I treated the engagement as a successful intervention. Only later did its significance become clear, not because it was an exception, but because it matched a pattern I had encountered repeatedly and could no longer ignore.

I left the work with a question that would not release its hold: How many problems leaders label as pricing issues, people issues, or process failures are, in fact, symptoms of how the enterprise moves—or fails to move—as a system?

That question did not resolve. It became the entry point to everything that follows.

These observations emerged through sustained fieldwork. Over more than two decades—the first decade in senior financial leadership roles inside midmarket enterprises, the second as a corporate strategist and CPA in private practice—I observed enterprises as they scaled, reorganized, and struggled to keep structure aligned with demand. Across industries and business models, the same dynamics repeated: Some enterprises advanced with comparatively little effort, while others worked harder quarter after quarter only to lose ground.

The difference came down to a structural condition I did not yet have language for—whether the enterprise reinforced itself in motion or quietly consumed its own energy through misalignment. What follows is grounded in that lived reality and in patterns that surfaced through repetition, observation, and watching structure either sustain performance or erode it.

THE FIRST CLUE: CONNECTION VS. COMPONENTS

The second time the pattern appeared, it could no longer be dismissed. Shortly after the software services engagement, I began working with another enterprise that was losing ground under a different set of surface conditions: churn in key accounts, rising delivery effort, and declining product quality. Each team could explain its actions. Each explanation was reasonable in isolation. And yet, taken as a whole, the enterprise could not produce consistent results. The familiarity of that contradiction was unmistakable.

What initially appeared as a series of unrelated problems

resolved into a single condition when viewed structurally. Teams were not failing in isolation; the breakdown lived at the interfaces between them, where assumptions diverged and handoffs absorbed energy instead of transferring intent. Communication existed, but it fractured at decision boundaries, allowing work to proceed without shared direction. Processes continued to operate, but they were carrying a load they had never been built to absorb, compensating for ambiguity introduced upstream. Customers responded inconsistently, not to effort or intention, but to motion that no longer operated as a whole across interactions. Economic pressure accumulated quietly as cost, pricing, and delivery logic stopped reinforcing one another.

Taken together, these signaled a failure of connection at the system level, not components underperforming.

To test that recognition, I mapped every issue the leadership team raised against patterns I had witnessed in prior enterprises. The result was immediate. Each issue aligned with the same five structural zones, without exception:

People: purpose definition, role boundaries, expectation logic, decision authority
Processes: interfaces, sequencing, structural fit
Execution: progression of work, variability, learning cycles
Customers: experience, meaning, relevance
Economics: viability, resource logic, enterprise value conversion

The enterprise had stopped operating as an integrated system, and symptoms were multiplying faster than leaders could address them individually.

The inverse proved equally instructive. As these five structural zones were reconnected, the enterprise resumed producing results. Communication did not recover because people tried harder, and performance did not recover through isolated correction. Both recovered because relationships between those five structural zones were reconnected.

This enterprise had not lost effectiveness because individual units failed. It had lost effectiveness because the relationships coordinating those units had weakened. After that became visible, I stopped examining enterprises as collections of parts and began reading them as systems.

Up to this point, the pattern can still be explained in two competing ways. One explanation treats enterprise problems as discrete failures—pricing issues, process breakdowns, execution gaps—each requiring its own fix. The other treats those same problems as downstream evidence of weakening relationships across the enterprise, where motion should transfer cleanly but does not. The surface diagnosis changes, but the governing condition does not.

The contrast in Table 1.1 clarifies that interpretive difference. It distinguishes between reading enterprise breakdown as a component failure and reading it as a systemic loss of connection.

Two Ways of Reading Enterprise Problems

Traditional Lens	Systemic Lens	What Changes
Problems are owned by functions	Problems emerge at relationships	Diagnosis shifts from blame to structure
Causes are linear and local	Causes are distributed and delayed	Fixes move upstream
Performance explains itself	Performance confirms prior conditions	Attention shifts to behavior
Improvement comes from fixing parts	Improvement comes from restoring coherence	Effort begins to compound

Table 1.1

Reading the enterprise as a set of parts produces a familiar cycle: leaders intervene when symptoms appear, only to see the same conditions re-emerge elsewhere. Reading it as a system shifts attention toward movement itself—how work advances, where decisions slow, where handoffs absorb energy, and where coordination becomes compensatory rather than reinforcing.

Motion as Evidence

Read as a system, the enterprise revealed motion as the primary evidence—not strategy, not intent, but how work moved. The enterprise was always in motion—work initiating, decisions propagating, responsibilities shifting, information advancing or encountering resistance. Some of this motion was assertive and deliberate; much of it was passive, ambient, or residual. Strategy and intent still mattered, but motion revealed what the system was actually doing once those intentions were released into the enterprise and encountered structure.

> **Motion** is the observable movement of work, decisions, information, and responsibility initiated by the enterprise and propagated across its relational fields over time.

Motion originates within the enterprise but extends through customers, markets, and partners, as those actors respond, adapt, and send signals that influence subsequent enterprise behavior. It is not what leaders intend; it is what occurs once decisions are introduced into a living system with constraints, interfaces, and accumulated patterns of behavior. Motion includes every form of movement the enterprise produces, whether purposeful or incidental, visible or background, accelerated or impeded.

Action is assertive by nature. It reflects deliberate effort: tasks performed, decisions made, initiatives launched, and interventions executed. Motion, by contrast, includes action but is not limited to it. Motion also includes the continuous, ambient activity that persists regardless of leadership focus: recurring coordination, habitual communication, automated processing, deferred decisions, standing routines, and work that circulates without resolution. These background movements consume capacity, shape load, and influence how effectively the enterprise operates even when no one is consciously "acting."

In the twentieth century, this would have been described simply as activity: people performing tasks and machines executing steps. In the modern enterprise, motion encompasses far more. It includes human and machine effort, communication signals, physical logistics, digital data transfer, automated workflows, platform interactions, and agentic activity operating continuously at machine speed. Work no longer moves only through people and processes; it moves through systems that sense, decide, communicate, transport, and act continuously—often without direct human initiation.

Because this motion never stops, the system condition it produces is never static. It is shaped not only by what leaders choose to do, but by how all forms of movement—assertive actions and ambient activity alike—interact with structure over time. The realization set the conditions for the discovery that would shape the next decade of my work.

Motion reveals what is moving, but it does not, by itself, explain how the enterprise is responding. As movement encounters structure, constraint, and consequence, the enterprise produces patterns of response that persist over time. Those patterns allow leaders to determine whether the system is reinforcing itself or working against itself.

> **Enterprise Behavior** is the observable pattern of response produced by an enterprise as work, decisions, information, and commitments move through people, machines, systems, customers, and markets over time.

Enterprise behavior is therefore evidence, not intention. It reveals how design, structure, coordination, and economics are interacting in practice.

THE NUMBERS NEVER TELL YOU WHY

After hundreds of month-end closes and executive reporting cycles, a single pattern became impossible to ignore: the numbers were consistently accurate, but they were never explanatory. Leadership teams reviewed dashboards filled with revenue, margin, utilization, cycle time, pipeline, churn, and operational measures, yet those figures captured only what had already occurred. They showed the shape performance had taken, not the conditions that had produced it. Long before outcomes appeared in financial or operational reports, patterns in enterprise behavior were already forming elsewhere.

When an enterprise accelerates or struggles, the numbers register the result with precision. Revenue rises or softens, margins expand or compress, utilization shifts, and operational indicators follow accordingly. What the numbers do not disclose is why those outcomes emerged. Metrics are reliable indicators of consequence, not explanations of cause.

Recognizing that gap changed how I approached leadership reviews. Attention shifted away from interrogating results and toward examining conditions: how priorities were being interpreted, where and why action slowed, where interfaces absorbed effort instead of transferring it, where customer experience varied despite consistent intent, and where commitments exceeded structural capacity. Financial review was not abandoned; it was repositioned within the system that produced the results being examined.

Across industries, sizes, and operating models, the same pattern repeated. Language, artifacts, and personalities differed across every enterprise. The signals did not. Misfit and disconnection surfaced through the same channels each time, regardless of context. Performance did not explain those conditions; it reflected how the enterprise was operating as a system.

Weakened coordination produced predictable deviation. Revenue softened, margins compressed, retention weakened, and operational stability declined. Restoring coordination reversed the pattern—

often more quickly than expected—because the conditions producing performance had changed upstream.

The pattern held across settings. In a manufacturing operation, on-time delivery fell from 94 percent to 81 percent. Operations attributed the change to staffing, human resources to turnover, and finance to cost pressure. In reality, the shift had begun months earlier, when cross-functional coordination weakened and structural fit no longer matched production load. In a forty-person professional services firm, utilization slipped and leadership cited motivation, while teams no longer shared a common definition of priority as market conditions changed. A rapidly scaling B2B software enterprise showed the pattern differently: pipeline volume declined amid internal debate over pricing, features, and positioning, while customers responded to inconsistent operations across the system rather than to any single decision.

Different symptoms appeared, accompanied by different explanations, yet the underlying structure was the same. The numbers were correct, but they arrived late, reflecting conditions that had already formed elsewhere. From that recognition emerged another consistent pattern: Financial signals are the last indicators of enterprise misfit, not the first. After this pattern repeated across dozens of enterprises, financial outcomes ceased to function as diagnostics and became confirmations. The shift in understanding made it possible to recognize when the enterprise was operating as an integrated system—and when it was beginning to separate—well before results forced recognition.

RECOGNIZING THE PATTERN ACROSS ENTERPRISES

Once I stopped treating symptoms as the problem, a pattern began to repeat itself everywhere I looked. I encountered it in a USD 25 million software company struggling to scale after rapid growth, in a manufacturing operation contending with variability on the production floor, in a consulting partnership losing ground as client expectations shifted, in a logistics firm facing rising exception rates, and in a healthcare company constrained by decision bottlenecks.

What leaders described always sounded specific. They spoke about needing to prioritize better, about teams feeling overwhelmed, about processes no longer keeping pace, about customers behaving unpredictably, about gaps in analytics, or about declining margins. Each description made sense in isolation, yet none captured the governing condition shaping performance. Beneath the surface variation, the same structure was present: The enterprise was beginning to separate as a system.

Across enterprises, the same five areas registered misfit first, and they did so in a consistent sequence. Shared meaning among people broke down first, allowing decision logic and expectations to diverge. Once interpretation fractured, process interfaces could no longer match the work they were required to carry; excess load accumulated and exceptions multiplied. Execution lost reliability as outcomes varied and learning cycles slowed or failed to close. Customer experience registered the shift next—value interpretation weakened, relevance declined, and interactions lost consistency. Economic signals followed last, as cost-to-serve increased, revenue stability fell, and the system's ability to operate as a financial whole weakened.

Industries expressed the separation differently—manufacturing through physical indicators, professional services through interpretive confusion, technology through relational signals—yet the enterprise-level order remained the same. What changed was surface expression, not structure.

As I continued to encounter this pattern, it became impossible to treat it as coincidental. The problem did not reside in any single function, industry, or cultural context; it was structural, and it repeated with remarkable consistency. The recognition changed how enterprises were examined. Instead of sorting problems by department or ownership, attention shifted to interaction—to the points where motion should have reinforced itself and did not. Those were the points where the governing condition consistently revealed itself.

Enterprises read this way revealed the pattern earlier and earlier, often well before a single metric deviated from plan. At that point, it was clear this was not the observation of isolated dysfunction, but the recognition of a recurring geometry of enterprise behavior—a stable shape that appeared across industries, scales, histories, and operating models.

NAMING COHERENCE AS A STRUCTURAL CONDITION

The pattern could no longer be dismissed. I needed language precise enough to name what I was observing: behavior that was repeatable, causal, and structural, pointing not to intent, effort, or aspiration, but to condition. What was missing was a term that could describe that condition without collapsing it into metaphor or judgment.

The word *coherence*[1] already existed in organizational language, but it was used loosely. Leaders spoke of coherent strategies, coherent cultures, and coherent narratives—usually as assessments made after the fact or as qualities they hoped to achieve. In practice, coherence was treated as a feeling, a virtue, or an outcome. It was rarely defined, and almost never anchored to how work, decisions, and information moved through the enterprise.

To discipline the term, I looked outside management language to a field that has long studied systems in motion. Physics does not explain enterprise behavior, but it does provide a precise way to describe what occurs when forces reinforce one another—and what occurs when they do not. In physics, coherence describes systems in which waves reinforce rather than cancel—an analogy that precisely mirrors what I was observing inside enterprises. When coherence weakens, energy does not disappear; it disperses, patterns lose integrity, and motion no longer compounds. The system remains active, but its output diminishes relative to the effort invested.

The description matched exactly what I was seeing inside enterprises.

> **Coherence** is the structural condition in which the enterprise's domains reinforce one another in motion, allowing effort, decisions, and information to compound rather than interfere. Coherence is verified through its observable consequences: declining coordination cost relative to output, quality that remains stable under increasing load, decisions that resolve without escalation, interfaces that carry work without repeated clarification, and enterprise value that accumulates across cycles rather than resetting with each one.

When people, processes, execution, customers, and economics moved together, effort began to reinforce itself. Less work produced stronger results. The enterprise appeared coordinated instead of constrained, reinforcing where it had previously been compensating, and capable of sustaining enterprise value over time.

As coherence weakened, the effects appeared in the same predictable sequence. Effort increased while returns diminished; processes demanded growing attention as exceptions multiplied. Execution lost continuity next—results varied from cycle to cycle, and learning loops slowed or failed to close. Customers registered the condition through inconsistent experience and weakening commitment, while financial signals confirmed the pattern later, expressing in numbers what the system had already been revealing in behavior.

These were not separate problems emerging independently. They were coordinated signals of a single structural condition: coherence was no longer operating across the system.

Seen this way, coherence resolved contradictions that had previously felt irreconcilable. It explained why enterprises could appear aligned yet remain ineffective, why others looked disordered on paper yet performed with force, why additional effort failed to correct misfit, and why leaders within the enterprise sensed hesitation and confusion long before performance declined.

Coherence is geometric, not soft. It describes the fit between purpose, structure, motion, and meaning—the way the parts of the enterprise relate as a system rather than as functions. Once coherence is understood as a structural condition, its implications become traceable rather than abstract. Across the enterprises I had observed, enterprise motion was continuous, shaped by alignment and the pathways through which work and decisions traveled. Those pathways depended on structure and interfaces, which in turn shaped experience. Experience formed interpretation, and interpretation ultimately determined performance.

Physics did not supply a business model. It supplied discipline—the ability to name what was already visible. The pattern was consistent: Enterprises that reinforced themselves in motion strengthened; enterprises that applied more effort without restoring structural connection did not. The distinction, once recognized, restructured how every subsequent enterprise was examined.

ALIGNMENT IS THE SNAPSHOT; COHERENCE IS THE VIDEO

Every leadership team pursues alignment. It is among the most familiar ideas in enterprise leadership, and among the least examined once declared.

> **Alignment** is the condition of interpretation in which people share a common understanding of purpose, priorities, and direction at a given moment. It reflects whether meaning is aligned—whether intent is understood similarly across individuals and groups—before work encounters structure, load, and consequence.

Leadership teams pursue it deliberately. Strategic off-sites exist to produce it. Alignment is present when goals are agreed upon, direction is affirmed, and commitment is declared.

What alignment captures is intention, not continuity. It reflects agreement at a point in time. It is a snapshot. Coherence, by contrast, is the sustained expression of that intention as work moves through real conditions. It is the video. Alignment organizes what leaders decide; coherence determines what happens once those decisions encounter structure, interfaces, and operating reality.

A leadership team can leave a conference room fully aligned and still preside over an incoherent enterprise. Strategy can be clear while interpretation diverges. Shared priorities do not prevent execution from proceeding at incompatible speeds. Roles can be defined while interfaces fail under load. The distinction becomes visible not in intent but in operation: Alignment produces agreement, while coherence produces performance. Whether alignment converts into coherence depends on what the enterprise is carrying and whether its structure can bear the weight.

> **Load** is the total demand placed on an enterprise's structure, people, and decision pathways at a given moment, relative to the system's capacity to carry that demand without loss of coherence.

Leaders are accustomed to thinking about load in familiar terms: work volume, workload, queue length, utilization, or backlogs. Those measures capture the amount of work present, but they do not fully describe how that work interacts with structure, variability, interdependence, and decision timing. In enterprise systems, load is not just how much work exists; it is how much pressure that work places on the system's ability to move coherently.

In coherent systems, decisions are resolved because interpretation is shared rather than negotiated repeatedly. Handoffs transfer intent instead of absorbing effort, allowing work to advance without rework or escalation. People anticipate one another's actions because meaning is stabilized, and coordination emerges from shared understanding rather than oversight.

Absent that coherence, the same direction is interpreted differently across teams, producing decisions that conflict rather than reinforcing one another. Work slows as meaning must be checked, clarified, and renegotiated at each interface, and meetings multiply to compensate for structural misfit rather than to advance action.

Coherence is a condition entirely different from alignment—the structural fit between intention and motion, not a softer expression of the same idea. That distinction became clear to me through a simple analogy.

Before an orchestra begins a performance, every musician tunes to the same reference pitch. That moment of tuning establishes alignment. Each instrument agrees on the note, and discord is temporarily removed. But tuning is not music. It is preparation.

Coherence appears only when the musicians begin to play. It is expressed through timing, balance, responsiveness, and the continuous adjustment each musician makes in relation to the others. The written score may be shared, and the pitch may be correct, but music exists only if the orchestra can hold tempo, sustain rhythm, adapt to dynamics, and move together through the piece in real time.

An orchestra can be perfectly aligned—in tune—and still fail to produce music if its structure cannot carry coordinated motion. When timing breaks down, sections overpower one another, or musicians cannot hear and adjust to the ensemble, shared intention remains intact, but the performance falls apart.

Enterprises behave the same way. Alignment is tuning; it establishes shared intention. Coherence is performing together; it determines whether that intention can be carried through coordinated action as conditions change. Weakening coherence produces predictable results: Effort scatters, timing breaks down, and execution requires constant correction. Coherence that remains intact produces a different outcome—motion sustains itself, and results emerge not from control, but from structure that carries the system as it moves together.

The orchestra analogy made the distinction operational. Enterprise leadership teams routinely confuse agreement with capability, and that confusion is why strategies that make sense in the conference room fail once work begins.

High-performing enterprises therefore attend not only to alignment but to its conversion into consistent interaction. That conversion—from intention to coordinated behavior—is where execution either persists or begins to separate. After this distinction became clear, a single question sat beneath every enterprise leadership challenge: Where is alignment failing to become coherence within the enterprise?

FROM FIXING PROBLEMS TO DESIGNING FLOW

For years, leaders contacted me only after something had already gone wrong—a strategy that misfired, a metric that was crashing, a team carrying an unsustainable load, or a customer relationship at risk. My role in those moments was to diagnose the issue, identify the cause, and help leaders repair what had broken. That work was necessary, but it was inherently reactive, focused on restoring stability after results had already begun to deteriorate.

Over time, the nature of the conversation began to change. Leaders were no longer asking how to fix the last failure; they were asking how to recognize vulnerability before failure appeared. One CEO captured the shift precisely when he said, "I don't want you to fix what broke last quarter. I want to know where we are exposed right now." His question redirected the work away from repair and toward design—from solving visible problems to shaping the structural conditions that determine whether problems emerge at all.

Instead of tracing backward from failure, I began examining how work was carried through the enterprise before misfit showed up as accumulated load, repeated intervention, and compensatory effort[2]. I looked at where organizational roles and leadership routines carried unnecessary load, where interfaces required repeated interpretation, where decisions accumulated resistance, and where teams relied on workarounds because structure no longer supported the work being asked of them. What emerged was a consistent pattern: Enterprises falter at the points where continuity of work has not been designed, or where existing design no longer matches the conditions the enterprise must operate within.

> **Flow** is the continuity of work as it moves through the enterprise—how decisions, tasks, information, and responsibility progress across

roles, teams, and domains without unnecessary interruption, reinterpretation, or rework.

It is a condition of design, not a mindset. It describes whether the enterprise's structure can support the movement required by its strategy and operating demands. When this condition is present, its effects are visible and consistent. Teams achieve the same outcomes with less compensatory effort, decisions propagate without distortion across boundaries, and workload stabilizes rather than oscillating unpredictably. Customer experience remains consistent across interactions, and financial indicators regain predictability because execution is no longer fragmented.

Loss of that condition forces the enterprise to compensate in equally predictable ways. Coordination overhead increases as meetings multiply, handoffs escalate to manage ambiguity, and exceptions accumulate as structure fails to carry the load. Fatigue builds as effort rises without a corresponding return, and leadership intervention intensifies to keep the system operating as a whole. The enterprise expends more energy while producing less enterprise value.

I began applying this structural logic inside enterprises that were not yet in visible trouble. The effect was immediate. One technology company preparing for rapid expansion was scaling sales, product, operations, and customer success simultaneously. Although performance metrics remained strong, misfit was already apparent in how work moved across interfaces and decision pathways. Together, we mapped interfaces, decision timing, execution load, and customer experience pathways. By redesigning the structure early—before misfit accumulated—the enterprise doubled revenue without the fragmentation that typically accompanies rapid growth.

Nothing extraordinary occurred. The enterprise simply preserved coherence during a period when most begin to separate. That experience made a final distinction unavoidable: fixing problems responds to breakdown after it occurs; designing continuity preserves coherence before breakdown appears.

After that shift, I could no longer approach enterprises the same way. I stopped asking what had failed and began asking where structural coherence was beginning to weaken. Because continuity of work consistently revealed coherence—or its loss—well before performance metrics registered the cost, that question marked the beginning of the next stage of discovery.

WHY TRADITIONAL PROBLEM-SOLVING FAILS

Most executives are trained to solve problems by isolating them: identify a cause, apply a fix, and move on. The approach is familiar—linear, efficient, and internally consistent. It is also poorly matched to how enterprises actually behave. In complex systems, performance degrades not because a single component stops working, but because relationships between components lose alignment.

Traditional problem-solving assumes that issues live inside functions. If sales underperforms, sales is fixed; if operations slows, operations is addressed; if product struggles, product is examined. The implicit belief is that repairing a part restores the whole. In enterprises operating as systems, that assumption rarely survives. Breakdown almost never originates inside a team; it forms at the points where interpretation, structure, and coordination intersect.

By the time a problem becomes visible in one area of the enterprise, the governing condition has usually taken shape elsewhere. What surfaces as a localized failure is already the downstream expression of an earlier misfit—in how priorities were interpreted, how structure carried work, or how decisions propagated across interfaces. Symptoms appear where pressure concentrates, not where causes originate.

To make this visible, I began using a simple diagnostic comparison with leadership teams, contrasting how problems were typically addressed with how they actually behaved across the enterprise system. The response was consistent: first recognition, then relief. Leaders were not ineffective; the interpretive lens they had been given for reading enterprise behavior was incomplete. The comparison clarified what linear analysis consistently misses: problems attributed to enterprises are expressions of enterprise system dynamics rather than isolated events.

Traditional problem-solving fails for three structural reasons listed in Table 1.2.

Structural Limits of Traditional Problem-Solving

Structural Reason	Examples	Mechanism	Consequence
Symptoms travel faster than causes	Revenue decline, deals pushed to later quarters, execution slowdown	Coherence weakens before metrics register the change	Attention anchors to the point of impact, not the point of origin
Problems rarely originate where they surface	Operational slowdown → priority interpretation; pricing pressure → customer experience; process failure → role ambiguity	Root condition is relational, not locational	Locational root-cause analysis cannot reach it
Additive fixes increase coordination load without restoring coherence	More meetings, more steps, more tools, more policies	Pressure is redistributed, not resolved	Resistance redirects from one interface to another

Table 1.2

When the enterprise is understood as a system in motion, the nature of problem-solving changes. Attention moves away from ownership and correction and toward condition and relationship. Instead of asking who owns an issue, which team needs to perform better, or what fix applies to a function, leaders begin asking where coherence is beginning to weaken, which interpretations no longer align, and which interfaces no longer fit the work being carried out. Those questions surface what traditional methods obscure.

That reframing prepared the ground for what followed, because it made clear that strengthening enterprise performance required not better fixes, but a different way of seeing how the system operated as a whole—or began to separate.

Why Traditional Problem-Solving Fails in Enterprises

Interpretive Habit	What It Obscures	Structural Consequence
Functional Isolation examining issues within a single team or domain	Cross-domain relationships and interface dynamics	Local fixes that displace strain elsewhere, increasing system-wide friction
Component Attribution assigning outcomes to owners instead of relationships	Interface behavior and dependency chains	Repeated failure despite corrective effort
Symptom Correction addressing visible pain instead of underlying structure	Recurring behavioral patterns produced by the system	Temporary relief while misfit persists
Metric Extrapolation treating indicators as explanatory rather than confirmatory	Upstream conditions shaping enterprise behavior	Late intervention and accelerating coherence loss
Linear Causality assuming cause and effect move in straight lines	Feedback loops, delays, and compounding effects	Interventions that introduce new resistance

Table 1.3

THE MOMENT THE PATTERN BECAME OBVIOUS

The pattern became unavoidable one evening as I stood in front of a whiteboard after a full day with a leadership team. We had spent hours cataloging issues that initially appeared unrelated—decisions that took too long, recurring process breakdowns, inconsistent customer experience, financial volatility, and visible leadership fatigue. The board was filled with arrows, notes, loops, points of resistance, and unresolved questions. It looked disordered, but the disorder was superficial.

When I stepped back, the structure resolved itself. Everything on the board clustered into five distinct fields of motion—five areas where the enterprise either reinforced itself or worked against itself:

1. People
2. Processes
3. Execution
4. Customers
5. Economics

These fields were not departments, functions, or boxes on an organization chart. They were systems of activity: the structural zones through which enterprise motion was being organized.

For the first time, I was no longer looking at a list of problems; I was seeing enterprise behavior directly. The same structure produced the same breakdowns, independent of industry, leadership personality, or declared direction. Across enterprises, symptoms varied, but breakdown consistently appeared in only two places:

1. Within a field whose structure no longer matched the work it was carrying, or
2. At the interfaces between fields, where motion should have reinforced itself but instead lost coherence.

That realization reframed everything. Enterprises were systems of motion, not collections of teams, processes, or objectives interpreted in isolation, and whether that motion compounded or degraded depended on how these five fields related to one another over time.

Seen clearly, the pattern surfaced everywhere. In a software enterprise losing customers, the separation appeared between Customers and Execution, where experience varied faster than execution could stabilize. A manufacturing operation facing quality decline revealed the misfit between Processes and Execution, where structure no longer carried production load. In a professional services firm overwhelmed by growth, tension accumulated between People and Economics, as leaders committed the enterprise to work its economics could not sustain. Different enterprises, different pressures, the same underlying geometry.

Over time, it became clear that I was not observing isolated conditions. Across size, industry, and operating model, the same structure governed how work advanced, how decisions formed, and how performance emerged. That structure persisted even as leadership changed, strategies shifted, and markets evolved. Natural Order was the only accurate name for it—not as a theory, but as the underlying structure that existed whether anyone recognized it or not.

> **Natural Order** is the consistent structural pattern through which enterprises organize motion, coordinate activity, and produce enterprise value. It describes the architecture that governs enterprise behavior—not the behavior itself. Enterprises may operate with or against this architecture, but they cannot alter the consequences. Enterprise motion that aligns with the Natural Order compounds enterprise value. Motion that does not produces rising coordination cost and declining performance that increase as misalignment persists.

After I began seeing the Five Enterprise Domains as interdependent forces rather than separate problem categories, the logic clarified. Misalignment traced back to interpretation rather than intent. Variability signaled structural misfit well before results deteriorated, while customer behavior exposed enterprise condition earlier than formal reporting ever could. Financial patterns followed later, confirming coherence or erosion only after the system had already shifted.

At that point, the pattern could no longer be dismissed. It was not a hypothesis or a model, but a structure—present across the industries, business models, and scales observed in the fieldwork.

> **The Five Enterprise Domains** are the five interdependent systems of activity through which enterprises organize motion, coordinate effort, and produce enterprise value. Together, they make the Natural

Order visible in daily operation: how people align, how work is structured, how execution behaves under pressure, how customers interpret value, and how financial outcomes emerge.

What I had given precise language to was not new—it was enduring. The pattern, once visible, restructured how every enterprise was subsequently examined.

VISUALIZING THE ENTERPRISE

The pattern that resolved on the whiteboard can be made structural. The five fields—People, Processes, Execution, Customers, Economics—were not categories I imposed on the enterprise. They were systems of activity the enterprise was already organized through. What remained was a way to see them operating simultaneously, across every part of the enterprise at once. The Activity Blueprint™ in Table 1.4 presents that view.

The rows are business functions—organizational units the enterprise recognizes on its own terms. The columns are the Five Enterprise Domains: the systems of activity that emerged from the whiteboard and that the subsequent chapters examine in depth. Where a row crosses a column, a business function participates in a domain. That intersection is the unit of observation.

No cell is empty. Service Delivery does not belong to Execution + Intelligence any more than Sales belongs to Customer + Interaction. Each function crosses all five columns. Sales operates within People + Alignment every time a new hire interprets the firm's value proposition differently from the founder intended. Finance operates within Execution + Intelligence when billing accuracy and project economics shape how engagement teams pace their work. Human Resources operates within Economics + Metrics when compensation decisions made without visibility into role economics quietly compress margins across the enterprise.

Activity Blueprint™ Domain and Business Function
Intangible Asset Enterprise / B2B Professional Services / USD 10–50 million

Business Function	People + Alignment	Processes + Integration	Execution + Intelligence	Customer + Interaction	Economics + Metrics
Service Delivery					
Sales					
Marketing					
Human Resources					
Finance					
Administration					

Table 1.4

Consider the USD 11 million software development services company from the opening of this chapter. Sales was discounting because shared interpretation of margin requirements had never formed—a People + Alignment condition operating inside the Sales function. Customer contracts locked in rates that could not absorb rising compensation costs—an Economics + Metrics condition, also operating inside Sales. Human Resources was granting raises disconnected from pricing models—an Economics + Metrics condition operating inside Human Resources. Each function could justify its logic because each function was reading only its own row. No one was reading down the columns. The domains revealed what no single function could see on its own.

The Activity Blueprint makes this visible in a way that narrative description alone cannot. It asks the leader to consider each intersection, not as a theoretical exercise, but as a structural question: What is happening here, and is it coherent with what is happening in the adjacent cells?

The five domains, their structural relationships, and the signals they produce are the subject of the chapters that follow. The complete Activity Blueprint instrument—including the enterprise signal tables it draws from and the weekly observation log it supports—appears in Appendix 1.

THE PATTERN BECOMES A PRACTICE

When the geometry of the enterprise came into focus, my work changed in a fundamental way. I stopped attempting to repair isolated issues or strengthen disconnected functions and began helping leaders see the enterprise as a system in motion, one whose performance was governed by how consistently its five domains reinforced one another over time.

Leadership teams worked together differently as a result. Instead of mapping symptoms in isolation, we began mapping interfaces—the points where interpretation, process, execution, experience, and economics met. Those interfaces did not obscure the truth; they made it visible. When an enterprise slowed, the behavior at its interfaces revealed why. Reinforcement produced equally visible evidence—the same interfaces showed where coherence was forming.

Another conclusion followed, unavoidable in its implications: what these enterprises revealed was that leadership, in practice, operated as the stewardship of coherence rather than the management of parts.

> **Stewardship** is the ongoing responsibility of keeping the enterprise aligned with its Natural Order as conditions change. It is visible in how leaders notice, interpret, and respond to the signals the system produces, and in their willingness to adjust structure, refresh interfaces, and sustain renewal so that information, intent, and learning continue to move reliably across the enterprise.

As leaders learned to see coherence as a condition, they began to recognize its state earlier, often before numbers, customers, or teams made the change explicit. The signals were subtle but consistent, appearing as decisions forming out of sequence across domains, teams interpreting the same priority in incompatible ways, and processes requiring repeated clarification simply to proceed. Execution grew more variable under similar conditions, customer expectations began diverging from actual enterprise behavior, and financial patterns lost comparability as coherence weakened.

These were not isolated issues. They were early indicators of structural misfit—evidence that alignment was no longer converting into coherent enterprise motion.

To make this visible, I began facilitating leadership mapping sessions in which teams saw how work moved across the five domains. We examined where work accumulated, where decisions slowed, and where continuity broke down. At first, leaders were surprised by how much became clear once structure was revealed. Over time, they learned to perceive coherence directly, without relying on dashboards or after-the-fact indicators.

That was the moment the pattern became a practice. The work repeated across enterprises, and its consistency became unmistakable. Across the enterprises observed, coherence governed whether performance compounded or eroded.

Coherence was a governing condition—observable, repeatable, and structurally determined—not a theory. The change extended not only to how I advised leaders, but to how they led. Their attention shifted first at the structural level.

WHAT EMERGED in this chapter was not a collection of problems, but a pattern that persisted across contexts. In each enterprise—including software services, manufacturing, professional services, and distribution—the same five structural zones either reinforced one another or worked against themselves. The sequence was consistent: Problems that appeared as pricing, people, process, or execution issues resolved into the same structural conditions once the enterprise was read as a system rather than as a set of parts. Across industries and leadership teams, the same structural signals appeared again and again—regardless of intent, intelligence, or effort. That recognition raises a deeper question: Why do enterprises behave this way at all? To answer it, we have to move beyond observation and examine the governing structure beneath enterprise behavior.

Chapter 2 turns to that problem directly. It introduces the concepts of enterprise energy, enterprise value, and breakdown as observable conditions that form well before metrics change. Energy is converted, reinforced, or dissipated as the enterprise moves—and learning to read those patterns is what makes misfit, pressure, and loss of coherence visible while response is still possible. What follows provides the interpretive vocabulary required to see what is already happening, long before results make it undeniable.

Endnotes

---

1. Enterprise coherence as a concept has significant prior art in the enterprise architecture literature. Roel Wagter, Henderik A. Proper, and Dirk Witte developed the Enterprise Coherence Framework (ECF) through the Dutch Government Enterprise Architecture (GEA) research programme, beginning in 2006. See Wagter, Proper, and Witte, *Enterprise Coherence Assessment* (Cham: Springer, 2012). Their framework defines coherence as "the extent to which all relevant aspects of an enterprise are interconnected to facilitate achieving desired results." Separately, David J. Teece, Richard Rumelt, Giovanni Dosi, and Sidney Winter addressed corporate coherence in "Understanding Corporate Coherence: Theory and Evidence," *Journal of Economic Behavior & Organization* 23, no. 1 (1994): 1–30, examining coherence through the lens of diversification strategy and organizational learning. The EA literature treats coherence as a design methodology objective: something to be achieved through architectural governance. The economic coherence literature addresses strategic portfolio coherence. "Coherence," as used here, describes an observable property of enterprise behavior in motion—how the Five Enterprise Domains reinforce or oppose one another in real-time operation. It is a behavioral condition, not a design objective or strategic portfolio characteristic.
2. *Compensatory effort* as used in this book describes the human behavioral cost of structural misfit—people working harder, longer, or less efficiently because the enterprise's structure no longer carries the work it was designed to support. The term has established but distinct usage in two adjacent fields. In cognitive psychology and neuroscience, compensatory effort refers to the increased mental exertion required to maintain performance under conditions of fatigue or impairment. In organizational design, Xiaowei Rose Luo and Lex Donaldson developed a theory of "compensatory misfits" that addresses how organizations offset struc-

tural under-fit through information-processing mechanisms. See Luo and Donaldson, "Compensatory Misfits: A Theory of Structural Adjustments in Groups and Organizations," *Journal of Organization Design* 2, no. 2 (2013): 5–16. The usage here is neither cognitive nor structural-design-focused; it describes the felt consequence—the additional effort required of people when the architecture around them no longer supports the work being asked of them.

2

WHAT THE FIELDWORK REVEALED

WHAT EFFORT ALONE CANNOT EXPLAIN

I have spent years inside enterprises where the math should have worked. The talent was present, the strategy was funded, and the leadership was experienced and engaged. Still, something refused to convert. Effort went in, but results came back lighter than they should have. Not catastrophically—these were not failing enterprises—but persistently. The gap between what was invested and what was produced never closed, and no one inside the enterprise could explain why.

Other enterprises—sometimes in the same industry, sometimes smaller, sometimes less resourced—produced results that exceeded what their inputs should have allowed. Work moved without the constant intervention that had become normal elsewhere. Decisions advanced without cycling. People stayed. The enterprise gained ground steadily, and the leaders running it often could not fully explain that, either.

The usual explanations never resolved the gap. Leaders in underperforming enterprises pointed to culture, to talent gaps, to market conditions, to legacy technology. Leaders in high-performing enterprises credited strategy, or hiring, or a particular initiative that seemed to have made the difference. None of these explanations survived contact with the next enterprise.

INSIDE FORTY ENTERPRISES

Over the course of nearly a decade, I worked inside more than forty midmarket enterprises—not as a consultant observing from the outside, but embedded in daily execution and communications. My firm manages finance, human resources, operations, and administrative functions while advising executive leadership teams on business strategy. That position provides full access to executive leaders, unrestricted financial and operational data, and a front-row seat for day-to-day decisions as they happen. These enterprises range from low eight to low nine figures in annual revenue. They are not small or unsophisticated, and nearly all of them are full of challenges.

The Enterprise-Level Pattern

What I see across these enterprises is remarkably consistent. Many do not produce the financial results their resources should allow—profits and cash flows fall below or are at industry benchmarks despite sufficient revenue, capable teams, and functioning operations. Most leadership teams cannot explain why the gap between what these enterprises earn and what they retain remains wider than it should be.

Enterprises in growth mode present a different version of the same pattern. Revenue increases, but the enterprise behind it becomes chaotic and reactive. Coordination breaks down as activity scales. Customer relationships suffer because the enterprise is too consumed by its own expansion to maintain what it already has. Growth creates motion without compounding what that motion produces.

Enterprises with declining revenue often present the opposite condition—not chaos, but inertia. Top-line contraction is accepted and blamed on markets. Marketing and sales strategies remain unchanged. The enterprise continues operating as it always has, even as the results no longer justify the approach.

Across nearly all of these midmarket enterprises, especially those with annual revenue below USD 25 million, a set of structural gaps recurs. Inbound lead generation is nonexistent. B2B sales teams rely on outbound efforts that take one to two years to produce a pipeline, with deals beginning to close only in the second year—if at all. Financial visibility into operations is limited, financial control is weak, and most of these enterprises are unprepared to present credibly to banks, investors, or regulators. Talent retention is questionable, with no deliberate strategy to address it. Decision-making is slow, unclear, or both. Meanwhile, functions operate in silos, with sales receiving the majority of leadership attention while everything else runs in isolation.

The Leadership Variable

These conditions are not random. They do not distribute evenly across enterprises, and they do not correlate reliably with industry, geography, or market position. What they correlate with is leadership.

The few enterprises in this population that grow enterprise value year over year share a recognizable leadership profile. Their leaders have typically built and sold enterprises before. They build leadership teams deliberately, recruit and pay top talent, maintain deep relationships with customers and industry, know how to scale operations and delivery to support additional revenue, and understand what enterprise value means because they have constructed it. The rest—the majority—are led by individuals whose capabilities produce a narrower range of enterprise outcomes.

Across more than forty enterprises observed over nearly a decade, leadership is the variable that separates enterprises that compound enterprise value from those that consume it.

Leadership Pattern and Enterprise Value Consequence

Value-Compunding Patterns	
The Enterprise Value Builder	Builds and sells enterprises deliberately; constructs leadership teams, compounds value across cycles, manages capital with discipline, and scales operations through organic growth and M&A
The Connected Seller	Deep industry relationships and personal credibility generate sustained revenue growth; evolves the sales approach across growth stages; enterprise value concentrates in the leader's network
The Developer	Invests deliberately in people and capability beneath them; delegates progressively; enterprise capacity expands through the leadership team rather than through one person
The Disciplined Operator	Maintains financial control, funds strategies deliberately, and keeps resources matched to activity; protects enterprise value but does not aggressively compound it
The Learner	Integrates mistakes into the next cycle; adjusts approach across growth stages; enterprise value is created but from correction rather than accumulated advantage
Value-Neutral to Value-Consuming Patterns	
The Mismatched Strategist	Has the instinct to build enterprise value but imports techniques from larger enterprises that don't fit the current scale; resources are consumed by structure that doesn't match the work
The Ceiling Leader	Builds to a growth stage and flatlines; controls decisions and processes through personal bandwidth; enterprise value stops accumulating as the enterprise reaches the leader's limit
The Technical Founder	Monetizable skill created the enterprise but now constrains it; cannot build teams, delegate, or evolve beyond personal capability; enterprise value asymptotes then declines
Value-Destroying Patterns	
The Wheel-Spinner	Does not learn from mistakes or implement proven advice; same failures recirculate across cycles; enterprise value erodes as the cost of repeated errors compounds
The Value Destroyer	Actively destroys enterprise value through financial mismanagement, failed planning, and uncontrolled spending; the enterprise earns but retains nothing; fastest path to value destruction

Table 2.1

These profiles represent what I have observed—not diagnostic categories, but recurring patterns positioned by their relative enterprise value consequence. Full profile descriptions appear in Appendix 6: Leadership Pattern and Enterprise Value Consequence.

The profiles in Table 2.1 are positioned along a spectrum ranging from compounding to consuming enterprise value. The positioning reflects patterns observed across the fieldwork population, not a diagnostic instrument.

> **Leadership Pattern and Enterprise Value Consequence** is the relative capability of a leader to create or destroy enterprise value over time. It reflects where a leadership pattern sits on the continuum between compounding and consuming enterprise value—estimating the probability of the leader's impact on enterprise value under a known or demonstrated pattern.

What the Pattern Revealed

Where leadership compounds enterprise value, the enterprise behaves differently at every level. Financial performance meets or exceeds what the enterprise's resources should produce. Growth, when it occurs, builds on what already exists rather than destabilizing it. Talent stays, decisions are made, and functions reinforce one another rather than operating in isolation. The enterprise converts what goes into it.

Leadership that consumes enterprise value—through misapplication, through ceilings, through repetition, through financial mismanagement—produces the opposite condition. Effort increases while results flatten or decline. Capable people leave, coordination deteriorates, and the enterprise works harder to produce less as the gap between investment and return widens with each cycle.

What struck me across these enterprises was not that some succeeded and others failed. It was that the difference between them could not be located in any single function, any single decision, or any single initiative. The difference operated across the entire enterprise at once. Something beneath the visible activity was either converting potential into performance or absorbing it before performance could form—and that something responded directly to how the enterprise was led.

This raised a question I could not answer with conventional language. If leadership determines whether an enterprise compounds or consumes, what exactly is being compounded or consumed? It is not effort alone—the struggling enterprises were full of effort. Credible strategies that never converted ruled out strategy as the explanation. Capable people were present on both sides of the divide, which ruled out talent. Something else was moving through these enterprises, and leadership was either directing that movement or obstructing it.

ENTERPRISE ENERGY AND ENTERPRISE VALUE

Every enterprise operates with a finite capacity for coordinated action, whether leaders name it or not. That capacity is enterprise energy: the combined potential of people, knowledge, systems, capital, and technology organized into motion. When this energy is connected and directed, execution operates as a whole, and performance progresses without constant intervention. Obstruction or absorption by misaligned structure slows execution regardless of team capability or stated priorities.

Most enterprise leaders believe they are governing people, processes, and technology. In practice, what is being governed is the movement of enterprise energy across the enterprise's interacting parts—its people, its structure, its execution, its customers, and its financial discipline. The enterprise behaves as it does depending on whether this energy converts across relationships or becomes trapped between misaligned parts of the system. What appears as smooth progress or persistent pressure is a consequence of how potential moves, not how hard individuals work.

The Enterprise Energy Definition

> **Enterprise Energy** is the total usable capacity of the enterprise to perform coherent, purposeful work—the combined human, structural, informational, financial, and technological resources operating in balance to create, amplify, and protect enterprise value.

For much of the twentieth century, enterprise performance was interpreted through an inputs-and-outputs model. Labor and materials entered the system, production transformed them, and finished goods exited. Value was assumed to be created by increasing efficiency within that transformation. This logic fit an era dominated by physical production, linear processes, and relatively stable conditions.

Modern enterprises still rely on inputs, but their performance cannot be explained by inputs and outputs alone. Enterprise value now emerges from coordination, interpretation, timing, learning, and interaction across people, systems, customers, and platforms. Enterprise Energy accounts for this shift by making visible how effectively effort, information, and capability move together as the system operates.

Enterprise Energy as Interpretive Construct

Enterprise Energy is an interpretive construct, not a physical measurement. It describes what leaders observe when the enterprise's combined capacity operates as a coordinated whole—and what they observe when that capacity fragments, disperses, or becomes trapped between misaligned parts of the system. The language of energy, conversion, and loss is borrowed from physical systems because it names what leaders already observe: capacity that is available, directed, converted, or consumed as the enterprise moves.

The parallel does not extend to quantification. Enterprise Energy cannot be measured in standard units the way electrical current or thermal energy can. It is inferred from the behavior the enterprise produces—the pace at which work converts, the consistency with which decisions advance, the degree to which effort produces proportional return. These are observable conditions, not instrument readings. The construct earns its place through what it makes visible: once enterprise energy is recognized as a system-level property, patterns that appeared unrelated resolve into expressions of a single operating condition.

What Enterprise Energy provides is integration—the ability to connect observations across the enterprise's interacting parts into a coherent account of enterprise condition, to distinguish effort that converts from effort that is absorbed, and to explain why enterprises with comparable resources produce divergent outcomes. What it does not provide is numerical measurement, and it does not require it. The construct operates at the level of structural interpretation—the level at which leadership decisions are made and enterprise condition is read.

Enterprise Energy: What Leaders See

Enterprise Energy appears to leaders as execution capacity. It is the capability that moves through people, processes, systems, and decisions as work advances. Execution progresses without continual correction where that capacity is available and aligned. When it becomes constrained or dispersed, effort fails to convert into results even when direction is clear.

Leaders encounter this distinction daily. Teams that advance work steadily and teams that lag behind targets often operate under comparable direction and comparable effort. Some decisions resolve quickly; others linger unresolved for months, with no visible difference in urgency. These differences are structural, not motivational. They reflect how enterprise energy is distributed, constrained, and converted across the enterprise.

Enterprise Value

Enterprise Energy describes what the enterprise carries. Enterprise Value describes what that carrying produces.

Enterprise value has already been operating in this chapter, as the thing that leadership either compounds or consumes. The definition that follows gives that observation structural precision.

> **Enterprise Value** is the capacity of an enterprise to produce, sustain, and renew meaningful outcomes over time. It emerges from the coherent interaction of people, structure, execution, customer experience, and financial discipline, and is preserved when the creation, amplification, and protection of enterprise value operate in balance.

While enterprise value is not limited to financial outcomes, it is ultimately expressed through them. Over time, the enterprise's ability to create, amplify, and protect enterprise value shapes valuation, market capitalization, and the cash flows available to owners. Financial measures do not define enterprise value on their own, but they reveal whether the system is producing value that persists rather than appearing briefly.

In practice, enterprise value is what remains when performance can be sustained, transferred, and relied upon—not merely achieved in isolated periods.

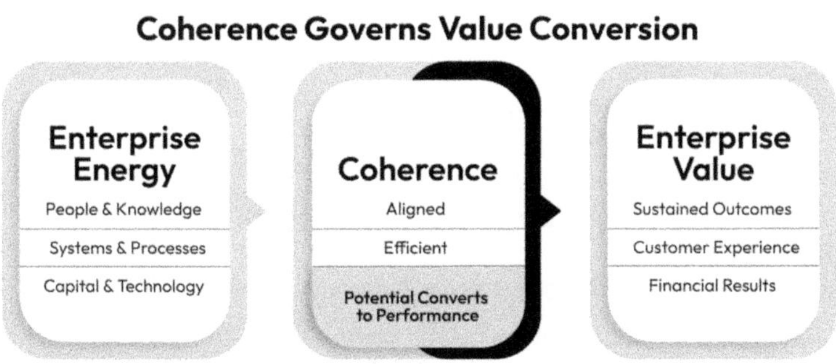

Figure 2.1

Enterprise energy moving through coherent structure compounds enterprise value—how much potential converts, how execution advances, and how reliably outcomes are sustained as conditions change. Weakening coherence redirects that energy into conflict, delay, and rework.

THE ENTERPRISE VALUE FUNCTION DUALITIES: HOW VALUE IS CREATED AND DESTROYED

Enterprise value does not move in a single direction. It is shaped by constructive forces that create, amplify, and protect enterprise value, and by countervailing forces that destroy, dilute, or erode enterprise value over time. These forces operate simultaneously, not sequentially, and their interaction determines whether enterprise value accumulates, stabilizes, or diminishes.

> **Enterprise Value Function Dualities** describe the paired constructive and destructive forces through which enterprise value is either compounded or depleted over time. For every constructive enterprise value function—Create, Amplify, and Protect—there is a corresponding counterforce—Destroy, Dilute, and Erode—that is simultaneously present within the enterprise system at the same time[1].

Create, Amplify, and Protect compound enterprise value when coherence is sustained. Destroy, Dilute, and Erode deplete enterprise value when coherence weakens. Enterprise performance reflects the relative strength of these opposing motions.

The Constructive Enterprise Value Functions

Every enterprise expresses three fundamental motions that determine how effectively potential is converted into enterprise value. These motions are always present—system behaviors rather than departments, initiatives, or phases of a plan. They appear wherever coherence is sustained and weaken wherever it erodes. Together, they describe how enterprise value is produced, expanded, and preserved.

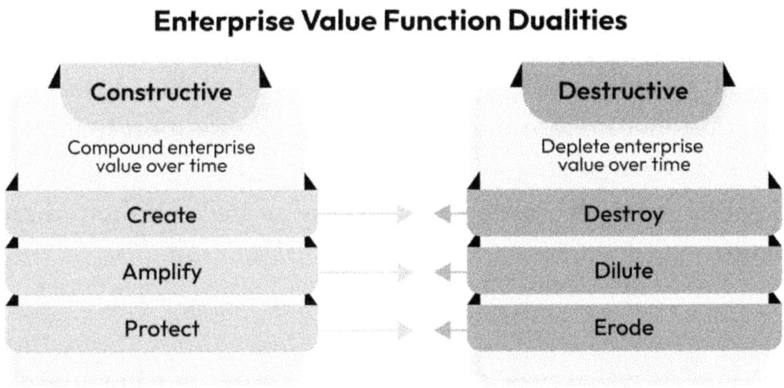

Figure 2.2

1. Create

Create occurs when ideas, effort, and resources are converted into new enterprise value—new customers, new capabilities, new capacity, and new opportunities. It is visible when the enterprise brings something into existence that did not previously exist, whether through innovation, initial execution, problem resolution, or first-time coordination. Creation expands the range of outcomes the enterprise can produce.

2. Amplify

Amplify extends existing enterprise value by strengthening integration, coordination, and execution across the enterprise. It converts isolated success into sustained performance by reducing repetition, aligning pathways, and reinforcing what already functions. Amplification increases enterprise value by converting reuse, consistency, and scale into compounding performance rather than repeated reinvention.

3. Protect

Protect preserves enterprise value already created by maintaining the conditions required for viability under pressure. It operates through economic discipline, governance, trust, and stability, ensuring that growth does not undermine the structures that support it. Protection operates as stewardship—preventing enterprise value from being diminished through overextension or neglect—rather than as restraint.

THESE FUNCTIONS APPEAR across the enterprise, but not uniformly: Different parts of the system carry different concentrations of creation, amplification, and protection. None operates independently, and none is optional.

Create, Amplify, and Protect in balance produce a coherent system. Enterprise value accumulates predictably, effort converts rather than dissipates, and capability strengthens rather than fragments. Imbalance—creation outpacing protection, amplification failing to keep pace with strategy—progressively weakens enterprise value through repetition, instability, and divergence.

These enterprise value functions make performance structurally legible. Seen this way, the forces that govern enterprise value—creation, expansion, preservation, and destruction—become visible as interacting dynamics rather than surface conditions.

The Destructive Enterprise Value Functions

Every enterprise works to create, amplify, and protect enterprise value. These constructive functions describe how potential is converted into outcomes, extended through integration and scale, and preserved over time. They represent the enterprise's capacity to impose structure, coordination, and continuity on its activity.

The Natural Order of enterprise behavior also includes opposing forces. When coherence weakens and the Protect function can no longer sustain structural integrity, countervailing motions appear. These motions are not deliberate actions or failures of intent. They appear as structural consequences—recurring wherever coordination and containment weaken as activity scales and interdependence increases.

Coherent structure contains dispersion and preserves continuity across the system. Weakening coherence releases three destructive motions—Destroy, Dilute, and Erode. These motions destroy enterprise value by fragmenting effort, dispersing energy, and replacing coordinated activity with inconsistency. They emerge wherever constructive enterprise value functions can no longer counterbalance loss of structure.

Every enterprise exists in constant tension between structure and dispersion. Enterprise performance depends on whether Create, Amplify, and Protect consistently counteract destructive motions, or loss of coordination accumulates faster than structure can contain it.

1. Destroy

Destroy is the sudden collapse of enterprise value through acute structural failure. It appears when essential containment gives way and the enterprise can no longer carry the activity moving through it. Destroy is the most visible and least subtle of the destructive motions because its effects are immediate and unmistakable. It surfaces when operational failure halts delivery, a governance breach erodes trust, a safety or product failure requires remediation, reputational damage erases accumulated equity, or a system outage interrupts revenue generation. Destroy consumes enterprise value at once. It signals catastrophic loss that requires recovery rather than refinement and indicates that structural integrity has failed completely.

2. Dilute

Dilute is the most common destructive motion and the most frequently underestimated. It appears when enterprise value spreads too thin to reinforce itself. Dilution emerges as effort disperses across competing priorities, processes fail to integrate, information accumulates in isolated pockets, initiatives overlap or conflict, and metrics reward local success at the expense of enterprise outcomes. In dilution, enterprise value is not lost suddenly but consumed gradually through dispersion. What could have been amplified becomes redundant effort, repeated work, and secondary activity. Over time, dilution prevents scale even when surface indicators appear stable.

3. Erode

Erode is gradual decay—the slow reduction of capability, relevance, or performance over time. Unlike Destroy, which is sudden, or Dilute, which is diffuse, erosion accumulates quietly and often goes unnoticed. It appears as processes age beyond current work, skills fall behind evolving demand, customer experience weakens incrementally, quality declines across cycles, decision timing slows, and unresolved issues recur. Erosion reflects sustained loss of renewal and maintenance. Left unaddressed, erosion compounds until it manifests as dilution or culminates in destruction.

These destructive enterprise value functions operate alongside the constructive ones at all times. Under coherent structure, Create, Amplify, and Protect counterbalance them. As coherence weakens, Destroy, Dilute, and Erode consume enterprise value faster than it can be renewed. These destructive motions reveal where enterprise value is being consumed rather than compounded and point directly to the structural conditions under which loss of coordination takes hold.

These six functions are not proposed as an exhaustive logical taxonomy but as the functions that appeared consistently across the fieldwork—the observable motions through which enterprise value was created, extended, preserved, consumed, dispersed, or diminished. Other characterizations are possible. Value may transform in character, concentrate in fewer nodes, or transfer between stakeholders. These motions can be described through the six functions already named: Transformation is creation in a new form; concentration is selective amplification; transfer is a redistribution that either preserves or erodes enterprise value, depending on whether coherence is maintained through the exchange. The six functions are sufficient to describe the observed dynamics. Each alternative proposed —transformation, concentration, transfer—resolves into a combination of the already established functions.

The Enterprise Value Balance: Structural Equilibrium

Enterprise condition reflects the relative influence of two sets of forces operating at the same time. Where Create, Amplify, and Protect exert greater influence, enterprise value strengthens and capacity expands; where Destroy, Dilute, and Erode predominate, enterprise value becomes harder to preserve and sustained performance is less certain. Across the fieldwork, this balance was present in every enterprise observed—expressed in how enterprise value accumulated or was consumed over time.

Leadership Implications

What distinguishes enterprises at the system level is how these opposing forces are regulated—and across the fieldwork, that regulation is traced back to leadership. The enterprises observed differed not because their leaders intended different outcomes, but because constructive and destructive enterprise value functions operated with different relative strength. In some, creation outpaced destruction. In others, dilution absorbed what amplification produced. In still others, protection maintained capability without constraining renewal. These relationships determined whether enterprise value accumulated, stabilized, or diminished as the system operated.

Regulating Polarity

Every enterprise operates under persistent opposition between enterprise value creation and enterprise value destruction. Capacity increases as constructive forces strengthen relative to destructive ones; constraint appears when that balance reverses and destructive forces accumulate faster than structure can counterbalance them. Changes in system state follow this relationship, not stated intent.

Enterprises that sustained enterprise value over time shared a recognizable pattern: Destructive forces were identified early and structurally constrained before they overwhelmed constructive motion. This directed attention to the conditions that weaken coherence—the conditions under which destructive dynamics take hold—without assigning blame, prescribing action, or implying failure.

The dualities describe what happens—enterprise value compounded or consumed, constructive and destructive forces in persistent opposition. They do not yet explain why the destructive side gains ground. Across the fieldwork, the answer was consistent: Coherence weakens under identifiable structural forces present in every enterprise observed, which intensify as scale, interdependence, and complexity increase. Those forces follow a recognizable sequence. What follows names them.

FORCES THAT WEAKEN COHERENCE

Coherence does not weaken randomly. Across enterprises, the same structural forces appear wherever the enterprise's operating condition deteriorates—recurring with enough consistency to be named. As enterprises grow, develop, and encounter new conditions, misalignment accumulates unless it is recognized and interpreted at the structural level. Coherence is not a fixed achievement but a condition that must be re-established as the enterprise continues to move.

These forces cannot be removed from the system—only observed, interpreted, and structurally regulated. What follows names the primary ways coherence weakens as enterprise activity increases in scale, density, and interdependence.

1. Structural Resistance

Every enterprise encounters resistance to motion. Some resistance is productive, exposing weak assumptions, surfacing gaps, and sharpening design. Structural resistance becomes problematic when it exceeds what the system can absorb and begins to require increasing effort simply to sustain existing outcomes.

> **Structural Resistance** describes the degree to which the enterprise's design impedes the movement of work, decisions, and information. It reflects the extra effort required to achieve the same outcome due to misfit, misalignment, or poorly configured interfaces[2].

As structural resistance rises, it becomes evident through persistent signals: meetings multiply, clarifications repeat, exceptions accumulate, cycles lengthen, and coordination burden increases. Work continues to be converted into outcomes, but only through compensatory effort as the system works around misfit rather than being carried by structure.

Structural resistance increases as information crosses excessive boundaries, processes accumulate exceptions and workarounds, decision authority loses clear definition, and shared goals are interpreted differently across domains. Under these conditions, meaning must be repeatedly renegotiated, and motion slows as dependency density increases.

Under the opposite conditions—clearly defined interfaces, processes that reflect actual work, information that propagates without distortion, and domains operating from a consistent interpretation of intent—structure carries load that would otherwise be absorbed manually.

Structural resistance does not indicate failure. It signals where coherence is weakening and where the enterprise's design is beginning to lose alignment with the work it supports.

Forces That Weaken Coherence

Force	Structural Description	Primary System Signal
Structural Resistance	Enterprise design impedes the movement of work, decisions, and information, requiring additional effort to achieve the same outcomes.	Rising coordination burden, repeated clarification, increasing effort without proportional gain.
Destructive Polarity	Opposing forces cease reinforcing one another and instead cancel their effect, converting natural tension into systemic opposition.	Persistent disagreement, competing priorities, energy expenditure without forward progress.
Structural Interests	Individuals or groups benefit from current arrangements of authority, information access, resource allocation, or decision rights in ways that resist structural renewal—even when renewal would restore coherence.	Sustained resistance to reorganization, repeated deferral of structural correction, renewal blocked where authority or resources would be redistributed.
Structural Misfit	Enterprise structure no longer aligns with current operational and relational demands, forcing work to rely on compensatory effort rather than design.	Improvisation, workarounds, decisions settling at inappropriate levels, loss of execution consistency.
Structural Decay	Prolonged loss of fit between structure and reality as misalignment persists, reducing the system's ability to carry work coherently.	Gradual degradation of coordination, reliability, and capacity without a single point of failure.

Table 2.2

2. Destructive Polarity

Every enterprise operates within inherent tensions. It must move quickly without becoming brittle, adapt without undermining reliability, and grant autonomy without losing coordination. When the system can sustain these tensions, adaptation and learning continue. Destructive Polarity emerges when that balance collapses.

> **Destructive Polarity** describes a condition in which opposing forces cease reinforcing one another and instead cancel each other's effect. Energy is expended, but conversion weakens. The enterprise remains active, yet forward progress diminishes.

As destructive polarity intensifies, it becomes visible through recurring patterns rather than isolated events. Competing priorities remain unresolved, discussions repeat without conclusion, strategic direction shifts across cycles, metrics reward opposing behaviors, and domains operate at cross-purposes. Effort persists, but enterprise value no longer compounds.

Destructive polarity signals that enterprise design can no longer contain tensions that were previously productive. As shared interpretation weakens, domains stop reinforcing one another and begin pulling in opposing directions.

3. Structural Interests

The forces described so far—structural resistance, destructive polarity—operate as conditions that weaken coherence through accumulated misfit. A different force operates alongside them, which is present in every enterprise of sufficient scale and rarely named: the persistence of arrangements that serve the interests of the people and groups who occupy them, regardless of whether those arrangements serve the enterprise as a whole.

> **Structural Interests** describe the condition in which individuals or groups within the enterprise benefit from the current arrangement of authority, information access, resource allocation, or decision rights in ways that resist structural renewal—even when that renewal would restore coherence across the system.

Structural interests do not require intent to obstruct. They operate through the ordinary mechanisms of enterprise behavior: accumulated authority that individuals are reluctant to redistribute, information advantages that confer influence, budget allocations that define departmental standing, and decision rights that establish professional identity. These conditions are not aberrations, but consequences of how enterprises distribute resources and responsibility over time.

Across the fieldwork, structural interests appeared wherever coherence had weakened and persisted uncorrected. An enterprise with redundant reporting layers that consumed coordination capacity retained those layers because the individuals staffing them held authority that would disappear under consolidation. A sales function that resisted pricing reform did so because existing arrangements protected commission structures that would not survive structural realignment. A leadership team that continued funding a product line producing declining returns maintained the allocation because discontinuing it would redistribute headcount and budget away from the executive sponsoring it.

In each case, the enterprise's operating condition had changed, renewal was structurally indicated, and the arrangements that would need to change served identifiable interests within the system. What persisted was not active sabotage but sustained resistance to renewal —a condition in which the enterprise continued compensating for misfit rather than correcting it, because the cost of correction was distributed differently than the cost of compensation.

Structural interests compound the effects of the other forces that weaken coherence. Resistance becomes self-reinforcing when the people experiencing it benefit from the conditions producing it.

Destructive polarity persists when the opposing forces are anchored in competing interests that neither side has reason to concede. Once structural interests take root, misfit accumulates faster—the structural renewal that would restore correspondence threatens the positions of those whose authority was shaped by the prior arrangement.

Recognizing structural interests as a force that weakens coherence does not assign blame. It identifies a condition that is present in every enterprise of sufficient scale and that compounds every other form of coherence loss described in this chapter. Enterprises that sustain coherence over time do so in part because their structures periodically redistribute authority, information, and access to resources as operating conditions change—accepting the internal friction of redistribution as a cost of renewal, rather than preserving existing arrangements at the cost of systemic correspondence.

4. Structural Misfit

Every enterprise depends on the fit between its design and the work it must carry. Where that fit is sustained, work and decisions are consistent—roles are clear, interfaces support coordination, and routines reinforce stable execution.

As conditions change, however, design and reality begin to separate. The structure that once matched the enterprise's scale, scope, or environment no longer fits the work it is being asked to support.

> **Structural Misfit** describes the condition in which enterprise design no longer aligns with current operational and relational demands. The enterprise continues functioning, but its structure no longer supports coherent motion. Work relies increasingly on compensatory effort rather than structural support.

Structural misfit appears gradually and is first recognized through recurring operational signals rather than discrete breakdowns. Workflows require repeated explanation, decisions settle at inappropriate levels, teams improvise to bridge structural gaps, and customer expectations exceed existing routines. These signals indicate a lack of fit between structure and work.

Structural misfit emerges when the enterprise evolves, but design remains anchored to an earlier cycle. Scale increases, technology advances, coordination density rises, and interfaces multiply while structure remains unchanged.

As misfit intensifies, domains lose alignment, processes lose carrying capacity, execution becomes inconsistent, and customer experience grows less predictable. Enterprise value becomes harder to protect because coherence no longer operates across the system.

Structural misfit marks the threshold where renewal becomes necessary rather than optional.

5. Structural Decay

No enterprise remains structurally aligned by default. Growth, turnover, increased scale, and accumulated complexity place ongoing pressure on design. What once supported coordination gradually begins to constrain it.

> **Structural Decay** describes the gradual loss of fit between the enterprise's structure and its current operating reality. As conditions change, the design that once supported coherent motion becomes increasingly misaligned. The system still functions, but it does so with rising resistance and diminishing ability to carry the work[3].

Structural decay becomes visible as processes no longer match how work is performed, interfaces lose reliability, routines lose meaning, and structural definition weakens across domains. These patterns indicate accumulated misalignment rather than isolated breakdown.

What differentiates sustained enterprise performance is whether structural renewal keeps pace with change. Enterprises that renew deliberately preserve coherence. Enterprises that compensate instead absorb rising resistance and steadily destroy enterprise value[4].

The Coherence Breakdown Progression

Enterprise coherence weakens in a recognizable sequence, and the earlier that sequence is identified, the lower the cost of restoring structural fit. Each stage produces observable signals that distinguish it from the others.

It begins with rising resistance, where greater effort is required to achieve the same outcomes. Meetings multiply, exception handling increases, clarification cycles lengthen, and coordination overhead rises—typically within months of the triggering misfit.

As resistance accumulates, destructive polarity appears, and natural tensions stop reinforcing performance. Teams begin operating on competing assumptions, priorities diverge across functions, and disagreements surface in execution rather than in conversation. At this stage, structural intervention can still arrest the progression.

Structural interests then anchor the resulting arrangements—individuals and groups whose authority, resources, or standing depend on the existing design resist the renewal that would correct it. Interests become visible as resistance to specific changes rather than as general organizational friction; information gatekeeping and decision routing begin serving positional preservation rather than enterprise function.

Structural misfit follows as design loses alignment with work and correction is deferred. By this stage, the enterprise is operating on borrowed structural margin, and restoration requires deliberate architectural correction rather than incremental adjustment.

When misfit persists without renewal, structural decay takes hold, and enterprise value destruction accelerates. The cost of restoration at this stage exceeds the cost of the original misfit, because the enterprise must now correct structure, rebuild interpretive conditions, and restore trust simultaneously.

The progression does not describe inevitable failure. It describes the sequence through which coherence weakens when the enterprise does not structurally respond to what these forces produce. At every stage prior to structural decay, renewal can arrest the progression—

but the form of renewal required escalates with each stage, and the window for low-cost correction narrows.

The Coherence Breakdown Progression

Stage	Structural Condition	Observable System Effect
1	Structural Resistance	Increasing effort required to achieve the same outcomes as structure begins impeding the movement of work, decisions, and information.
2	Destructive Polarity	Natural tensions cease reinforcing performance and instead cancel one another, causing energy expenditure without forward progress.
3	Structural Interests	Existing arrangements serve the interests of occupants, resisting the renewal that would restore coherence
4	Structural Misfit	Enterprise design no longer aligns with current operational and relational demands; work relies on compensatory effort rather than structural support.
5	Structural Decay	Prolonged loss of structural integrity as misfit persists; coordination weakens and the system functions with rising resistance and diminishing capacity.
6	Enterprise Value Destruction	Cumulative outcome in which enterprise value can no longer be sustained, preserved, or renewed due to unresolved coherence loss.

Table 2.3

Structural Interests and the Political Economy of Coherence

Structural interests warrant further examination because they resist correction differently than the other forces that weaken coherence. The arrangement that produces current performance also produces the positions from which that performance is governed, and those positions carry interests that are structurally embedded in the current architecture. Renewal alters architecture, altered architecture redistributes access, and redistribution encounters resistance from positions favored by the current architecture. The people positioned to recognize that renewal is necessary are often those whose positional interests are most affected by the changes it would require. Information that would surface the need for renewal may be filtered, reinterpreted, or delayed by the same decision pathways that renewal would restructure.

Structural interests operate through several predictable mechanisms. Information gatekeeping occurs when those who control access to performance data, customer signals, or execution intelligence shape what leadership sees—not through deliberate deception, but through the tendency to present conditions through the lens that preserves current authority. Decision routing concentrates when renewal threatens to redistribute decision rights, and existing holders slow or complicate the routing to preserve their position. Coalition formation solidifies as groups whose interests are served by the current architecture align to resist changes that would redistribute access, even when those changes would restore coherence across the system.

The consequence for the Five Enterprise Domains System is direct: Recognizing that the enterprise is a system in motion is necessary but not sufficient. Leaders must also recognize that the system contains interests that resist the renewal it requires. A framework that diagnoses structural misfit without accounting for the structural interests that prevent its correction produces accurate diagnosis and incomplete action.

Renewal that ignores structural interests is blocked or absorbed. Renewal that addresses them—by accounting for the redistribution of authority, information, and access that structural changes produce—creates change that persists because it simultaneously realigns the architecture and the interests embedded within it.

RENEWAL AS STRUCTURAL NECESSITY

Renewal is the enterprise's structural response to misfit. It is not a finite reaction or an event-specific corrective effort; it is the ongoing work of refreshing enterprise design so that fit is restored and coherent motion is sustained as conditions change. As enterprises grow, evolve, and encounter new demands, misfit accumulates unless structure is deliberately renewed—making renewal the continuous counterpart to the forces described in the preceding section.

Enterprises that sustain coherence share a common pattern: Their structures are periodically realigned. Interfaces are adjusted, information pathways clarified, and decision logic updated as operating reality changes. Renewal preserves alignment between the Natural Order of enterprise behavior and the conditions the enterprise inhabits. Without it, structure gradually loses its ability to carry work coherently.

Renewal Defined

> **Renewal** is the enterprise's capacity to restore coherence by adapting structure, routines, and interfaces in response to misfit as conditions change. It sustains the enterprise's ability to create, amplify, and protect enterprise value by ensuring that design continues to match scale, interdependence, and environment.

When renewal is absent, misfit accumulates. Interfaces lose reliability, processes lose relevance, coordination weakens, and the system no longer matches the work it is expected to carry.

Why Renewal Matters

Enterprises that renew continuously remain aligned as conditions change. Structure adjusts before misfit compounds, and routines update before inconsistency hardens into failure—coherence is maintained without requiring crisis to force correction.

Renewal that occurs only after breakdown produces a different result. Motion returns without reliability, accumulated misfit is corrected without addressing its source, and the conditions that produced incoherence remain intact. The distinction is between coherence sustained through continuous adjustment and coherence recovered after its loss: the first compounds, the second repeats. Renewal is distinct from the corrective activities that enterprises routinely perform. Process correction addresses inefficiency within existing structure; renewal asks whether the structure itself still fits the work it must carry. Transitional coordination moves people through known changes, but renewal identifies that the change is structurally necessary before the enterprise has named it. Incident resolution corrects specific failures, whereas renewal addresses the conditions that made failure structurally probable. Each of these activities may accompany renewal, but none constitutes it. Renewal operates at the level of structural fit—the relationship between enterprise design and the conditions that design must serve.

The Pattern of Renewal

Renewal follows a repeatable pattern of reassessment. What distinguishes renewal is continuity—the persistent examination of whether enterprise design still matches the work it must support—rather than any fixed cadence.

Renewal present in the enterprise sustains coherence; absent renewal, misfit compounds and enterprise value destruction accelerates.

STEWARDSHIP AND THE LEADERSHIP ROLE

What this chapter has constructed—enterprise energy, enterprise value, the forces that weaken coherence, and the necessity of renewal—converges on a single structural position: the leader. The domains are already active wherever enterprise work, decisions, and relationships advance, and what distinguishes enterprises that sustain coherence is whether leadership maintains fit, connection, and reinforcement across them rather than attempting to control each one in isolation.

Stewardship is the ongoing responsibility of keeping the enterprise aligned with its Natural Order as conditions change. It is visible in how leaders notice, interpret, and respond to the signals the system produces, and in their willingness to adjust structure, refresh interfaces, and sustain renewal so that information, intent, and learning continue to move reliably across the enterprise.

Stewardship carries structural weight. It is visible in enterprises where behavior is monitored and intervention occurs at the level of design and relationship as coherence begins to weaken—not in enterprises where leadership reacts to symptoms after misfit has already taken hold.

Leadership effectiveness is expressed through the conditions leaders maintain. Enterprise behavior emerges from the interaction of people, processes, execution, customer signals, and financial discipline, and enterprise condition depends on whether these elements remain aligned and mutually reinforcing as the system operates.

Coherence does not persist without attention. It is preserved where fit between structure and work is maintained, where behaviors that create enterprise value are supported by ones that preserve enterprise value, and where the enterprise's interacting parts operate as a single, interdependent system rather than in isolation.

Stewardship present in the enterprise keeps motion coordinated; structure, connection, and renewal stay aligned with how work moves. Without it, alignment weakens over time as structure no longer fits the work it is required to carry, connections lose reliability, and the Natural Order of the enterprise loses coherence as a consequence of unattended misfit.

THIS CHAPTER ESTABLISHED that enterprises signal their condition long before the results record the cost. Value, energy, and breakdown become visible upstream, revealing coherence or misfit well in advance of performance metrics. Leaders sense these signals, but recognition alone raises a practical question they cannot ignore: Where do these signals originate, and why do their effects propagate so quickly across the enterprise?

Chapter 3 introduces the Natural Order of Enterprise Behavior—the system-level reality that explains why these patterns are inevitable, how coherence forms or collapses, and why enterprises move the way they do, long before results become visible.

Endnotes

1. The Five Enterprise Domains System proposes that enterprise value moves through six integrated functions organized as three complementary dualities: Create/Amplify/Protect and Destroy/Dilute/Erode. This is a novel theoretical contribution. Individual dynamics of creation, amplification, protection, destruction, dilution, and erosion appear throughout management, economic, and organizational literature, but no prior framework integrates them as complementary value-function dualities. This framing here treats these six functions as inherent to all enterprise behavior—the system cannot eliminate the destructive polarity; it can only manage the ratio of value-building to value-degrading forces.
2. The concept of resistance within organizations has a long history, most prominently in the change management literature. Michael T. Hannan and John Freeman introduced the theory of structural inertia, arguing that organizations develop internal resistance to change as a byproduct of reliability and accountability. See Hannan and Freeman, "Structural Inertia and Organizational Change," *American Sociological Review* 49, no. 2 (1984): 149–64. That literature frames resistance as an organizational response to proposed change—people and systems resisting transformation. Structural resistance as used here describes something different: how the enterprise's design itself impedes the movement of work, decisions, and information, regardless of whether change is being attempted. It is an engineering concept applied to enterprise architecture—impedance in the system's design—rather than a behavioral response to disruption.
3. The concept of organizational decay has been explored by several scholars, most notably Howard S. Schwartz in *Narcissistic Process and Corporate Decay: The Theory of the Organization Ideal* (New York: New York University Press, 1990). Schwartz examines how narcissistic organizational dynamics produce institutional decline. The broader literature on organizational decline treats decay as a pathological condition of institutional deterioration. Structural decay, as defined here, is more specific and less pathological: It describes the gradual, natural loss of fit between an enterprise's structure and its current operating reality as conditions evolve. It is framed not as dysfunction but as an inevitable characteristic of living systems—design decays as conditions change, requiring ongoing renewal to restore coherence.
4. The concept of organizational and strategic renewal is well-established. Rajshree Agarwal and Constance E. Helfat provided a comprehensive treatment in "Strategic Renewal of Organizations," *Organization Science* 20, no. 2 (2009): 281–93.

Michael Tushman and Charles O'Reilly have written extensively on strategic renewal through organizational ambidexterity—the ability to simultaneously exploit existing capabilities and explore new ones. That literature frames renewal as episodic strategic transformation or as a capability to be developed through leadership design. Structural renewal, as used here, is more specific: It describes the ongoing, continuous recalibration of processes, interfaces, roles, and economic architecture required to restore fit as conditions evolve. It is not an initiative or a transformation program; it is a necessary response to the natural decay of fit in living systems.

3

THE NATURAL ORDER OF ENTERPRISE BEHAVIOR

THE NATURAL ORDER OF THE ENTERPRISE

Every enterprise operates as a system long before anyone attempts to manage it. Well before org charts, budgets, or job descriptions exist, work is being coordinated through relationships that have no formal name, decisions are moving through paths no chart describes, customers are responding to an experience no one designed as a whole, resources are constrained by commitments already made, and learning is either compounding or being lost. These patterns arise from coordination itself, not from intention or design. They are the mechanics of enterprise behavior—observable across the industries, scales, and leadership conditions encountered in the fieldwork—and they determine whether effort compounds or disperses across competing directions.

The order is already present. It governs how the enterprise converts effort into outcome, whether anyone has named it or not. The Five Enterprise Domains, introduced in the next section, do not create this order; they make it visible. What this section establishes is the condition the reader already recognizes: an enterprise that behaves as a system before anyone attempts to describe it as one.

> **Enterprise System** describes the enterprise operating as a unified whole—the totality of its domain interaction, relational field participation, and structural behavior governed by the Natural Order. References to "the system" mean this: the enterprise as an integrated, continuous pattern of motion across its five domains and three relational fields, producing enterprise value through their interaction. The Enterprise System is the enterprise as it operates when its structural behavior is read as a whole rather than decomposed into parts.

Most leaders recognize these dynamics before they can name them. They notice teams working hard without moving together, tension accumulating in meetings without a clear source, progress in one area quietly negating progress in another, and decisions that make sense in isolation colliding in practice. These signals originate at a structural level that most leadership frameworks do not reach—deeper than people problems or process issues. What shows up as behavior is the surface expression of structural misalignment.

The enterprise is already behaving as a system. The structure producing these patterns has no name in most leadership vocabularies, and effort and intelligence alone cannot resolve what they cannot describe. Without that name, the same conditions recur, the same corrective responses repeat, and the same explanations fall short.

This chapter establishes that Natural Order. Not the individual domains—those are examined individually in Chapters 6 through 10—but the system that ties them together. This is the architecture beneath execution: the structure that shapes behavior, governs coherence, and explains why leadership approaches built for the twentieth century fail inside twenty-first-century enterprises. The sections that follow name the system, locate it historically, and prepare the reader to interpret enterprise behavior through it rather than around it.

THE FIVE ENTERPRISE DOMAINS DEFINED

The Structural Architecture of Coherence

Coherence emerges from structure—not from luck, leadership charisma, or the accumulation of good intentions. Every enterprise contains a limited number of interdependent systems of activity that determine how it performs, learns, and sustains enterprise value. The Five Enterprise Domains name these systems and make visible the Natural Order that already governs how purpose is interpreted, work is carried, execution is tested, experience is received, and economic consequences are accumulated. What appears emergent or unpredictable becomes readable as a consequence of the system's arrangement.

Each domain contributes to the creation, amplification, and protection of enterprise value, but not evenly or identically. Their influence varies by position and interaction, not by leadership intent. Taken together, the domains form a continuous system of exchange—how the enterprise converts resources into performance and performance into renewal. Coherence persists not because any single domain performs at its theoretical maximum, but because the interaction between them remains consistent.

The Performance Topology of the Enterprise

The Five Enterprise Domains operate simultaneously, not sequentially. Their interaction forms the enterprise's performance topology[1]—the structural pattern that determines how enterprise value moves, interacts, and compounds. Mutual alignment across the domains produces a recognizable condition: Effort reinforces itself, coordination remains intact, and performance compounds. As that alignment erodes, the enterprise compensates predictably—meetings multiply, handoffs escalate, reporting expands, exceptions accumulate, and leadership intervention intensifies.

Over time, these compensatory responses increase load rather than restoring coherence. Enterprises that sustain coherence over time exhibit a different pattern. They attend not only to results, but to connection—to how consistently their systems move together and convert effort into outcome. Coherence, understood this way, is the structural condition that emerges when the domains convert effort into outcome rather than into corrective activity—a condition produced by interaction, not by control.

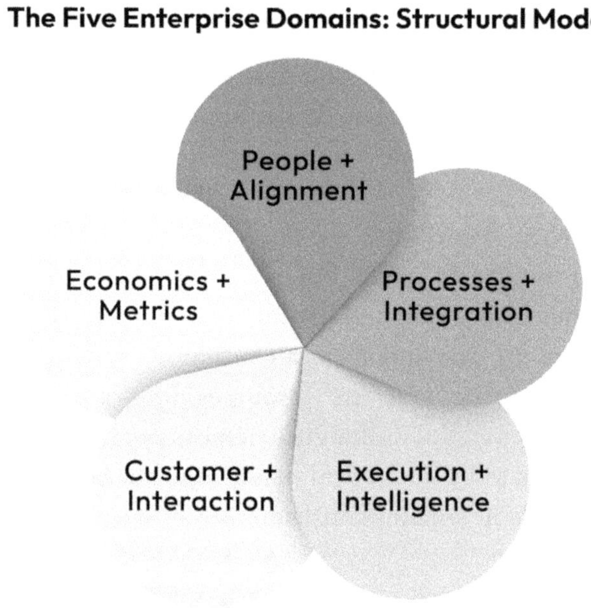

Figure 3.1

The Five Enterprise Domains as Enterprise Systems of Activity

Every enterprise organizes its activity through recurring systems, regardless of how it is designed or what language it uses to describe itself. These systems exist because work must be interpreted, carried, executed, exchanged, and sustained under constraint. Over time, these functions resolve into five distinct but interdependent enterprise domains.

The Five Enterprise Domains function as fields of enterprise activity—not as functional groupings or leadership assignments—through which motion is organized, and coherence is either reinforced or weakened.

1. **People + Alignment** is the domain where interpretation forms—how purpose is understood, expectations propagate, and decision authority is established.
2. **Processes + Integration** is the domain where work is carried—how workflows connect, interfaces function, and structure fits the work it must support.
3. **Execution + Intelligence** is the domain where the system reveals itself under load—how decisions translate into action and what execution exposes about reality.
4. **Customer + Interaction** is the domain where enterprise behavior becomes experience—how consistency, reliability, and delivered value are interpreted by those who benefit from its products and services.
5. **Economics + Metrics** is the domain where constraint is enforced—how resources are allocated, tradeoffs are made, and continuity of enterprise value is sustained.

The Five Enterprise Domains operate simultaneously as overlapping systems of enterprise activity. Coherence does not reside within any single domain, but converges at their intersections—where interpretation, structure, execution, market response, and economic constraint reinforce one another in motion. In Figure 3.1, convergence at the center indicates the zone of systemic coherence.

These domains are always present and always active. Enterprises may emphasize them to different degrees, misunderstand them, or attempt to manage around them, but they cannot remove them. Together, they form the Natural Order through which enterprise behavior takes shape.

The domains are the structure that determines whether solutions produce a lasting effect. What that effect looks like—and what its absence signals—is the subject of the sections that follow.

The Five Enterprise Domains as Systems of Activity

Domain (Dominant EV Function)	System of Activity	Illustrative Enterprise Motions
People + Alignment (Create)	The system through which purpose is interpreted, expectations are formed, and decision authority becomes legible across the enterprise.	Interpretation of purpose, role clarity, leadership signaling, expectation alignment, trust formation.
Processes + Integration (Amplify)	The system through which work is carried—how workflows, interfaces, and structure support the continuous movement of effort without loss or distortion.	Workflow connection, interface design, handoff integrity, integration of systems, structural fit to load.
Execution + Intelligence (Amplify)	The system through which decisions convert into action and reality is revealed through feedback, variability, and learning under load.	Action progression, operational feedback, performance variability, learning cycles, signal capture.
Customer + Interaction (Create)	The system through which enterprise behavior becomes experience and value is interpreted externally by customers and markets.	Experience consistency, value signaling, responsiveness to demand, relationship continuity, market interpretation.
Economics + Metrics (Protect)	The system through which constraint is enforced—how resources, tradeoffs, and measurement sustain continuity of enterprise value over time.	Resource allocation, economic tradeoffs, performance measurement, risk containment, value continuity.

Table 3.1

Why Five Domains and Not Another Number

The question arises naturally: why five? If the domains were observed rather than designed, what prevents a sixth from appearing or two of the five from collapsing into one? The question is structural, and it deserves a structural answer.

Each domain governs a distinct phase of how enterprise energy converts into enterprise value. People + Alignment governs interpretation: how purpose, priority, and expectation form before work begins. Processes + Integration governs carriage: how work, decisions, and information connect and sequence as they advance. Execution + Intelligence governs conversion, the phase where structure becomes motion under real conditions and where that motion reveals what the enterprise actually is. Customer + Interaction governs exchange: how the enterprise's output encounters external response and where value is recognized or rejected. Economics + Metrics governs constraint: how resources are allocated, trade-offs accumulate, and continuity is sustained or consumed.

These five phases are the minimum distinct functions required for enterprise energy to complete a full cycle of conversion—from potential to motion to exchange to renewal. Remove any one, and the cycle breaks. Merge two, and a structural distinction disappears that the enterprise cannot operate without.

Consider the alternatives. If People + Alignment and Processes + Integration were combined, the distinction between interpretation and carriage would collapse. Shared understanding and the structural sequences that carry work would be treated as the same function. Every enterprise I have observed contradicts that merger: Teams that share a common interpretation of purpose still fail when the structure carrying their work loses fit. Alignment and integration are related—one conditions the other—but they are not the same activity, and they do not degrade through the same mechanisms.

If Execution + Intelligence were separated into two domains (one for execution, one for intelligence), the system would lose the connection that makes both functions consequential. Execution without the intelligence it generates is activity without learning—and intelligence that never reaches execution is observation without consequence. Across the fieldwork, these two functions never operated independently. What execution produced and what the enterprise learned from that production were always the same motion, registered at different timescales. Separating them would describe the enterprise as if action and learning occur in different places—but across the fieldwork, they occurred in the same domain, through the same motion, simultaneously.

If a sixth domain were added—strategy, for instance, or technology—the system would require that domain to govern a phase of energy conversion that the existing five do not already cover. Strategy operates through every phase at once: through interpretation in People + Alignment, structural decisions in Processes + Integration, execution choices in Execution + Intelligence, market positioning in Customer + Interaction, and resource allocation in Economics + Metrics. Elevating strategy to domain status would duplicate what the five domains already govern, because strategic activity is distributed across the full conversion cycle rather than concentrated in one phase. The same reasoning applies to technology, data, culture, and every other candidate for a sixth domain that surfaced across the fieldwork: Each one operates through the existing five rather than alongside them.

The number five is therefore neither arbitrary nor theoretical. It represents the minimum number of structurally distinct conversion phases required to account for what enterprise energy does as it moves from potential to enterprise value and back to renewal. Fewer domains collapse distinctions the enterprise cannot afford to lose; additional domains duplicate functions the existing five already perform. Five is the number at which the system accounts for everything observed without redundancy—the point where each domain governs something no other domain governs, and together they cover the full cycle without remainder.

Structural Simultaneity and Directional Dependence

The Five Enterprise Domains exist simultaneously. At any moment, an enterprise is governed by all five at once: interpretation, structure, motion and learning, relationship, and economic constraint are always present. There is no point at which one domain "turns off" while another begins—the simultaneity is structural, describing what the enterprise is at any given time.

> **Structural Simultaneity** is the system property by which all five Enterprise Domains are present and operative at the same time in every moment of enterprise activity. It explains why coherence or misalignment cannot originate in a single domain in isolation, because the enterprise always exists as an integrated whole rather than as sequential parts.

At the same time, the effects of coherence and misalignment do not appear simultaneously. They propagate. While the domains coexist, the consequences of how they function emerge in a consistent order as enterprise activity progresses across domains. Interpretation shapes structure, which in turn shapes motion; motion shapes experience, and experience shapes economic signal. This sequence is directional in consequence, even though no domain ranks above another in importance.

> **Directional Dependence** is the predominant pattern by which the consequences of enterprise activity propagate across domains under sustained operating conditions. Interpretation conditions structure, structure conditions execution, execution conditions customer response, and customer response conditions economic signal. Directional dependence describes the primary causal pathway, not the only one. External events, discontinuities, and downstream shocks can simultaneously restructure conditions across domains.

This sequence appeared consistently across the fieldwork and accounts for why the effects of misalignment are detected downstream from their origin.

As a result, leaders often encounter problems first in customer response or financial results, not because those domains are primary, but because they are where accumulated consequences become visible. Understanding the enterprise therefore requires reading both properties at once: the domains as an interdependent system that exists in full at every moment, and as a directional system in which effects accumulate and become visible over time. Simultaneity explains where coherence resides. Directional dependence explains when its loss becomes observable—though not, as the next section addresses, the only way that loss originates.

Directional Dependence and Reverse Causation

Directional dependence describes how consequences propagate under sustained operating conditions. That sequence—interpretation conditioning structure, structure conditioning execution, and so on through to economic signal—appeared consistently across the fieldwork, across the industries and scales observed.

It does not follow that causation originates exclusively in the first domain. Downstream events can directly restructure the interpretive conditions in People + Alignment without passing through the forward sequence in reverse. A significant customer departure generates new misalignment by disrupting the assumptions on which shared interpretation was formed—the event does not merely reveal what was already present. A regulatory change imposed on Economics + Metrics does not wait for its effects to propagate backward through customer response and execution before altering how people interpret enterprise priorities. The interpretive shift is immediate and direct.

Directional dependence describes the propagation of consequences through the system under its own motion—one causal pathway, not the only one. External events, internal shocks, and discontinuities can enter the system at any domain and restructure conditions across multiple domains simultaneously. When that occurs, the enterprise experiences a system-wide reconfiguration of interpretive, structural, and operational conditions at once—not a sequential cascade.

The distinction matters because leaders who read directional dependence as the only causal pathway will search for upstream origins when the actual cause entered downstream. A financial constraint that forces reallocation of resources across the enterprise does not originate in People + Alignment, even though its effects appear there. Reading the system accurately requires recognizing both properties: Consequences propagate directionally under sustained conditions, and discontinuities can restructure the system from any point of entry. Together, these two system properties produce three structural consequences for leadership. Because all five domains operate simultaneously, leaders cannot address any one domain in isolation. Correcting execution without aligning interpretation or economic discipline will fail because the domains the intervention ignores continue conditioning the one it addresses. Because effects propagate directionally under normal conditions, leaders can read where misfit originates by tracing consequences back through the sequence: Customer inconsistency that traces to execution instability that traces to process misfit that traces to interpretive divergence points to the human domain as the structural origin. And because reverse causation operates through discontinuity rather than through the forward sequence, leaders must distinguish between symptoms that accumulated through directional propagation and conditions that entered the system directly—a distinction that determines whether the correct response is upstream renewal or immediate structural accommodation at the point of entry.

THE FIVE ENTERPRISE DOMAINS AND THE TWENTY-FIRST-CENTURY ENTERPRISE

From Machines to Networks

The Five Enterprise Domains arose from observing how modern enterprises behave: faster, more interconnected, and less predictable than the industrial organizations of the past. The Natural Order of today's enterprise operates as an interconnected system of motion and response, shaped by continuous interaction rather than the fixed sequences that governed industrial production.

For much of the twentieth century, enterprises were designed for a different operating reality—one defined by physical production, linear processes, and relatively stable markets. Enterprise structures and leadership practices were built for predictability, repetition, uniform output, and centralized control, because those conditions made large-scale coordination possible. People were treated primarily as labor, vendors as suppliers, and customers as end users. Coordination relied on hierarchy and formal authority rather than on continuous connection across relationships.

Work moved step by step through fixed functions—strategy downward, reporting upward—and control kept the system operating as a whole. This design excelled at stability, and for most of the twentieth century, stability was the operating problem that mattered.

The twenty-first-century enterprise operates under different conditions. It behaves as an interconnected network—an arrangement of platforms, interfaces, relationships, and exchanges that adjust continuously. Work no longer advances in fixed sequences. It moves across technologies, decisions, and relationships that reconfigure as demand, information, and constraint change.

Just as importantly, the modern enterprise is no longer composed solely of employees. Its performance depends on a wider field of participants—contractors and vendors, service providers and strategic partners, channel alliances, automation systems, and software platforms—that directly participate in enterprise motion. Distributed operations interact continuously with customer-generated signals and data-rich environments, eliminating any stable distinction between organizational roles and relational participation. All of these participants operate within the same field of motion, shaping outcomes as work, decisions, and information advance, whether or not leadership formally recognizes their influence.

Hierarchy did not disappear; it ceased to be the primary organizing force. In the modern enterprise, coordination depends on connection across relationships rather than on control through hierarchy.

Why Old Logic Fails

Industrial-era management logic was designed for the earlier world. It assumed stable demand, clear boundaries, linear cause-and-effect relationships, and top-down oversight. Planning occurred in cycles, and learning followed the same sequential logic. Performance depended on extracting efficiency from well-contained functions.

That logic no longer matches how enterprises operate. Networked enterprises function in real time, with adaptation occurring continuously as conditions change. Learning is recursive rather than sequential, and consequences appear sooner because interdependence transmits effects across the system faster than linear processes ever did. Cause and effect arise from interdependence across teams, technologies, partners, and customers. Enterprise value is rarely created in isolation; it emerges through coordinated interaction across a distributed system.

As interdependence increases, information moves instantly, and coordination becomes unavoidable. Management approaches built for repetition cannot govern systems defined by connection. The limitation is a mismatch between logic and reality, independent of leadership competence. Twentieth-century enterprises succeeded by mastering repetition; the enterprises that sustain performance now do so by maintaining renewal and coherence across interdependent systems. The logic itself is mismatched—built for conditions that no longer define how enterprises operate.

WHAT THE FIVE ENTERPRISE DOMAINS REPRESENT

The Five Enterprise Domains are present from the first day an enterprise exists, because coordination, execution, exchange, and enterprise value do not wait for formal structure. From inception, the enterprise is already moving through all five at once. The only question is whether that motion reinforces itself or pulls in opposing directions.

Each domain expresses a distinct kind of motion that is always present, whether named or not. Human energy aligns around purpose and belonging, while work organizes through processes and interfaces. Execution, simultaneously producing results and generating the information the enterprise uses to understand itself, converts both into the experience that markets receive and the economic commitments that sustain or constrain what follows. These motions interact continuously, establishing the enterprise's behavioral pattern long before anyone attempts to manage it.

When these motions reinforce one another, decisions align because signals remain consistent across the system, work converts cleanly as handoffs retain meaning, and learning paths remain intact. Performance compounds because effort reinforces itself rather than cancelling out. These conditions are visible in how work, decisions, and information move through the enterprise over time.

The contrast between reinforcing motion and weakening connection is difficult to hold through narrative alone. Table 3.2 condenses these conditions into a set of observable signals, allowing the reader to see how coherence expresses itself—and how its loss becomes visible—before outcomes register the cost.

Observable Signals of Coherence and Misalignment

When Coherence Holds	When Coherence Weakens
Decisions propagate cleanly	Decisions fragment or conflict
Handoffs transfer intent	Handoffs absorb effort
Feedback returns quickly	Feedback lags or dissipates
Performance compounds	Effort increases without proportional return

Table 3.2

When these motions become unbalanced, discontinuity appears not as a sudden failure, but as a consequence. Signals stop reinforcing one another, and decisions lengthen as causes blur. Work begins to repeat as boundaries lose definition; customer response weakens as experience no longer reflects intent. Financial results weaken—not from a single event, but because execution and economics are no longer connected to the same assumptions.

What often appears as a collection of unrelated conditions is, at its root, one domain no longer moving in concert with the others. The domains themselves are related, not managed—leadership influence shows up in how consistently these fields of motion remain synchronized, not in directing any single domain. Patterns that look like isolated performance variance are almost always relational effects: people decisions disconnected from process reality, operational insight that never reaches strategy, market signals that fail to register economically, and financial choices made without visibility into execution. Behavior follows the structure of these relationships.

Seen this way, the Five Enterprise Domains render visible a layer of the enterprise that has always been present. They allow the enterprise to be read as a single system in motion—preparing the ground for understanding how the domains relate to each other, depend on one another, and shape enterprise value together.

WHY THE FIVE ENTERPRISE DOMAINS FIT TODAY'S WORLD

The Five Enterprise Domains describe connection—the Natural Order of motion, interaction, and coordination inside modern enterprises—rather than hierarchy, reporting lines, or authority. They fit today's world because interdependence increases naturally and becomes manageable only when it is given structure rather than suppressed by control. Functional and hierarchical models address how enterprises are organized; the Five Enterprise Domains address how they behave once in motion.

Through this lens, differences between enterprises become visible. Some move with coordinated motion, while others compensate with additional oversight, repeated clarification, and corrective activity. The distinction holds across the range of enterprises observed in the fieldwork. What twentieth-century enterprises maintained through control, the enterprises that sustain coherence now maintain through connection—through the consistency of interaction across domains rather than the authority of any single position. When leaders understand the Natural Order of the enterprise, what previously appeared as unrelated operational problems becomes recognizable as a structural condition—the presence or absence of connection across domains. Coherence, sustained through structure that matches how modern enterprises operate, is the condition this chapter has been building toward.

HOW TO READ THE FIVE ENTERPRISE DOMAINS

The Five Enterprise Domains use familiar language—coherence, alignment, renewal—to describe interdependent enterprise behavior. These terms correspond to conditions leaders encounter repeatedly, often without formal explanation. What has been missing is a disciplined way to interpret what those conditions are signaling; the awareness itself was never the problem. Reading the domains requires treating these experiences as structural indicators rather than isolated events: signals of how the system is configured and moving.

The domains provide a method for interpreting those signals without collapsing into reaction. Delays point to structural conditions rather than individual error; breakdowns at boundaries reveal how interfaces are configured rather than how people are performing. Changes in pace—acceleration, deceleration, irregular conversion of effort into outcome—reflect how alignment is expressed through execution. These observations are concurrent expressions of the same system operating across domains. When the interactions between domains are made visible, patterns that once appeared unrelated can be examined together, and conditions previously treated as chaotic can be understood in context because their causes are no longer obscured.

This chapter has been about changing how the enterprise is read. When the Five Enterprise Domains become the interpretive frame, leadership shifts from forcing outcomes through direct intervention to maintaining the conditions under which coherence persists. The enterprise stops appearing as a collection of problems to be solved and begins to appear as a system whose logic is already present, already operating, and now observable.

THIS CHAPTER ESTABLISHED that enterprise behavior is not arbitrary. It follows a Natural Order—one governed by motion, structure, interaction, and coherence rather than by intent or design alone. Once that order becomes visible, enterprise performance no longer feels mysterious. What remains unclear is how to read it before results harden into consequences.

Answering that question requires looking beyond internal structure. Chapter 4 turns to the environment in which enterprise behavior operates, examining the unwalled conditions under which modern enterprises function and explaining why coherence can no longer be understood—or sustained—within internal boundaries alone.

Endnotes

---

1. *Performance topology*, as used in this book, describes the structural pattern that determines how enterprise value moves, interacts, and compounds across the Five Enterprise Domains. Mutual alignment across the domains produces a recognizable condition: Effort reinforces itself, coordination remains intact, and performance compounds. The use of "topology" to describe structural patterns in organizational contexts has recent precedent. Matthew Skelton and Manuel Pais developed a framework of "team topologies" to organize technology teams for fast flow. See Skelton and Pais, *Team Topologies: Organizing Business and Technology Teams for Fast Flow* (Portland, OR: IT Revolution Press, 2019). Jay R. Galbraith

addressed how organizational structural configurations determine information flow and performance in *Designing Complex Organizations* (Reading, MA: Addison-Wesley, 1973). The Skelton-Pais usage refers to team organization patterns for software delivery; Galbraith addresses information-processing structures designed to manage uncertainty. Performance topology, as defined here, is neither. It describes the value-flow dynamics of the entire enterprise system—how the enterprise's configuration either enables compounding or produces dissipation—rather than a team-organization or information-processing concept.

4

THE UNWALLED ENTERPRISE

THE ILLUSION OF INSIDE AND OUTSIDE

For more than a century, leaders were taught to view the enterprises they led as contained systems. Planning, process design, and coordination were treated as centralized activities, while customers, competitors, vendors, regulators, and communities were treated as distinct points of interaction rather than continuous participants in enterprise motion. This separation felt intuitive because it mirrored the industrial conditions of the time—factories, linear supply chains, predictable exchanges, and tightly constrained forms of coordination.

That operating reality no longer applies. Today's enterprise does not function within fixed walls, but within a continuous field of relationships shaped by people, platforms, customers, partners, and technologies that interact without pause. Work moves across networks rather than corridors, and information travels through systems the enterprise does not fully own or control. Customers shape products before transactions occur. Through direct participation in enterprise motion, vendors and partners condition operational capability, extend reach, and expand capacity. Communities amplify meaning and reputation while regulators alter market conditions directly, all participating in enterprise performance within a single system of motion.

In practical terms, the distinction between inside and outside, or internal and external, no longer describes how enterprises operate. What remains is the enterprise itself and the relationships through which it operates. The internal-external divide belonged to a twentieth-century abstraction—useful in an era of linear processes, physical production, and controlled environments. In a twenty-first-century enterprise defined by constant interdependence, that abstraction no longer accounts for how the enterprise functions.

The operating conditions of the modern enterprise are predominantly unwalled—structurally, even where legal boundaries remain. Regulated industries, classified operations, and enterprises subject to mandated information barriers may retain structural walls in specific domains. Even within these enterprises, however, the relational forces described in this chapter act on the portions of their operation that interact with customers, partners, platforms, and markets. The unwalled condition is not absolute, but it is the prevailing structural reality across the enterprises observed in this work and across the operating conditions most midmarket enterprises now inhabit. Customer behavior becomes part of the enterprise's learning loop, and market signals register as immediate indicators of enterprise condition rather than delayed or indirect feedback.

> **The Unwalled Enterprise** describes the structural condition in which the enterprise no longer depends on fixed physical, geographic, or structural separations to govern how work, decisions, and information move. It operates through interconnected systems rather than isolated functions, with partners, platforms, vendors, customers, and automated capabilities participating directly in enterprise motion[1].

Leaders accustomed to managing within clear boundaries encountered something different. Customer difficulty could no longer be contained as a service complaint; instead, it exposed how the enterprise was performing across its relationships. Vendor breakdowns rippled through execution in ways that could not be attributed solely to the vendor. Execution quality registered in customer interpretation before it appeared in internal reporting, and financial stability shifted with market conditions the enterprise had no capacity to wall off.

In my work with midmarket enterprises, nearly all leaders were applying models learned and reinforced through training for bounded enterprises that no longer exist. Customers, vendors, contractors, data partners, platform providers, and distributed teams all participate in the same system of motion. What leaders once treated as "external factors" now shape enterprise performance as directly as any internal decision or process.

Across dozens of enterprises, I watched the assumption that an enterprise could function as a self-contained coordinating construct collapse under the speed and relational interdependence of modern operating reality. The boundaries leaders believed they were managing had already lost their organizing power. What remained was an enterprise whose performance was determined by how effectively alignment was sustained across its relational field.

The enterprises I worked with had already crossed into this condition. The question was whether their leaders could see it—and what would become visible once they did.

WHY THE INTERNAL-EXTERNAL PARADIGM NO LONGER WORKS

For most of the twentieth century, enterprise self-understanding was shaped by assumed separations between planning, coordination, and execution on one side and customers, markets, and constraints on the other. Leaders spoke in terms of operations versus markets, contrasting internal priorities against external pressures and measuring capabilities against threats, treating these as distinct realms rather than as interacting conditions of enterprise motion.

Over time, this separation became so embedded in management thinking that it ceased to be examined and began to function as an accepted truth rather than a design assumption.

What that model described, however, was a specific historical operating environment, not enterprise reality as a permanent condition. It reflected a world in which workers shared physical space and information traveled slowly—processes followed largely linear paths, production was centralized, and supplier relationships were primarily transactional. Customer interaction remained limited and delayed. Competitive moves played out over extended horizons, and markets changed at a pace that leadership could reasonably anticipate and plan around. In that environment, separation between coordination and response was tangible and operationally meaningful, and the distinctions that later hardened into doctrine accurately reflected how work and interaction were structured at the time.

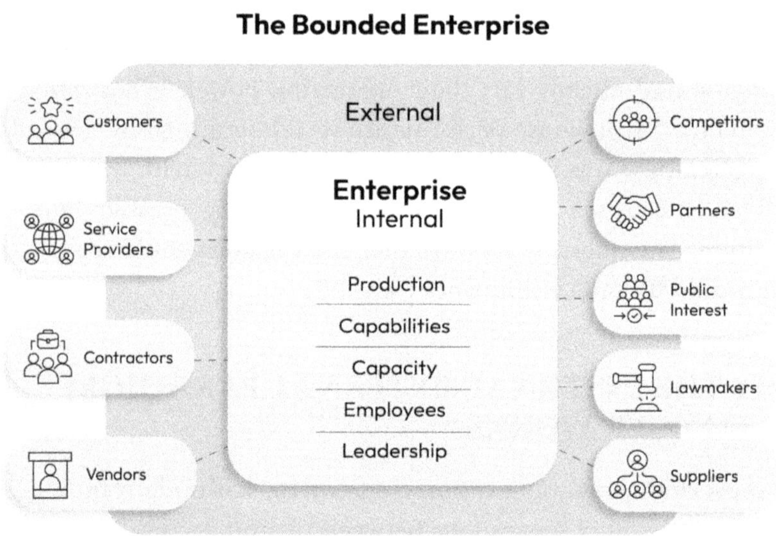

Figure 4.1

Modern enterprises no longer operate under those conditions. Today's enterprise exists within a continuous, interconnected field in which performance emerges through interaction rather than isolation. Customers, partners, platforms, suppliers, regulators, and technologies condition outcomes directly and continuously. The model applied as long as the operating environment remained stable enough to sustain its assumptions.

The Modern Enterprise Is a Network

The twenty-first-century enterprise no longer behaves like a bounded machine. It operates as a networked system in which work moves across digital platforms, communication systems, geographic distance, and partnership layers, with customer expectations shifting continuously and vendors participating directly in capability creation. Platforms mediate exchange and connect teams across continents, while social signals shape enterprise meaning in near real time.

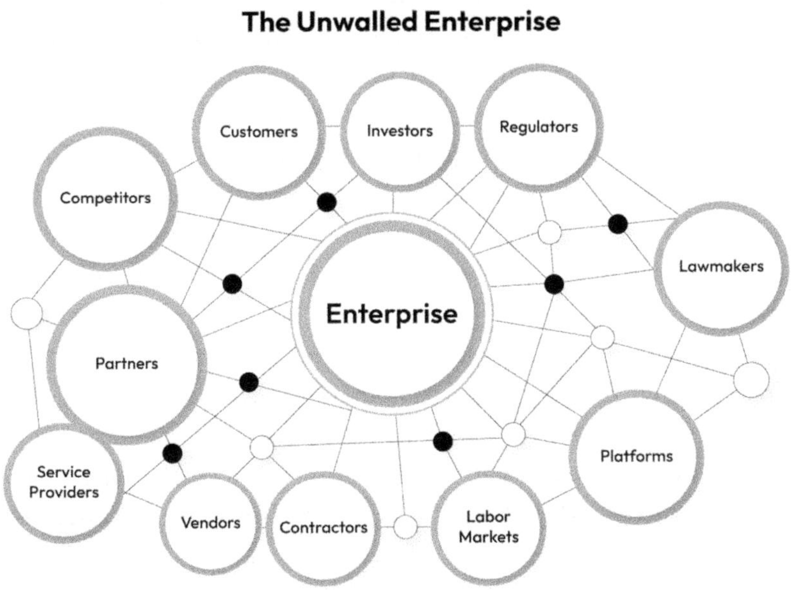

Figure 4.2

Performance emerges at permeable interfaces rather than within isolated execution. Customer interpretation conditions product design while partner capability shapes operational capacity. Platform architecture conditions how coordination occurs. Regulatory constraints alter strategic possibilities in ways that reach well beyond compliance.

No stable "inside" remains to optimize in isolation. The enterprise participates in a shared environment, and its performance takes shape through that participation.

The enterprise operates as a participating node within a dense field of customers, partners, competitors, suppliers, contractors, platforms, regulators, labor markets, and public interests. Enterprise behavior emerges from continuous interaction across this field rather than from activity contained within its formal boundaries.

The Consequences of Using an Outdated Model

Leaders who continue to rely on the internal-external paradigm encounter predictable limits. Signals arriving through customers, vendors, partners, and markets are sorted into "internal" or "external" categories and handled accordingly—customer signals analyzed after the fact, vendor reliability treated as someone else's problem, market shifts recognized late. Processes are redesigned in isolation, without regard for the relational system in which the enterprise operates.

Most critically, the internal-external divide obscures coherence. Leaders who hold inherited boundaries in place lose sight of how the enterprise actually behaves. Internal performance is calibrated against internal metrics while customers evaluate relational consistency. The market shapes shared priorities that internal planning has not accounted for. Teams get aligned around enterprise logic even as relational forces destabilize the conditions that alignment depends on.

The unwalled enterprise is the operating environment observed across every industry, scale, and business model in the fieldwork.

Only by releasing the internal-external paradigm does the enterprise become visible as it actually operates.

THE ENTERPRISE AS A RELATIONAL FIELD OF CONTINUOUS EXCHANGE

Enterprises do not operate as isolated entities. They exist within a continuous relational field—a dynamic pattern of interaction through which people, teams, customers, partners, platforms, technologies, and market forces participate simultaneously. Legal boundaries remain, but the distinctions that once separated coordination from response have lost their explanatory power.

This relational field behaves differently than the models built on separation and control. Connection replaces centralized coordination as the primary mechanism of adaptation. Learning travels through continuous feedback; hierarchical reporting no longer describes how learning moves. Shared signals—not formal directives alone—govern how adjustment occurs. Enterprise motion moves through interdependent relationships, and coherence depends on how effectively those relationships reinforce one another as conditions change.

Within this field, the enterprise operates through continuous exchange. Work, decisions, and information move between leadership and teams, systems and platforms, strategy and market movement, and execution and customer interpretation without pause. These exchanges shape both performance and perception, determining how enterprise motion propagates through the system and how enterprise value is created, interpreted, and reinforced over time.

The enterprise does not act and then await response. It participates continuously in a shared pattern of signals and consequences. Actions taken by the enterprise propagate through this relational field, while signals arising elsewhere reshape enterprise behavior in return. Performance emerges from this reciprocal interaction—shaped by the exchange itself, not by any single participant's activity, intent, or control.

Customers Are Not "External": They Are Participants

In the unwalled enterprise, customers do not sit outside the system. They participate directly in it. They condition product evolution, service delivery, brand interpretation, operational expectations, innovation priorities, and enterprise learning. Customer feedback directly expresses enterprise coherence. Customers who encounter inconsistency are experiencing structural misfit; those who encounter consistency are encountering coherence in action. Customer behavior shapes enterprise priorities because customers are embedded within the same relational system.

Partners and Vendors Extend Enterprise Capability

Partners, vendors, and platforms function as extensions of enterprise capability, conditioning delivery performance, service quality, financial predictability, customer experience, innovation cycles, and capacity. Their performance is inseparable from enterprise coherence—treating them as outside contributors misreads the relational structure. A partner's system that slows down slows execution across the enterprise. Enterprise design that fails to account for partner workflows produces consequences customers experience directly.

Capability in a relational system is distributed rather than contained. Coherence is sustained through connection and alignment across the system.

Information Has No Borders

Information no longer moves according to formal coordination pathways or inherited separations. Signals propagate instantly through relational connections, traveling across digital channels at network speed and shaping interpretation and behavior well before structured response mechanisms engage.

Customer comments, partner delays, competitive actions, and regulatory adjustments can register as immediate system signals, while social platforms amplify their reach, converting what once would have remained localized operational information into broadly shared market meaning within minutes.

Perception now changes faster than planning cycles. Market shifts routinely outpace formal communication as weak signals become decisive through rapid amplification across networks. The enterprise that filters information through internal-external distinctions loses the capacity to interpret signals as they form—signals that carry meaning and consequence simultaneously.

Relational Fields of the Unwalled Enterprise

Relational Field	Description	What Moves Through the Field	What the Field Reveals
Enterprise Field	The relational system through which work, decisions, and learning are coordinated	Direction, interpretation, execution routines, feedback, load	Whether alignment, structure, and execution reinforce one another or compensate for misfit
Customer Field	The relational space where enterprise behavior is interpreted as value, reliability, or friction	Experience, response, trust, hesitation, adoption, renewal behavior	Whether enterprise motion is coherent from the customer's perspective
Market Field	The relational context that conditions relevance, viability, and constraint	Competitive signals, platform dynamics, regulatory conditions, expectation shifts	Whether the enterprise's economic and strategic posture remains viable
Interfaces (Across Fields)	Structural interfaces where work, decisions, or information transfer connect	Handoffs, coordination, interpretation, capacity	Where misfit, friction, and incoherence appear first
Relational Signals	Observable patterns emerging from interaction across relational fields	Variability, pacing changes, hesitation, load concentration	Early indicators of coherence strengthening or weakening

Table 4.1

Behavior, meaning, and value emerge through continuous interaction across these fields, and coherence is tested at their interfaces.

Interfaces Replace Boundaries

In an unwalled enterprise, what were once considered boundaries become interfaces—points where relationships meet and interaction occurs. These are connection points where priorities converge, signals travel, and coherence is either reinforced or weakened. They exist between teams, between the enterprise and customers, between the enterprise and partners, and across systems, platforms, and workflows.

Well-designed interfaces sustain coordinated enterprise movement. Weakened interfaces produce friction in execution and interpretation. The enterprise is defined by how it participates in its relational system—by the quality of its interfaces, not by the rigidity of its boundaries. Coherence across the full system depends on that participation.

THE UNWALLED ENTERPRISE MODEL

The Unwalled Enterprise describes how modern enterprises actually operate, not a philosophical position to be adopted. Every enterprise observed in the fieldwork, whether it acknowledged it or not, operated within overlapping relational fields that shaped performance, perception, and potential.

> **Relational Field** is described as a continuous, dynamic pattern of interaction through which people, teams, customers, partners, platforms, technologies, and market forces participate simultaneously in enterprise motion. The enterprise exists within three interdependent relational fields—the Enterprise Field, the Customer Field, and the Market Field—each of which shapes behavior differently and none of which operates in isolation[2].

These fields interact continuously, conditioning priorities, expectations, and outcomes across the entire system. Enterprise behavior emerges from these interactions—isolated internal decisions do not account for it.

The twenty-first-century enterprise functions as a participant within a multilayered, interconnected environment rather than as a self-contained entity. The Unwalled Enterprise describes that environment without relying on outdated internal-external distinctions.

From Bounded Enterprises to Unwalled Systems

Bounded (20th-Century) Assumption	Unwalled (21st-Century) Reality
Coordination occurs inside organizational boundaries	Coordination occurs across relational interfaces
Customers are external recipients	Customers are participants in enterprise motion
Vendors and partners are outside contributors	Vendors and partners extend enterprise capability
Information flows through internal channels	Information propagates across relational networks
Control preserves stability	Connection sustains coherence
Performance is optimized internally	Performance emerges relationally
Misalignment is managed within functions	Misfit appears first at interfaces
Change is planned and deployed	Change is sensed and responded to through interaction

Table 4.2

The Three Relational Fields

Each field shapes enterprise behavior through a distinct mode of interaction, and the three operate as an interdependent system rather than as separate environments.

1. The Enterprise Field

The Enterprise Field describes the relational context in which the Five Enterprise Domains interact—people, processes, execution, customer interaction, and economics[3]. It reflects how coherence is produced through their interaction: how shared meaning is established, how work is structured, how decisions propagate, and how enterprise value is created, amplified, and protected.

This field governs how the domains coordinate with one another, determining whether effort reinforces itself or dissipates. It does not exist in isolation, but is continuously shaped by interaction with the Customer Field and the Market Field, which condition and reshape enterprise behavior in real time.

Unwalled Enterprise Relational System

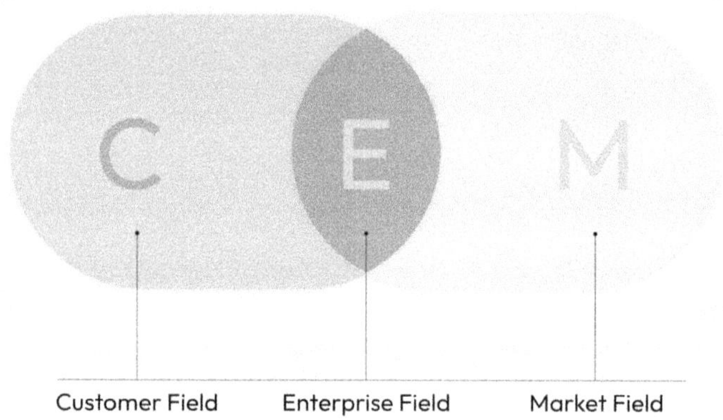

Figure 4.3

Conventional representations place customers within the market. This model separates them because the distinction is structural: Customers are relational participants within one field. The Market Field encompasses every other relational participant operating within the same system: labor markets, suppliers, vendors, partners, service providers, platforms, investors, regulators, technologies, competitors, substitutes, and adjacent industries. The separation is the point.

2. The Customer Field

The Customer Field represents the expectations, interpretations, and behaviors of those the enterprise serves. Customers are not external observers. Their actions directly shape enterprise priorities, quality standards, timing expectations, capability requirements, and strategic viability.

Customer signals register structural misfit directly, because customers participate in the enterprise as it actually operates. Customer behavior therefore functions as a structural indicator of coherence. The Customer Field operates as a structural force within the enterprise system.

3. The Market Field

The Market Field encompasses all contextual forces beyond individual customer relationships: labor markets, suppliers, vendors, partners, service providers, platforms, investors, regulators, technologies, competitors, substitutes, and adjacent industries[4]. This field shapes what is possible, acceptable, and sustainable, determining how differentiation emerges, how quickly the enterprise must adapt, and how enterprise value is interpreted.

The Market Field operates within the same environment of interdependence as the enterprise, shaping how enterprise motion is directed to maintain coherence and relevance.

Exogenous Forces and the Limits of the Relational Field

The unwalled condition describes how relational participants—customers, partners, platforms, distributed teams, and vendors—

shape enterprise behavior through continuous interaction. Their influence operates through the same fields of motion that govern enterprise activity, registering across domains in real time.

A different category of force also acts on the enterprise: regulatory change, macroeconomic contraction, geopolitical disruption, technological displacement, supply chain discontinuity, and pandemic. These forces affect enterprise behavior—often severely—but they operate differently than relational participants. A customer's purchasing decision shapes execution and economic signal simultaneously, through the enterprise's own activity. A regulatory mandate imposed by a government does not flow through enterprise motion; it restructures the constraints within which that motion occurs.

The distinction separates forces that interact through the enterprise's relational field from forces that act upon the enterprise from outside that field. Relational forces are unwalled by nature—flowing through interfaces, shaping execution, and generating the feedback the enterprise uses to adjust. Exogenous forces alter the operating conditions without participating in the activity that those conditions produce.

Both categories demand enterprise response. The difference lies in how the response forms. A customer shift is absorbed through existing interfaces and feedback mechanisms—the same systems the enterprise uses for ongoing activity. A regulatory mandate requires structural accommodation (adjustments to constraint, resource allocation, or operating scope) before the enterprise can respond through its domains.

The unwalled condition remains the governing reality of the modern enterprise. Relational participants operate within the enterprise's field of motion and continuously shape its behavior. Exogenous forces restructure conditions from outside that field. The enterprise encounters both forms of pressure persistently, and how it responds to each differs: relational correspondence is sustained through the ongoing activity of the system; structural accommodation precedes that activity, adjusting the conditions under which correspondence can be maintained.

Patterns of Exchange Across Relational Fields

Pattern	What It Describes	Coherence Condition
Intent and Expectation	Enterprise direction encounters customer and market interpretation—purpose, priorities, and promises meet needs, experiences, and constraints across the relational system.	Whether intent and expectation remain aligned as conditions change, or meaning diverges before the enterprise recognizes it.
Signal and Response	Behavior in one field generates adjustment in another—enterprise actions produce signals that customers and markets interpret and act on, returning as new signals that shape enterprise interpretation and action.	Whether the speed and precision of exchange sustains coordination or allows misalignment to compound.
Design and Experience	Structural decisions meet lived outcomes—processes, roles, interfaces, and incentives shape how work is experienced by customers, partners, and teams, feeding back as information about fit, relevance, and reliability.	Whether experience informs renewal or reinforces misfit.
Action and Feedback	Execution generates learning—every action produces information about what worked, what failed, and where assumptions no longer apply. Feedback loops determine whether that information is reintegrated or dissipates.	Whether the speed and fidelity of exchange governs how quickly the enterprise adapts.
Value and Perception	Value mechanisms meet interpretation—economic, functional, or relational value must be perceived, trusted, and reinforced by those who experience it if coherence is to persist.	Whether gaps between value creation and value perception weaken coherence.

Table 4.3

The Patterns of Exchange

The three relational fields—Enterprise, Customer, and Market—interact through recurring patterns of exchange rather than linear cause-and-effect sequences, shaping how meaning, action, and value circulate across the enterprise and its environment. These exchanges operate continuously and simultaneously, with each field constraining how the others are interpreted and acted upon.

Together, these patterns form a relational operating system rather than a sequential process, determining how meaning stabilizes, action coordinates, and enterprise value is sustained or eroded through continuous interaction.

Why Coherence Requires Unwalled Thinking

Coherence depends on the full relational field through which enterprise motion moves—internal coordination alone does not sustain it. Because enterprise behavior propagates through customers, partners, platforms, and markets, coherence is preserved only when those relationships are treated as integral to system performance.

Leaders who adopt unwalled thinking find that familiar signals take on a different meaning. Conditions previously sorted into "internal" or "external" categories register instead as system information—relational data about how the enterprise and its environment interact. The specific interpretive shifts that follow from this reframing are addressed in the next section.

The Unwalled Enterprise describes modern enterprise reality more accurately than earlier models—reflecting how performance emerges through interconnected motion and response, rather than how those models imagined coordination and control to operate.

WHAT LEADERS SEE WHEN THEY ADOPT THIS VIEW

The internal-external distinction, released, gives way to enterprise behavior that is more intelligible rather than more complex. Patterns that once appeared random can be read as related effects, signals that previously felt disconnected begin to resolve into structure, and issues handled as isolated dysfunctions reveal their origin in relational mismatch across the system.

Adopting an unwalled perspective does not alter the environment itself—it recalibrates how leaders interpret enterprise conditions so that signals register as expressions of system behavior rather than as local problems. The shift is decisive, because coherence can only be sustained where structure and relationship are visible together.

What follows are the consistent shifts in interpretation that occur when leaders begin seeing the enterprise as part of a relational system.

Customer Inconsistency Becomes an Enterprise Signal

In the twentieth-century model, customer complaints were addressed after the fact, treated as downstream conditions encountered once work was already complete. In an unwalled enterprise, customer inconsistency is interpreted differently. It is read as an enterprise signal that reflects structural misfit across the system, not as a discrete service failure confined to a single function.

Unclear roles, inconsistent processes, execution variability, communication breakdowns, quality issues, and misaligned priorities surface first through customer experience, often well before they appear in formal reporting. Customer response becomes the earliest indicator that coordination is weakening, because customers encounter the enterprise as it actually operates rather than as it intends to operate. Leaders who adopt this view stop treating customer difficulties as issues to be resolved in isolation and begin examining them as evidence of how the enterprise is functioning structurally.

Market Shifts Become Renewal Triggers

Market changes were long framed as disruptive events that arrived after plans were set. In an unwalled enterprise, market shifts are read as renewal triggers, providing early information about emerging expectations, changing interpretations of value, new capability requirements, and shifts in competitive context.

Demand changes, competitor moves, platform updates, and regulatory adjustments are interpreted as relational data that surfaces mismatches sooner than internal reporting can. Renewal can therefore occur before misfit compounds—structure adjusting in response to evolving relationships instead of correcting course after performance has already deteriorated.

Partner and Vendor Problems Become System Weaknesses

Partner and vendor problems were often treated as failures that belonged elsewhere—someone else's system, someone else's responsibility. In an unwalled enterprise, that separation no longer applies. Partners, platforms, and vendors contribute directly to execution quality, capacity, predictability, and customer experience, operating as part of a single, interdependent system.

Delays propagate and inconsistencies compound. What first appears as a partner issue is revealed as a system weakness, pointing to integration gaps rather than individual fault. This shift reduces attribution and redirects attention toward design. Leaders stop asking who failed and begin examining how coordination across the system is being carried.

Social and Environmental Signals Become Immediate Feedback

Digital platforms have removed the delay that once separated signal from response. Information now travels across the relational system faster than formal communication cycles can engage, shaping perception and behavior almost immediately. A customer review, market reaction, regulatory adjustment, or competitor announcement can register as a system signal in real time.

Signals that were once discounted or deferred become, through the unwalled view, immediate feedback. Leaders read social and environmental signals as early indicators of emerging patterns, inputs to renewal, and evidence of how meaning is forming across the system.

Instead of buffering or postponing response, leaders use these signals to realign structure with changing conditions.

Leadership attention moves accordingly—toward maintaining alignment within the relational system rather than shielding the enterprise from it.

Leadership Attention Shifts From Control to Connection

The most significant change is perceptual. Leaders who accept that the enterprise operates without walls find that control ceases to function as a primary mechanism of influence. Control belonged to a bounded world in which stability could be enforced through hierarchy and separation. In an unwalled enterprise, coherence depends on connection, integration, and shared interpretation.

Leadership attention therefore moves toward strengthening relationships, designing interfaces, interpreting signals, and sustaining alignment across the relational system. Enforcing compliance within assumed boundaries gives way to maintaining coordination across interactions. Leaders operate from within a system of relationships—attending to how those relationships carry enterprise motion.

This shift reshapes how the Five Enterprise Domains are understood and led, which is examined in the next section.

IMPLICATIONS FOR THE FIVE ENTERPRISE DOMAINS

The Unwalled Enterprise is the structural condition under which the Five Enterprise Domains become intelligible. Without this perspective, leaders unconsciously interpret the domains through inherited assumptions about separation and containment, flattening their meaning and weakening their ability to explain enterprise behavior. Once the unwalled condition is recognized, the domains resolve into dynamic, interconnected fields of enterprise activity whose behavior is shaped by continuous relational interaction, rather than resolving as functionally isolated constructs inherited from outdated coordination models.

1. People + Alignment: Human Understanding as a Relational Condition

Alignment in a bounded enterprise was treated as internal consensus —teams aligning with one another, leaders aligning around strategy, the entire process understood as inward-facing agreement.

The unwalled enterprise surfaces a different condition. People align not only around enterprise purpose, but around customer priorities, partner realities, and shared outcomes that span platforms and the relational system. Leadership alignment is shaped as much by relational signals as by internal logic, and trust extends across the relational system rather than remaining confined to internal teams.

People + Alignment becomes the interpretive center of the enterprise, where human understanding forms at the intersection of enterprise intent and relational reality. Shared understanding is sustained across the relational field—not assembled from internal consensus alone.

2. Processes + Integration: Structure That Fits the Relational System

Structural fit in a relational system requires more than internal efficiency and functional calibration. Processes are shaped by customer timing as much as by enterprise sequencing, and integration accounts for technological, contractual, and relational interfaces wherever coordination is required. Structural fit is therefore evaluated against patterns of relational interaction and consequence, not against convenience, legacy design, or inherited coordination assumptions. The bounded model's emphasis on coordination among internal teams captured only a portion of what integration entails.

Processes + Integration, understood within the unwalled condition, operates as an architecture of continuity across the relational system, structuring how work is carried through interfaces; contained workflows no longer describe how integration operates.

3. Execution + Intelligence: Execution as Relational Coordination

The unwalled nature of the enterprise becomes unmistakable at the point of execution. Execution quality is shaped by customer expectations, partner reliability, platform constraints, regulatory conditions, and market dynamics, all interacting simultaneously. What leaders experience as execution difficulty frequently stems from relational conditions that the enterprise has not accounted for.

Interpreting execution therefore requires reading signals from across the relational system, not only from internal reporting. Execution reveals coherence (or its loss) within the enterprise's own activity before other domains can report it, because it is where structure meets reality in real time. The domain functions as the enterprise's primary discovery mechanism—the place where what is actually happening becomes visible.

4. Customer + Interaction: A Relational Field, Not an External Function

The distinction between internal operations and external customer-facing activity collapses in an unwalled enterprise. Customer + Interaction is the relational alignment field where enterprise priorities encounter customer interpretation and market meaning. Experience reflects coherence; relational tension exposes structural misfit. Market signals inform how the enterprise renews itself. Value is coproduced with customers through continuous interaction—shaped by both parties rather than delivered from one to the other.

The customer field operates within the relational system of the enterprise. Treating it as external misreads both the customer's role and the enterprise's structure.

5. Economics + Metrics: Economic Stewardship Across the Relational System

Financial condition is shaped by relational dynamics as directly as by internal efficiency. Customer adoption, partner stability, platform economics, regulatory context, and operational consistency across the relational system all condition cost, margin, risk, and enterprise value. Separating economic systems from the relational conditions that produce financial outcomes renders the metrics incomplete—measuring internal performance while relational forces determine the results.

Economics + Metrics, understood within the unwalled condition, functions as the economic interpreter of the full enterprise system—reading financial signals as expressions of relational condition; isolated internal outcomes do not account for what the metrics describe.

The Five Enterprise Domains Through the Unwalled Lens

Domain	Unwalled Function
People + Alignment	Interpretive center of the enterprise—human understanding formed at the intersection of enterprise intent and relational reality, sustained across the relational field
Processes + Integration	Architecture of continuity across the relational system—structuring how work is carried through interfaces rather than diagrammed within contained workflows
Execution + Intelligence	Primary discovery mechanism—where structure meets reality in real time and coherence or loss of coherence becomes visible earliest
Customer + Interaction	Relational alignment field—where enterprise priorities encounter customer interpretation and market meaning, and value is co-produced through continuous interaction
Economics + Metrics	Economic interpreter of the full enterprise system—reading financial signals as expressions of relational condition across the system

Table 4.4

The Structural Insight

Coherence is produced through coordinated interaction across the enterprise, its customers, its partners, and its markets. Leaders who adopt unwalled thinking interpret the domains as interdependent forces whose alignment with the broader relational field determines enterprise behavior and enterprise value. Leaders who do not attempt to refine the domains independently—and consistently—misread the signals that matter most.

HOW THE INTERNAL–EXTERNAL DIVIDE DISTORTS AND DELAYS

Internal-external thinking constrains how leaders interpret enterprise behavior—and that interpretive distortion shapes every subsequent decision. By dividing reality into artificial categories, it obscures how work actually advances, how decisions form, and how coherence is either sustained or weakened. The outcome is predictable: Leaders misread relational signals, intervene in the wrong places, and diagnose structural conditions as tactical, cultural, or interpersonal problems.

Understanding the Five Enterprise Domains requires releasing this inherited paradigm entirely. The internal-external divide is one of the most persistent—and least examined—limitations shaping modern enterprise leadership.

How the Old Model Distorts Interpretation

A customer issue that appears to originate outside the enterprise frequently signals misfit within People + Alignment, Processes + Integration, or Execution + Intelligence. A partner delay attributed to a supplier reflects misalignment at enterprise interfaces. A market shift dismissed as an external threat carries information the enterprise requires for renewal. Each interpretation that relies on the internal-external divide steers attention away from the relational conditions that produced the signal.

The distortion compounds over time. Coherence depends on alignment across relationships—customer expectations shaping priorities, partner capabilities conditioning operational capacity, platform constraints conditioning how work is designed and carried, market conditions informing strategic direction. These forces operate simultaneously within the same relational system. Maintaining an internal-external divide fragments coherence by misrepresenting how interaction occurs.

The divide also delays renewal. In a bounded view, renewal occurs only after performance degrades enough to create urgency. Relational signals—the early indicators that structure and conditions are diverging—register before formal reporting catches up. Leaders operating within the internal-external frame discount those signals because the frame classifies them as external interference rather than system information. Structural resistance accumulates and misalignment expands. Customer disappointment deepens as partner instability intensifies; execution diverges, and financial volatility follows. The sequence is connected—each condition feeding the next rather than arising independently.

Structural decay follows not because leaders failed to act, but because the interpretive frame prevented early signals from being read as what they were: evidence that the enterprise and its relational field were moving apart. The internal-external divide delays renewal by muting the enterprise's capacity to register change as it forms; misfit hardens before correction occurs.

The Five Enterprise Domains describe how the enterprise behaves as a coherent system. That system cannot be recognized through a divided interpretive frame. Only when the enterprise is seen as unwalled do the domains resolve into the relational system they describe. The internal-external distinction is what prevents that resolution.

. . .

THIS CHAPTER DISSOLVED the assumption that enterprises operate within stable boundaries. It established the unwalled condition as the reality in which modern enterprise behavior now operates—one defined by continuous interaction, rapid signal propagation, and relational dependence that no longer pauses for coordination to catch up. Once that condition is visible, a new question becomes unavoidable: If all enterprises now operate unwalled, why do they still encounter pressure in fundamentally different ways?

The answer lies in the nature of the enterprise value being carried, which imposes different constraints across the enterprises observed—independent of leadership quality or the specific industry in which they operated. Enterprises built around physical assets encounter different limits than those built around intangible ones, even as both operate within the same relational field. Chapter 5 introduces the Two Enterprise Archetypes, clarifying how distinct modes of value creation shape motion, load, coherence, and breakdown, and why understanding this distinction is essential before examining how coherence is formed or lost within the Five Enterprise Domains.

Endnotes

---

1. The concept of enterprises operating without traditional boundaries has a well-known history. Jack Welch and GE popularized "the boundaryless organization" in the 1990s as an aspirational management philosophy—a goal of removing vertical, horizontal, and external barriers. Ron Ashkenas, Dave Ulrich, Todd Jick, and Steve Kerr formalized this in *The Boundaryless Organization: Breaking the Chains of Organizational Structure* (San Francisco: Jossey-Bass, 1995). The term *unwalled enterprise* was chosen deliberately to make a different point. "Boundaryless" describes something leaders aspire to create. "Unwalled" describes a condition that already exists—a structural reality in which the enterprise no longer depends on fixed physical, geographic, or organizational separations to govern how work, decisions, and information move, whether leaders have chosen it or not. The distinction matters because it reframes the leadership task: not to remove boundaries, but to design coherence across an enterprise that is already operating without them.
2. The concept of a relational field draws from several established intellectual traditions. In Gestalt psychology, Frederick Perls, Ralph F. Hefferline, and Paul Goodman introduced the relational field as the context within which experience emerges between organism and environment. See Perls, Hefferline, and Good-

man, *Gestalt Therapy: Excitement and Growth in the Human Personality* (New York: Julian Press, 1951). Kurt Lewin's field theory (1952) and Pierre Bourdieu's sociological field theory further established the concept of fields as structured spaces of interaction. In organizational theory, Paul J. DiMaggio and Walter W. Powell's work on organizational fields ("The Iron Cage Revisited," *American Sociological Review* 48, no. 2 [1983]: 147–60) and Jody Hoffer Gittell's relational coordination framework ("Organizing Work to Support Relational Co-ordination," *International Journal of Human Resource Management* 11, no. 3 [2000]: 517–34) address related territory. The Gestalt usage is therapeutic. Bourdieu and DiMaggio examine sociological fields of power and institutional behavior. Gittell focuses on task-level coordination through communication and relating. *Relational field*, as used here, is structural and enterprise-wide: it describes a persistent, dynamic pattern of interaction—encompassing people, teams, customers, partners, platforms, technologies, and market forces—through which the enterprise exists and operates simultaneously across three specific fields: the Enterprise Field, the Customer Field, and the Market Field.

3. The use of "field" as an organizing concept in social theory is well-established, most notably through Bourdieu's field theory and DiMaggio and Powell's concept of organizational fields (see note 2 above). Neil Fligstein further developed the concept of "strategic action fields" as arenas of socially structured interaction. The specific phrase "enterprise field" does not appear in the published literature as a defined concept. As used here, the enterprise field describes the internal relational context in which the Five Enterprise Domains interact—how shared meaning is established, how work is structured, how decisions propagate, and how enterprise value is created, amplified, and protected. It is distinct from the sociological usage, which examines competitive and institutional dynamics across organizations.
4. The term "market field" appears in organizational and institutional theory. The AMS Review has published work on "Markets and Institutional Fields," drawing from Bourdieu's field theory, DiMaggio and Powell's organizational fields, and Fligstein's strategic action fields. In that literature, market fields are examined as institutionally structured competitive arenas. As used here, the market field describes one of three interdependent relational fields surrounding the enterprise —encompassing labor markets, suppliers, vendors, partners, service providers, platforms, investors, regulators, technologies, competitors, substitutes, and adjacent industries. The emphasis is on how these contextual forces shape what is possible, acceptable, and sustainable for the enterprise, rather than on the institutional structure of markets as a sociological phenomenon.

5

THE TWO ENTERPRISE ARCHETYPES

TWO WAYS ENTERPRISES CREATE VALUE

Across my work with enterprises, I observed that they do not face identical structural challenges. Conditions that appeared similar on the surface behaved very differently depending on whether enterprise value depended primarily on physical assets or on intangible, knowledge-based capability. Enterprises grounded in physical production, such as manufacturing, logistics, and retail, encountered limits related to load, sequencing, and material constraint. Enterprises grounded in intangible assets, such as software enterprises, professional services firms, and digital platforms, encountered limits related to interpretation, coordination, and relational dependency. The consistency of these patterns across enterprises made the distinction impossible to ignore.

The two enterprise archetypes are not theoretical categories; they reflect the operational physics I encountered repeatedly in midmarket enterprises, making asset base one of the most reliable indicators of where load will surface, how quickly misfit accumulates, and what forms of structural response will sustain enterprise performance.

Structural Signatures of the Two Enteprise Archetypes

Structural Dimension	Physical Asset Enterprise	Intangible Asset Enterprise
Primary motion	Physical movement of matter	Movement of meaning and decisions
Constraint type	Hard physical limits	Interpretive and relational limits
Capacity logic	Fixed and asset-bound	Elastic but coordination-bound
Interfaces	Physical handoffs	Digital and relational interfaces
Failure mode	Bottlenecks, delays, breakdowns	Misinterpretation, fragmentation
Renewal trigger	Physical misfit and wear	Interpretive misfit and decay

Table 5.1

Across the industries and scales observed in the fieldwork, every enterprise creates enterprise value through one of two structural archetypes:

1. **Physical Asset Enterprises** are those that require physical assets to produce and deliver physical value.
2. **Intangible Asset Enterprises** are those that require intangible assets to produce and deliver intangible value.

The distinction is structural. It reflects the underlying substance an enterprise works with and the mechanics through which enterprise value is produced—determining how people align, how processes are organized, how work is executed, how customers are engaged, and how financial performance is sustained.

Physical Asset Enterprises depend on factories, machines, facilities, inventory, and physical workflows to produce and deliver enterprise value. They move matter through space, and their operations are governed by capacity, throughput, load, sequencing, and physical constraints. Historically, these enterprises defined the industrial economy, and their structures evolved to reliably manage material movement at scale.

Intangible Asset Enterprises work with fundamentally different substance. Knowledge, expertise, relationships, data, software, and intellectual property constitute their primary assets, and enterprise value moves through nonphysical systems rather than material workflows. These enterprises coordinate meaning, judgment, and information—governed by interpretation, learning, decision timing, and relational coordination. They form the core of the knowledge economy.

Two Enterprise Archetypes

Enterprise Archetype	Primary Asset Base	Mode of Value Creation	Governing Constraint
Physical Asset Enterprise	Tangible assets (facilities, equipment, inventory, infrastructure)	Transformation and movement of physical matter	Capacity, throughput, load, physical constraint
Intangible Asset Enterprise	Intangible assets (knowledge, expertise, IP, data, relationships)	Creation and application of meaning, judgment, and information	Interpretation, coordination, relational fit

Table 5.2

Although these archetypes differ in origin and mechanics, both now face conditions that no longer respect the boundaries their original structures assumed. Customers, partners, platforms, technologies, and regulators interact continuously with both archetypes. Digital interfaces and relational exchange act on both systems, and the distinction between internal operations and external forces has dissolved for each.

This chapter examines why these two archetypes exist and how each behaves under unwalled conditions, making visible why enterprises that appear dramatically different on the surface—manufacturers and consulting firms, retailers and SaaS enterprises, logistics networks and design agencies—are governed by the same Natural Order beneath those differences.

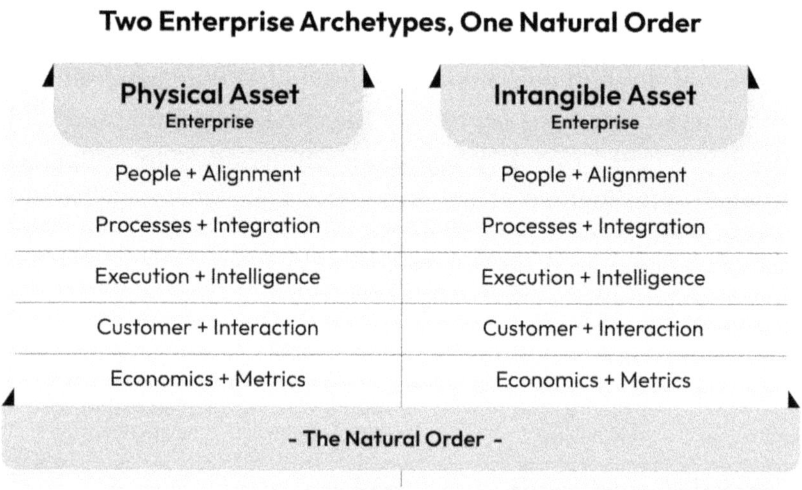

Figure 5.1

PHYSICAL ASSET ENTERPRISES: DEFINED BY TANGIBLE PRODUCTION

Physical Asset Enterprises create enterprise value through the movement, transformation, and coordination of physical assets rather than through interpretive or digital systems. Their assets are not knowledge or intellectual property but physical capital:

- Buildings and facilities
- Equipment and machinery
- Vehicles and logistics infrastructure
- Inventory and raw materials
- Physical workflows and production systems

These enterprises formed the backbone of the industrial economy and continue to underpin global infrastructure today. They span manufacturing plants and production facilities, wholesale distribution networks, retailers and omnichannel stores, logistics and transportation operations, construction and industrial services, energy and utilities, healthcare facilities, hospitality and real estate operations, and physical infrastructure providers.

Their defining characteristic is not industry but dependence on physical capital as the primary medium through which enterprise value is created. Whether manufacturing products, transporting goods, constructing infrastructure, operating retail environments, or delivering healthcare services in physical settings, matter moves through space in every case. Constraints are imposed by physical reality, and performance is governed by capacity, throughput, timing, availability, and load.

Their Structural Signature

Because they operate through physical assets, Physical Asset Enterprises share a distinctive structural signature shaped by physical reality. Operational continuity depends on sequencing, timing, load management, and physical interfaces. Capacity places hard limits on what can be produced—space, equipment, throughput, and staffing levels directly constrain enterprise value creation. Safety and reliability function as systemic requirements because failure in a physical system can halt operations entirely and place both people and enterprise value at risk.

Physical interfaces—warehouses, production lines, treatment rooms, delivery fleets, and store layouts—directly constitute customer experience, while asset leverage introduces long-term consequences through depreciation, maintenance, utilization, and life-cycle management. Misfit in this archetype appears through predictable mechanisms: Bottlenecks form, delays accumulate, inventory becomes imbalanced, capacity no longer matches demand, equipment downtime increases, and handoffs fail because work is constrained by the physics of the environment.

The Unwalled Transition

Although their assets remain physical, enterprise motion is no longer confined to physical boundaries. Physical Asset Enterprises now depend on e-commerce interfaces, digital customer journeys, omnichannel fulfillment, real-time data flows, platform systems, distributed operational networks, partner relationships, and predictive analytics. Customer behavior operates independently of location, partner performance determines operational outcomes, and digital systems mediate core workflows. Market signals now reach operations faster than physical assets can adjust.

The physical plant remains. Warehouses, factories, and facilities are tangible, fixed, and constrained by geography. But the systems that determine how those assets produce and deliver value—supply chains, demand signals, customer relationships, platform dependencies—operate without those same constraints.

In this archetype, the Natural Order expresses itself in physical terms: constraint, sequencing, load, and coordinated material motion. The governing structure is not different, but the medium through which it operates is.

The Twenty-First-Century Condition

Physical Asset Enterprises were the first to confront the collapse of the internal-external divide. E-commerce disruption, omnichannel expectations, digitally mediated customer experience, and globalized supply chains forced these enterprises into unwalled operation not by strategic choice but by structural necessity.

Physical constraints continue to govern production. Relational forces now govern whether that production reaches the right customers, through the right interfaces, at the pace those customers expect. This archetype carries industrial foundations into unwalled conditions—revealing how enterprises built on material systems encounter the same domain-level forces that govern knowledge-intensive enterprises, expressed through fundamentally different mechanics.

INTANGIBLE ASSET ENTERPRISES: DEFINED BY KNOWLEDGE

Intangible Asset Enterprises create enterprise value through knowledge, expertise, creativity, relationships, and digital capability rather than physical infrastructure. Their assets are not factories or fleets, but:

- Insight and judgment
- Intellectual property
- Creativity and expertise
- Data, algorithms, and software
- Digital products and platforms
- Content, brand, reputation, and relational capital

These enterprises form the backbone of the knowledge economy and represent the fastest-evolving segment of modern enterprise operating reality. They span professional services firms in law, accounting, engineering, consulting, architecture, and advisory; design, marketing, creative, and communications firms; financial services across banking, insurance, investment management, wealth advisory, and fintech; healthcare knowledge enterprises in diagnostics, telehealth, clinical decision support, and biotech research; SaaS and software enterprises; digital platforms and online marketplaces; education, training, and research institutions; content, media, and publishing enterprises; IP-based and licensing enterprises; and AI, data, and analytics-driven enterprises.

Regardless of sector, their shared identity is consistent: They produce and deliver enterprise value through intangible systems. Products may be experienced physically or digitally, but the enterprise value itself is intellectual, relational, or informational—the medium of enterprise value creation is interpretation, meaning, and digitally mediated coordination rather than physical production.

Their Structural Signature

Because their assets are intangible, these enterprises share a distinct structural profile shaped by interpretation rather than physical constraint. Knowledge and expertise are the primary instruments of enterprise value creation, with problem-solving, creativity, and learning constituting the observable activity of the enterprise. Information replaces inventory, making insights and relationships function as both inputs and constraints. Where physical enterprises coordinate material through space, intangible enterprises coordinate decisions through time—coherence depends on the speed and accuracy of interpretation rather than material handling. Interfaces are digital and relational, so that performance depends on communication quality, collaboration, and connection rather than physical throughput. Scalability follows from capability design, not machinery, with capacity constrained by talent, workflow architecture, and knowledge-sharing systems.

Misfit in this archetype appears as interpretive breakdown. Communication becomes unclear, assumptions diverge, decision timing slows, quality becomes inconsistent, digital interfaces fragment, and coordination across distributed teams degrades into isolated effort.

The Unwalled Transition

Unlike physical enterprises, Intangible Asset Enterprises did not evolve into unwalled systems; they emerged that way. Their operating structure has always been relational and digital. Teams collaborate across locations and time zones, work occurs asynchronously, and customers engage primarily through digital channels. Expertise moves through relationships, technology mediates every interaction, and markets change faster than planning cycles can absorb. What physical enterprises encountered as disruption has been the native operating reality of intangible enterprises from the beginning.

Because enterprise value in this archetype moves through knowledge, judgment, and relationship rather than through material production, the Natural Order governs through interpretation—how meaning converges, how decisions move, how coordination persists across distributed effort, and how relational coherence sustains or fractures. The governing structure is the same one that acts on physical enterprises; the medium through which it operates is not.

Domain Expression Across the Two Enteprise Archetypes

Enterprise Domain	Physical Asset Enterprise	Intangible Asset Enterprise
People + Alignment	Operational understanding, safety, role clarity	Shared meaning, trust, expectation alignment
Processes + Integration	Sequencing, load, physical continuity	Knowledge pathways, tool integration
Execution + Intelligence	Throughput, cycle time, telemetry	Responsiveness, insight quality, learning
Customer + Interaction	Physical reliability and availability	Interpretive experience and perception
Economics + Metrics	Capital utilization, depreciation, cost-to-serve	Utilization, pricing logic, capability investment

Table 5.3

The Twenty-First-Century Condition

Intangible Asset Enterprises represent the most dynamic segment of the global economy. They scale faster, adapt more quickly, face higher expectations, experience faster competitive cycles, and depend heavily on coherence across distributed teams. That dependence makes the governing forces of enterprise behavior visible in their most concentrated form—where misfit cannot hide behind physical buffers, and where the consequences of interpretive breakdown register immediately in enterprise value, customer retention, and competitive position.

Whether enterprise value moves through physical assets or intangible ones, the same domain-level forces act on both archetypes. This archetype surfaces that reality at speed, because the absence of physical structure removes every buffer between coherence and its loss.

HOW BOTH ARCHETYPES CONVERGED INTO THE UNWALLED ENTERPRISE

Physical Asset Enterprises and Intangible Asset Enterprises emerged as distinct archetypes shaped by fundamentally different modes of enterprise value creation. One archetype organizes enterprise motion around the movement and transformation of physical goods—through factories, fleets, and facilities. The other organizes motion around the creation, interpretation, and application of knowledge, meaning, and expertise—through relationships, judgment, and information systems. For much of the twentieth century, treating these archetypes as distinct operating realities was both accurate and practically useful.

Their strategies, operating models, and constraints differed because each archetype was built for a specific form of enterprise value creation, and that distinction held as long as the surrounding environment reinforced it.

In the twenty-first century, that separation ended—not because enterprises became the same, but because the operating conditions they faced did. Across the industries and scales observed in the fieldwork, every enterprise now participates in the same relational field: one in which customer priorities shift continuously, platforms mediate interactions, technology accelerates feedback, and market signals propagate faster than enterprise coordination structures can absorb. Physical Asset Enterprises and Intangible Asset Enterprises now operate under the same unwalled conditions, even though their modes of enterprise value creation remain distinct.

The End of the Internal-External Divide

In the industrial era, enterprises largely controlled the conditions of enterprise value creation. Customer engagement occurred at defined points of interaction rather than as continuous participation in enterprise motion. Partner relationships were structured as discrete exchanges rather than ongoing coordination. Information moved in predictable cycles, and feedback arrived slowly enough to be absorbed through formal review. Separation provided stability because operating conditions remained stable enough to support it.

Those assumptions no longer hold. Customers shape expectations continuously. Partners integrate directly into operational workflows, platforms govern both visibility and exchange, and information propagates instantly through digital systems. Talent collaborates across geography and time zones without waiting for instruction. The distinction between "inside" and "outside" no longer maps to how enterprises behave.

Relational Dependence and Shared Signals

Both archetypes have become dependent on extended relational systems, though the components and constraints of those systems differ. Physical Asset Enterprises sustain performance through interconnected supply networks, logistics platforms, distributed production partners, digital coordination tools, and real-time demand signals. For Intangible Asset Enterprises, coordination depends on cloud infrastructure, distributed talent networks, digital collaboration platforms, global knowledge flows, partner systems, platform algorithms, and continuous customer feedback.

In both cases, coherence can no longer be maintained solely through enterprise coordination; it must be preserved across permeable interfaces where work, information, and enterprise value move through relational interactions rather than through contained handoffs.

Despite the different mechanics of each archetype, both are now governed by immediate signals that act on performance as they arise. Supply disruptions, demand shifts, platform changes, competitive movements, regulatory updates, talent dynamics, and learning curves all register as actionable conditions rather than delayed feedback. The source and timing of these signals vary by archetype, but the structural requirement does not: Enterprises must sense, interpret, adjust, and renew under continuous conditions. Periodic recalibration no longer matches the speed at which operating conditions change for either archetype.

Convergence Without Erasure

Physical Asset Enterprises express the Five Enterprise Domains through physical sequencing, capacity management, timing, safety, and reliability. Intangible Asset Enterprises express the same domains through interpretation, relational coordination, decision movement, responsiveness, and value perception. The modes of motion differ, but the governing structure does not.

Coherence originates through People + Alignment in both archetypes, though its expression differs: shared understanding of physical workflows in one, interpretive convergence across distributed teams in the other. Processes + Integration then organizes enterprise motion, whether that motion takes the form of material sequencing or knowledge coordination. The conversion of motion into performance falls to Execution + Intelligence, surfaced through throughput and defect rates in physical enterprises and through responsiveness and learning cycles in intangible ones. Customer + Interaction is where that performance becomes enterprise value; availability and consistency define the experience in one archetype, perception and meaning in the other. Economics + Metrics close the cycle by conserving and extending enterprise value, governed by capital discipline and asset utilization in physical enterprises and by pricing logic, retention, and capability investment in intangible ones.

As conditions changed, the archetypes began absorbing elements from one another. Manufacturing firms adopted data platforms and digital twins, professional services firms implemented workflow systems and analytics, and retailers became omnichannel platforms. On the intangible side, SaaS enterprises built global service operations, logistics firms applied predictive technologies, and consulting firms developed productized digital assets. This borrowing accelerated structural convergence without erasing the differences in how each archetype creates enterprise value.

Customers completed the convergence. They no longer distinguish between physical and intangible value flows; they evaluate coherence. Retail customers expect seamless digital and physical integration; manufacturing customers expect visibility and responsiveness. A SaaS customer evaluates human understanding alongside technical reliability, while a consulting client measures structured delivery supported by digital tools. Experience now moves through platforms, relationships, social signals, and instantaneous feedback, requiring every enterprise—regardless of asset base—to operate without walls.

Both archetypes now operate within the same structural reality: coherence across relational fields, immediate sensing, continuous renewal, permeable interfaces, customer-interpreted value, and integrated motion across people, process, execution, customer, and economics. The governing structure did not change as enterprise conditions evolved. The archetypes converged because the conditions surrounding them became unwalled—and the structure that had always governed both became visible.

HYBRID ENTERPRISES: OPERATING ACROSS BOTH ARCHETYPES

Many enterprises do not sort into a single archetype. A software enterprise that maintains physical distribution infrastructure operates as an Intangible Asset Enterprise in product development and as a Physical Asset Enterprise in logistics. A manufacturing enterprise whose revenue increasingly depends on service contracts carries both physical load in production and intangible load in customer relationships. Healthcare enterprises deliver physical care through facilities and equipment while simultaneously operating digital platforms that govern scheduling, records, and patient interaction. In each case, the enterprise contains both archetypes simultaneously—often within different business units, product lines, or value streams.

The domains through which physical load concentrates—typically Processes + Integration and portions of Execution + Intelligence—behave according to the physical archetype: Load is tangible, variability is constrained by material limits, and capacity is governed by throughput. Intangible load concentrates differently, typically through People + Alignment, Customer + Interaction, and portions of Economics + Metrics. There, load is interpretive, variability follows meaning rather than material, and capacity depends on coordination density.

Because the Five Enterprise Domains behave differently under each archetype, the same domain within the same enterprise may require different structural conditions depending on which archetype governs it. People + Alignment in a physical-asset division depends on shared understanding of capacity, sequencing, and physical constraint. In an intangible-asset division within the same enterprise, People + Alignment depends on interpretive convergence across distributed judgment. Both are People + Alignment. Each requires different structural conditions to sustain coherence.

The structural consequence of hybrid operation is that archetype-specific pressure acts on different domains simultaneously. Physical constraints in one part of the system interact with interpretive variability in another, and the interfaces between them—where a manufactured product depends on software-mediated customer experience, or where a knowledge service depends on physical infrastructure—carry load that neither archetype alone can account for. Because the structural logic on each side differs, these cross-archetype interfaces carry the highest coordination load. A manufacturing enterprise whose service contracts generate the majority of its revenue cannot read customer response through a physical production lens; customer meaning in the service relationship operates through intangible dynamics even though the underlying product is physical. The archetype that governs a domain's behavior is determined by the load that domain carries, not by how the enterprise is classified at the entity level.

The two archetypes apply at the domain level, not the enterprise level. In a hybrid enterprise, each domain's behavior is governed by whichever archetype characterizes its load, and coherence depends on whether the interfaces between archetype-governed domains sustain correspondence as both forms of load interact.

Three structural signals indicate that a hybrid enterprise's cross-archetype interfaces are failing to carry the coordination they require.

Inconsistent decision logic is the most visible: Decisions made under physical archetype assumptions—throughput discipline, capacity scheduling, material sequencing—collide with decisions made under intangible assumptions of interpretive alignment, knowledge circulation, and relational positioning at the same interface.

A second signal appears as mismatched renewal timing: The physical domains renew on equipment cycles, facility constraints, and supply continuity, while the intangible domains renew on interpretive shifts, capability evolution, and relational repositioning. When these cycles operate independently, the interface between them accumulates misfit that neither side's renewal addresses.

The third signal—load translation failure—presents when the output of a physical domain enters an intangible domain without structural translation: Production data crosses into customer relational systems without interpretive conversion, or knowledge-intensive design crosses into manufacturing execution without material specification.

Each of these signals indicates that the interface between archetype-governed domains is carrying coordination it was not built to sustain.

WHAT CONVERGENCE DEMANDS

The convergence described in this chapter creates a structural problem that recognition alone cannot resolve. The two archetypes share the same governing structure, but that structure expresses itself differently depending on the substance of enterprise value being carried. The same domain—People + Alignment, Processes + Integration, Execution + Intelligence, Customer + Interaction, Economics + Metrics—behaves one way when enterprise value moves through physical systems and another way when it moves through interpretation, knowledge, and relational coordination. Generic examination of how enterprises operate will not account for that difference.

When leaders misread their asset base, the consequences are structural. Physical Asset Enterprises that adopt interpretive coordination methods without addressing material constraints do not become more responsive, but lose operational continuity. Intangible Asset Enterprises that impose physical sequencing logic on knowledge work do not gain discipline, but slow the interpretive movement on which enterprise value depends. The asset base determines which signals indicate misfit, which forms of renewal restore coherence, and which structural responses produce results. In physical enterprises, misfit registers as demand variability, supply disruption, capacity bottlenecks, and system wear. In intangible enterprises, misfit registers as expectation shifts, knowledge decay, capability mismatch, and coordination breakdown. Both archetypes require continuous renewal, but the triggers differ—and so does the form renewal must take.

This means that domain-level examination cannot proceed generically. Each of the Five Enterprise Domains must be understood in terms specific enough to account for how physical and intangible asset bases shape its expression, its constraints, and its failure modes. That examination begins at the point where coherence originates—the domain through which enterprise motion first takes form.

. . .

THIS CHAPTER CLARIFIED that enterprises do not encounter structural limits for the same reasons, even when they operate under the same unwalled conditions. The nature of the enterprise value being carried—physical or intangible—shapes how motion behaves, where load accumulates, and how coherence weakens. Yet across both archetypes, one fact remains constant: Coherence originates with people, not with structure, execution, or markets.

Interpretation must converge before work can be sequenced, before learning can compound, before enterprise value can be recognized or protected. Meaning and direction must stabilize together. Regardless of asset base, every enterprise enters coherence through its human field—or fails to. Chapter 6 begins the examination of the Five Enterprise Domains at that origin point: People + Alignment, the domain in which enterprise motion first takes form and value potential is created.

PART II

THE FIVE ENTERPRISE DOMAINS

6

PEOPLE + ALIGNMENT

THE HUMAN ENGINE AS THE FIRST FIELD OF MOTION

Every enterprise begins with people. In this domain, people are not limited to employees: They include all individuals whose actions, decisions, or interpretations shape how enterprise motion takes form.

Before strategy exists, before structure is defined, and before processes, technologies, or metrics are introduced, human interpretation is already forming the preconditions for enterprise value creation or loss. Individuals encounter one another around intent and constraint, bringing prior experiences, assumptions, incentives, fears, and judgments. Meaning is negotiated through interaction, and coordinated action emerges only after that meaning stabilizes. Enterprise value is therefore conditioned here before it can be created, amplified, or protected elsewhere. This occurs before the enterprise acquires formal shape or designation.

> **People + Alignment** is the enterprise domain through which interpretation, trust, and shared meaning form wherever the enterprise

comes into contact with people, establishing the conditions for coherent human motion.

People are the origin point of enterprise motion and the first determinant of enterprise value flow. The convergence or fragmentation of early action, the compounding or cancellation of effort, and the operational compatibility of intent are all determined here. How attention is allocated, which priorities are deferred, and what is disregarded altogether take form through human interpretation, establishing the enterprise's initial allocation of attention, effort, and economic energy before any formal mechanism intervenes. The capacity to interpret direction, commit under uncertainty, and adjust to consequence determines whether work reinforces itself or dissipates. Where shared interpretation converges, enterprise energy converts into enterprise value with less corrective cost; as it fragments, resistance accumulates early and shifts downstream, increasing the cost of coordination, execution, and value realization.

Interpretation precedes all other forms of organization, and the enterprise domains reflect this. The Five Enterprise Domains do not activate through leadership choice; they are present from the moment coordinated activity exists. People + Alignment establishes the initial conditions of coherence by stabilizing interpretation before work is structured. It determines the form decisions take, the way authority is understood, and the conditions under which coordination becomes possible at all.

The other domains—Processes + Integration, Execution + Intelligence, Customer + Interaction, and Economics + Metrics—respond to the interpretive conditions established here. Each depends on the degree to which meaning is shared and trust is present before work is carried or executed. Where coordination proceeds from a common reference, downstream domains require less manual intervention and compensatory effort; as interpretation fragments, load shifts outward, and other domains absorb it to sustain performance.

What People + Alignment Stabilizes

Condition Established	What Stabilizes Here	Downstream Effect
Shared interpretation	Meaning of purpose and priority	Compatible decisions
Trust	Willingness to commit under uncertainty	Reduced coordination cost
Decision authority	Who resolves what, when	Predictable timing
Expectation alignment	Pace, urgency, and accountability	Synchronized action
Interpretive norms	What is treated as signal vs distraction	Reduced rework

Table 6.1

People do not simply supply effort to the enterprise; they generate its usable energy. Decision timing, certainty of action, information movement, priority interpretation, trust formation, and conflict resolution are all functions of how meaning persists among people—and together they determine the enterprise's learning capacity. These dynamics are governed less by formal policy than by the informal rules that emerge through repeated interaction. Those rules determine the pace and quality of work.

People + Alignment is a structural condition, not a leadership activity. Coherence originates in human interpretation, misalignment forms before it is visible elsewhere, and the domain's interpretive conditions govern every other domain that follows. All downstream behavior is conditioned by the interpretive patterns set here.

Across every enterprise I have observed, this domain appears first. Before process disconnects, execution variability, customer inconsistency, or financial instability become visible, there is a shift in how purpose, priorities, and expectations are interpreted. That shift may appear as decision timing losing consistency, assumed agreement that fails to persist in action, or actions that are individually rational but collectively incompatible. People + Alignment consistently surfaces as the earliest structural indicator of enterprise condition. As interpretation fragments at the source, the effects register across every other domain; where shared expectations remain intact, the scale and coordination demands that overwhelm other domains remain absorbable.

People + Alignment: The Origin of Enterprise Motion

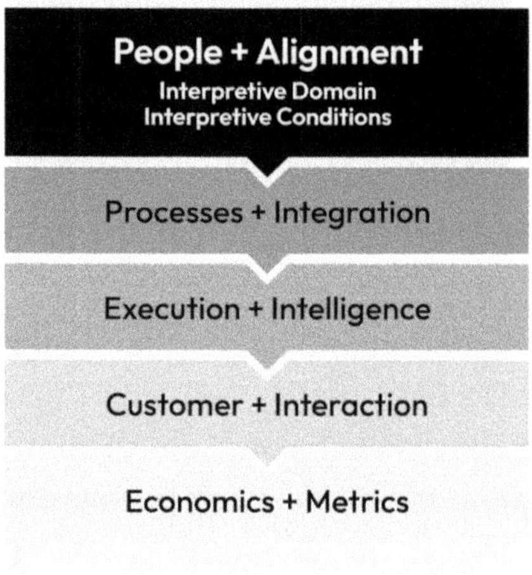

Figure 6.1

THE ROLE OF PEOPLE + ALIGNMENT IN THE NATURAL ORDER

People + Alignment is not a department, function, or initiative. It occupies the first position in the Natural Order because no other domain can begin operating until interpretive conditions have formed. In this domain, interpretation settles before work is organized, expectations form before structure is imposed, and interaction patterns consolidate before any formal mechanism regulates behavior. Whether the enterprise moves as a single system or fragments into incompatible motion is determined by what stabilizes here.

The Governing Role of People + Alignment

Aspect	What This Domain Governs
Domain position	First domain in the Natural Order
Primary function	Interpretation of purpose, priority, and authority
What it receives	Intent, aspiration, strategic direction
What it performs	Meaning-making, expectation setting, trust formation
Governing condition	Interpretive coherence

Table 6.2

The moment two or more people commit to a shared outcome, interpretation begins forming through interaction rather than design. Purpose is interpreted differently across participants, roles separate through assumption as much as design, and norms form through repeated interaction. Communication patterns, expectations of pace, and assumptions about authority consolidate early and persist, often long after conditions change. These early interpretive conditions become durable constraints on how the enterprise can operate.

As additional participants enter the enterprise's operating field, those interpretive conditions shift. New assumptions are introduced—some reinforcing shared meaning and others fragmenting it—causing alignment to consolidate or erode through accumulated interaction over time.

What This Domain Governs

People + Alignment governs the practical interpretation of purpose, the sorting of priorities under pressure, the formation of trust through experience, and the inference of decision authority before it is formalized. It determines whether people share a common understanding of what matters, how quickly decisions should form, and how responsibility is assumed or avoided. Where these interpretive conditions remain stable, coordination emerges without enforcement and downstream domains operate with predictability; as they destabilize, coordination must be imposed, and downstream domains rely on substitution to proceed.

Where decision logic is shared and trusted, decisions form with consistency, accountability consolidates without enforcement, and meaning circulates ahead of formal guidance. As that logic fragments, delays and contradictions emerge in decision-making, expectations diverge, and every downstream domain absorbs additional load to sustain motion through compensatory effort.

How This Domain Receives from the Enterprise System

People + Alignment is the first domain in the Natural Order, but it is not closed to the rest of the enterprise system. Interpretation, trust, and shared meaning form in response to conditions that already exist. People do not align in a vacuum; they interpret purpose and priority through the structures, experiences, and consequences they encounter as the enterprise moves.

Processes + Integration shapes People + Alignment through structural feasibility. Where structure fits the work, roles remain coherent, decisions resolve with grounding, and expectations stabilize. As structure loses fit, people encounter confusion, delay, and ambiguity long before they can name the cause. Interpretation adjusts to what structure permits, not to what leadership asserts.

What People + Alignment Receives From Other Domains

Upstream Domain	What Registers Interpretively
Processes + Integration	Structural constraints on intent and feasibility
Execution + Intelligence	Evidence of what holds under real conditions
Customer + Interaction	Buyer interpretation of enterprise meaning
Economics + Metrics	Limits, tradeoffs, and sustainability signals

Table 6.3

Execution + Intelligence shapes alignment through lived evidence. Where execution proceeds without intervention or compensatory effort, trust builds and interpretation converges because experience reinforces meaning. As execution increasingly depends on escalation or compensating controls, meaning fragments and people revise their assumptions about what is possible.

Customer + Interaction shapes People + Alignment through relational response. Customer adoption, resistance, appreciation, or disappointment becomes a powerful interpretive signal that shapes how people understand whether their work matters and whether enterprise priorities are credible. These signals condition interpretation more powerfully than formal messaging.

Economics + Metrics shapes People + Alignment through financial constraint and enterprise viability. When economic signals are coherent, people interpret tradeoffs through margin, capacity, and capital limits, and adjust expectations based on what the enterprise can sustain financially. As those signals conflict or lag, alignment fractures as assumptions diverge about cost, risk, and economic feasibility.

People + Alignment is therefore the interpretive boundary where structural, operational, relational, and economic conditions are translated into meaning. Interpretation is reinforced or destabilized here before any downstream domain can correct for it.

Systemic Consequence

Where shared interpretation remains consistent, enterprise behavior stabilizes as a single system. Information circulates without loss of meaning, decisions remain compatible across contexts, and accountability consolidates without enforcement. As interpretive fragmentation begins at the source, instability is displaced into every other domain. Process structure loses fit with the work it carries, execution loses consistency across contexts, customer experience loses continuity, and economic signals lose comparability across the system. Leadership response shifts toward oversight, escalation, and corrective intervention—structural indicators that coherence has begun to give way.

The positioning of People + Alignment at the front of the Natural Order reflects a structural fact, not a claim of importance: The interpretive conditions that form here govern the operating state every other domain inherits.

People + Alignment in the Relational Fields

People + Alignment governs wherever the enterprise comes into contact with people. That scope does not end at the organizational boundary. The enterprise operates continuously within two relational fields—the Customer Field and the Market Field—and both are populated by people whose interpretation, trust, and shared meaning condition how enterprise motion reaches and returns from those fields.

In the Customer Field, People + Alignment does not govern the relational field itself: That is the structural territory of Customer + Interaction. It governs the interpretive conditions of every person the enterprise deploys into that field. Whether customer-facing people share a common understanding of commitment, responsiveness, and value before they enter the Customer Field determines whether the enterprise's relational position is coherent or variable at the point of contact. Where interpretive conditions among customer-facing people are coherent, consistent behavior across interactions follows. As those conditions fragment, variability enters the Customer Field that Customer + Interaction's governing mechanisms must absorb before the relational position can stabilize.

In the Market Field, People + Alignment operates through the same mechanism: governing the interpretive conditions of the people the enterprise engages across that field, not the field itself. Partners, vendors, suppliers, and other market participants form working interpretations of the enterprise through repeated interaction. Those interpretations—whether the enterprise is reliable, whether its commitments are credible, whether its people share a common operating frame—determine the structural integrity of the coordination the enterprise can sustain across the Market Field. Shared meaning does not require formal employment; it requires sufficient interpretive convergence for coordinated action to form and persist. Where that convergence exists across market relationships, the enterprise's relational reach extends without compensatory effort. Without that convergence, the enterprise encounters the same substitution dynamic across its market relationships that it encounters within the Enterprise Field when interpretive conditions degrade.

People + Alignment governs the full span of the enterprise's relational system: not only the Enterprise Field. Leaders who read this domain as an internal condition—governing employees, teams, and organizational culture—are reading it correctly but incompletely. The interpretive conditions this domain governs travel wherever the enterprise's people go: into every customer interaction in the Customer Field, and into every working relationship with partners, vendors, and suppliers in the Market Field. Those fields are not governed by People + Alignment in the way the Enterprise Field is—but they are conditioned by the quality of interpretation, trust, and shared meaning that the enterprise's people carry into them. The reach of this domain is the reach of the enterprise itself[1].

That reach, however, does not guarantee what it produces. The domain extends wherever the enterprise's people go—but whether the interpretive conditions those people carry constitute genuine alignment, or only the appearance of it, determines whether coherence follows. That distinction is structural—it determines whether the enterprise's interpretive reach produces coherent motion or only its appearance.

ALIGNMENT VS. COHERENCE: A FOUNDATIONAL DISTINCTION

Alignment is frequently claimed by leadership teams and rarely tested. Agreement reached in discussion is often mistaken for compatibility in operation. Leaders may affirm priorities and depart assuming shared direction persists, yet divergence may appear once decisions encounter real conditions.

Alignment and coherence are not equivalent. Alignment describes agreement at a point in time. Coherence describes whether that agreement remains operationally compatible as the enterprise moves, scales, and encounters pressure. The distinction is not one of degree: Alignment is a precondition; coherence is the structural state that follows only when interpretation converts into sustained compatibility of action.

Alignment and Coherence: Distinct Operating Conditions

Alignment	Coherence
Agreement at a point in time	Compatibility across ongoing interaction
Expressed through intention	Revealed through behavior
Achieved through discussion	Sustained through structure
Can exist without integration	Requires integration
Provides direction	Provides capacity to act

Table 6.4

An enterprise can be aligned and still incoherent; agreement does not ensure integration. Where alignment fails to convert into coherence, the consequences compound in sequence: Decision timing diverges first, then interpretations conflict across coordination points, and effort accumulates without reinforcement until enterprise energy is absorbed through correction rather than converted into motion.

Enterprises do not underperform because agreement is absent. They underperform when agreement never converts into operational compatibility across the system. Alignment establishes a directional target; coherence is the condition that determines whether the enterprise can move toward it without compensatory effort, or whether every subsequent domain must absorb the cost of unresolved interpretation.

That conversion boundary sits squarely within the People + Alignment domain, governing whether the system carries more of its own load or begins generating destructive polarity through competing interpretations and duplicated efforts that accelerate structural decay.

LEADERSHIP AS THE SYNCHRONIZATION FUNCTION

Leadership is neither management nor authority. In the People + Alignment domain, leadership functions as the synchronization mechanism that stabilizes human interpretation, enabling coordinated action without continual correction. It is where coherence becomes visible in behavior rather than asserted through intent, and where every other enterprise domain inherits its interpretive conditions.

People infer how to operate by observing leadership behavior under real conditions rather than relying on formal statements. They register the treatment of priorities under pressure, the structure of communication, the resolution of disagreement, and the pace at which decisions form. From these signals, expectations consolidate and patterns of action take form. Where those signals remain consistent, coherence reinforces itself; as they lose consistency, variance enters shared interpretation.

Leadership synchronization operates through five recurring structural signals—direction, decision timing, strategic focus, communication structure, and adaptability—that regulate interpretive convergence within the People + Alignment domain in Table 6.5. These signals are structural behaviors, not techniques or preferences, and they directly condition enterprise motion. Each signal functions as a point at which leadership behavior either contains variance or introduces it into the system.

Leadership and Interpretive Variance

The primary structural effect of leadership in this domain is the introduction or containment of interpretive variance. Where shared meaning is stabilized through consistent signals, action reinforces itself without continual correction. As variance accumulates, coherence weakens first in the human domain, then becomes visible elsewhere.

Variance amplification is the most common way leadership misoperates in this domain[2]. It arises because leadership interaction is a high-gain signal source operating across multiple interpretive surfaces at once. Small differences in emphasis, timing, or resolution expand without coordination, producing locally rational action that becomes globally incompatible. The enterprise remains active, but shared meaning fragments. The mechanism operates through compounding stages. When leadership signals contradictory timing expectations across separate meetings—accelerating one initiative while extending deliberation on a related one—team leads interpret priority differently based on which signal they received. Those divergent interpretations produce incompatible process handoffs: One team advances work that the receiving team is not prepared to carry at the pace at which it is delivered. Execution quality becomes inconsistent as the downstream team compensates through effort rather than through structure. The customer encounters the inconsistency as variable responsiveness: the same enterprise delivering at different speeds depending on which internal pathway the request follows. By the time the inconsistency registers in financial reporting as margin compression or delivery cost variance, the originating signal—a timing contradiction in two separate leadership conversations—is invisible. Each stage of the cascade is locally rational; the systemic effect is structurally produced.

Leadership Synchronization Signals and Variance Introduction

Signal	Structural Function	How Variance Enters
Direction	Establishes what is treated as immediate, deferrable, or nonessential through repeated attention and decision resolution	When direction is interpreted inconsistently across leadership interactions, individuals substitute personal judgment for shared meaning; interpretive load increases and action slows
Decision timing	Governs whether work accumulates or converts by determining the pace at which decisions resolve	Unresolved decisions expand dependency across coordination points; decisions resolved without shared context generate rework downstream — both introduce variance into timing and priority
Strategic focus	Determines whether leadership attention is oriented toward structural design or embedded in execution cycles	Where leadership attention remains embedded in execution, interpretive authority contracts around immediate activity and coherence narrows to what is locally visible
Communication structure	Determines how information moves, how context accompanies decisions, and where meaning is resolved	Confusion originates in communication pathways that fragment interpretation, not in individual failure; variance enters where pathways lose structural definition
Adaptability	Determines whether interpretation is recalibrated through structural adjustment as conditions change	Where structural revision is resisted, coherence constricts around prior conditions; variance enters as the gap between operating reality and established interpretation widens

Table 6.5

This condition first appears in leadership interactions because leaders are the primary stabilizers of interpretation under uncertainty. As synchronization demand exceeds the capacity of leadership interaction to converge meaning, leadership behavior increases interpretive spread rather than containment. At this stage, the system remains functional, but without a uniform interpretive reference.

As variance accumulates, the effects compound through coordination, not through isolated failure. Decision resolution concentrates instead of distributing, dependency increases as teams reconcile incompatible timing manually, and priorities stabilize locally while fragmenting across the enterprise. These effects are not yet costs; they are early distortions of coordination.

These conditions are not leadership styles or failure modes. They are system expressions that appear when synchronization demand exceeds the capacity of leadership interaction to converge meaning, passing variance into downstream domains rather than resolving it here.

Leadership coherence weakens not through incorrect decisions, but when leadership behavior increases variance at the point where the system requires convergence. In the People + Alignment domain, this distinction determines whether enterprise energy converts into coordinated action or enters later domains without a shared baseline for coordination.

ORGANIZATIONAL DESIGN AS HUMAN FLOW ARCHITECTURE

Many enterprises approach organizational design through boxes, reporting lines, layers, and titles—the visible arrangement of the enterprise. That arrangement is real, but it does not reveal what the design actually governs: how human effort converts into coordinated action, how work advances, how decisions form, how information moves, and how people coordinate across the enterprise. Structure does not merely sustain motion; it constrains or carries it. The enterprise behaves according to the design it inhabits, whether that design is intentional or accidental.

People experience organizational design long before they see it. They encounter it through the effort required to complete work, the presence or absence of decision authority, and the reliability with which issues are resolved and returned. Where design fits the work, coordination proceeds without explanation, and effort converts directly into outcomes. As design loses fit, interpretive burden increases—repeated clarification, escalation, and substitution of effort become necessary simply to maintain motion.

The relationship between design and variance is structural. Design fitted to the work being carried absorbs upstream variance through structure itself: Decisions resolve predictably, coordination requires less intervention, and corrective activity recedes. As design falls behind the work, variance amplifies: Roles blur, authority loses definition, and performance becomes dependent on added coordination rather than structure. No increase in effort can offset a structure that no longer matches the enterprise's operating reality.

Design is not a one-time event; it is architecture that changes as scale, scope, and operating conditions change. Structures that function at a small scale cease to carry load as coordination demands increase. The Natural Order of the enterprise requires design to remain fitted to coordination demand, and the cost of that lost fit appears as variance amplification before it appears as performance degradation.

The architecture of organizational design operates through five structural elements—span of control, decision rights, interfaces between teams, cross-team integration, and scalability—each of which determines whether variance is absorbed or amplified at a specific point in the system in Table 6.6. These elements do not describe preferred configurations or design conventions. They describe the structural points at which the enterprise's capacity to absorb variance is either preserved or exceeded.

What determines whether variance is absorbed is not the quality of any single design element but the fit between the full architecture and the work the enterprise is now required to carry. When span, authority, interfaces, integration, and scalability remain fitted to operating demand, the architecture absorbs variance structurally, and leadership intervention recedes. As that fit erodes—through growth, reorganization, market shift, or accumulated structural neglect—variance passes through design rather than being contained by it, and every downstream domain inherits the amplified load.

Organizational Design Elements and Variance Behavior

Design Element	Structural Function	Variance Consequence When Misfit
Span of Control	Coherence bandwidth constraint—determines how much interpretive consistency a leader can sustain across teams	Wide spans lose synchronization capacity; narrow spans concentrate decision resolution and accumulate dependency
Decision Rights	Determines who resolves, when resolution occurs, and what logic governs resolution	Ambiguity in decision authority produces resistance, resurface cycles, and bypassed resolution—inconsistency spreads into downstream domains
Interfaces Between Teams	Governs how handoffs, shared ownership, escalation, and cross-team dependency transfer work across boundaries	Undefined interfaces absorb energy through rework, duplication, and interpretive reconciliation at boundaries
Cross-Team Integration	Determines whether coherence is maintained across functional boundaries or confined within them	Functional excellence without integration weakens the system—teams perform well in isolation while generating incompatibility
Scalability	Determines whether structure evolves in step with coordination demand as the enterprise grows	Structures designed for prior scale lose carrying capacity—decision authority, interfaces, and responsibility fail to redistribute

Table 6.6

COMMUNICATION FLOW AS THE HUMAN FEEDBACK LAYER

Communication is not a matter of volume; it is a matter of structure—the direction, timing, and pathways through which information, meaning, and interpretation move. Every enterprise generates extensive communication, yet few maintain coherent communication across interfaces.

Communication functions as the feedback layer of the enterprise—the structural mechanism through which people register conditions, interpret direction, coordinate action, and convert experience into adjustment. Where communication pathways preserve a common reference, the enterprise adjusts with minimal delay because meaning circulates without loss. As those pathways fragment, the enterprise becomes reactive and increasingly dependent on escalation to resolve conditions that should have stabilized locally.

The conversion sequence that communication carries is structural, not metaphorical: Alignment converts into shared understanding, which converts into coordinated action, which converts into performance, which converts into learning. When these conversions remain intact, the enterprise stays responsive to reality instead of becoming trapped in retrospective correction. Without reliable feedback pathways, the enterprise loses its ability to register conditions accurately and respond before interpretive lag accumulates.

Variance enters communication flow through the same structural channels it enters every other part of the human domain—but communication is where variance becomes visible as signal degradation[3]. The interpretive variance introduced through leadership behavior and amplified or absorbed through organizational design now travels through the enterprise's communication pathways. Where those pathways remain structurally intact, variance is contained because meaning circulates with sufficient context to preserve shared reference. As pathways lose structure, variance compounds: Meaning degrades across handoffs, direction loses context in transit, and feedback arrives too late or too distorted to correct the conditions it registers.

Communication flow operates through four structural pathways—vertical flow, horizontal flow, relational flow, and feedback loops—each of which carries a distinct form of signal and degrades in a distinct manner as variance accumulates in Table 6.7. What matters for the People + Alignment domain is not the volume of communication traveling through these pathways but the structural integrity of the pathways themselves.

Communication Pathways and Signal Degradation

Pathway	Structural Function	How Variance Degrades Signal
Vertical Flow	Coherence bandwidth constraint—determines how much interpretive consistency a leader can sustain across teams	Wide spans lose synchronization capacity; narrow spans concentrate decision resolution and accumulate dependency
Horizontal Flow	Governs coordination across teams without requiring leadership intermediation	Where lateral coordination breaks at interfaces, handoffs fracture, effort duplicates, and customer experience loses consistency—most communication breakdowns originate at boundaries, not within teams
Relational Flow	Connects the enterprise to its external environment —customers, partners, regulators, markets	As external signal connection weakens, execution loses correspondence with real-world demand while internal indicators lag, sustaining assumptions that no longer reflect operating reality
Feedback Loops	Determines how quickly the enterprise recognizes patterns, corrects error, and converts experience into interpretation	Where feedback circulates continuously, response time compresses and coherence reinforces itself; as feedback delays or breaks, learning slows, outdated behavior persists, and resistance accumulates without correction

Table 6.7

The consequence of signal degradation is the progressive loss of shared reference across the enterprise, not miscommunication in the colloquial sense. Vertical flow narrows first: Leadership decisions form without adequate contact with operating reality. Horizontal flow fractures next, and coordination between teams shifts to escalation, where shared context once sufficed. Relational flow weakens in parallel as execution separates from external demand. Delayed feedback compounds the other three, leaving the enterprise operating under assumptions that no longer reflect its conditions. Each pathway degradation reinforces the others, and the cumulative effect is an enterprise that generates increasing communication volume while extracting decreasing interpretive value from it. Vertical flow degradation presents as decisions that do not translate into action and front-line conditions that do not reach leadership—the enterprise plans without contact and executes without direction. Horizontal flow degradation produces duplicated effort across teams, failed handoffs, and coordination that requires managerial escalation for conditions that should resolve laterally—teams that share interfaces cannot share context. When relational flow degrades, enterprise behavior diverges from customer and partner expectations without internal detection—the enterprise loses contact with the relational field it depends on. Feedback loop degradation compounds the other three: Repeated mistakes persist, lessons go unincorporated, and structural conditions survive review cycles without correction. The enterprise registers its own condition without adjusting to it. Where multiple pathways degrade simultaneously, the diagnostic priority is vertical flow, because it governs whether leadership interpretation remains in contact with the conditions that produce all other pathway failures.

Communication flow does not create variance. It transmits and compounds the variance that originates upstream. The structural condition of communication pathways determines whether the People + Alignment domain can sustain shared meaning under load, or whether meaning degrades faster than the enterprise can restore it.

TALENT ARCHITECTURE AS ENTERPRISE CAPACITY FORMATION

Talent is not a roster of people—it is the enterprise's system for forming capacity. Skills, roles, development pathways, and succession logic are structural components that determine how much enterprise energy can be generated, how effectively that energy can be directed, and how much structural continuity the enterprise can sustain as conditions change.

People + Alignment establishes the initial conditions of enterprise motion; talent architecture determines how far that motion can be carried and sustained. It governs how much work the enterprise can absorb, how rapidly capability can adapt, and how reliably performance is maintained over time. Enterprises without coherent talent architecture encounter a capacity ceiling well before a market ceiling.

The variance that enters through leadership behavior, passes through organizational design, and degrades communication pathways eventually reaches the enterprise's capacity structure. Talent architecture is where that variance encounters structural limits: the points at which the enterprise can no longer absorb additional load through effort alone.

Three structural questions determine where those limits appear: whether the enterprise possesses the capabilities required by its work, whether those capabilities are assigned to roles that match decision and delivery demand, and whether future capacity is being built before constraints arise. Enterprises that cannot resolve these questions encounter rising limits regardless of process discipline or technology investment. Capability gaps function as structural ceilings, misplaced talent slows conversion at critical coordination points, and absent capability renewal reduces the enterprise's capacity to sustain continuity. Talent architecture therefore determines whether the enterprise sustains continuity or enters cycles of structural reset as demand outpaces capacity.

Talent architecture operates through five structural components —skills and capability mapping, role design, career pathways, succession logic, and learning and development—each of which governs a distinct dimension of enterprise capacity (Table 6.8). These components do not describe talent management preferences. They describe the structural points at which capacity is either sustained or exceeded.

Talent Architecture Components and Capacity Constraints

Component	Structural Function	Capacity Constraint When Misfit
Skills and Capability Mapping	Ongoing structural discipline that clarifies what capabilities exist, what is required, and where constraint will emerge	Where capability expands faster than placement, effort disperses; where demand expands faster than capability, execution cannot convert intent into results—unacknowledged gaps function as structural limits
Role Design	Structural definition of success criteria, boundaries, decision authority, and the relationship between responsibility and accountability	Vague, overly broad, or inconsistently defined roles become sources of interpretive variance and dependency—duplicated effort, delayed resolution, and eroded trust across interfaces
Career Pathways	Signal whether the enterprise compounds capability over time by connecting contribution to expanded scope	Where pathways are absent, high performers exit when contribution can no longer expand in step with enterprise demand—talent exits faster than it can be developed, and renewal capacity constricts
Succession Logic	Preserves interpretive continuity at moments of role transition by sustaining institutional knowledge and decision patterns	Without succession logic, role transitions produce turbulence—institutional knowledge dissipates, decision patterns fracture, and coherence resets at the point of highest leverage
Learning and Development	Renews structural fit within the human domain by evolving capability in correspondence with changing demand	Where capability renewal stalls, skills that supported prior performance become insufficient—the enterprise loses adaptive capacity as conditions change, and structural fit degrades from within

Table 6.8

The capacity limits exposed by talent architecture are not resource constraints in the conventional sense. They are structural constraints on the enterprise's ability to carry the work its conditions now require. When talent architecture remains fitted to operating demand—capabilities matched to work, roles defined to carry decisions, pathways sustaining renewal, succession preserving continuity, and learning evolving fit—capacity absorbs variance and the enterprise sustains motion without structural reset. When fit deteriorates, capacity limits surface before performance declines: Conversion slows in critical areas, institutional knowledge concentrates in too few roles, decision authority exceeds the bandwidth of the people carrying it, and renewal falls behind the pace of change.

These limits are not visible in engagement scores or retention metrics until well after they have constrained the enterprise's operating capacity. They surface first as increased effort required to sustain prior performance levels—a structural tax that compounds as the gap between talent architecture and operating demand widens.

CULTURE AS THE PATTERN OF HUMAN COHERENCE

Culture is not an HR initiative, an engagement score, or a set of values displayed on a wall. Culture is pattern: the consistent, repeatable way people behave when guidance is absent or incomplete. It is the lived expression of the People + Alignment domain. What leaders describe as "culture" is the accumulation of behaviors the enterprise reinforces, tolerates, or leaves unaddressed over time.

Culture is the cumulative consequence of the interpretive conditions established upstream—the interpretation of direction, the resolution of decisions, the treatment of disagreement, and the signals people absorb about what is rewarded, avoided, or ignored. As these underlying patterns shift, culture follows; where they remain unchanged, behavior persists regardless of stated intent.

Because culture forms through accumulation rather than design, it absorbs variance the same way it absorbs everything else—gradually and without announcement. Normalization occurs when accumulated variance ceases to register as a condition requiring correction and is instead absorbed into the enterprise's accepted operating patterns. The enterprise does not decide to normalize; it normalizes because the patterns people rely on adjust incrementally to accommodate the variance they encounter, until the adjusted state becomes indistinguishable from intended operation.

Cultural Patterns and Normalization of Variance

Pattern Type	What It Governs	How Variance Normalizes Through It
Behavioral Norms	The unwritten rules governing how people engage, respond, and follow through	As variance persists, norms adjust to accommodate it—caution, inconsistency, territorial behavior, or silence become expected rather than recognized as degradation
Decision Habits	The observable ways choices resolve in practice—concentration, distribution, pace, and context sufficiency	Where decision habits absorb variance without correction, resolution patterns stabilize around delay, insufficient context, or concentrated authority—and the enterprise treats those patterns as its operating rhythm
Conflict Patterns	Whether disagreement surfaces and resolves or is deferred, softened, or suppressed	Deferred conflict accumulates as unresolved tension that the enterprise absorbs as a normal operating cost; over time, suppression is treated as cooperation rather than as interpretive loss
Psychological Safety	Whether people surface risk, uncertainty, and early indicators of trouble without reprisal	Where psychological safety erodes, silence normalizes—truth takes longer to surface, and the enterprise loses its earliest correction mechanism without registering the loss
Learning Appetite	How quickly error converts into adjustment rather than concealment or rationalization	Where learning slows, the enterprise normalizes repetition of error—the same conditions recur without triggering structural correction, and adaptation stalls
Openness Under Pressure	Whether coordination is preserved or narrows as conditions tighten	Under pressure, defensive patterns replace open ones—communication contracts, resolution slows, and the enterprise normalizes escalation and manual intervention as its default operating mode

Table 6.9

Decisions that once resolved in hours now take weeks, and no one remarks on the change. Escalation that was once exceptional becomes the default path. Workarounds introduced as temporary measures persist without review. The enterprise works harder to produce the same results and treats the additional effort as the cost of doing business rather than as evidence that operating conditions have shifted beneath it.

Interpretive variance does not remain visible indefinitely. Variance that enters through leadership behavior, passes through organizational design, degrades communication pathways, and exceeds talent architecture eventually ceases to register as variance. Culture is the mechanism through which the enterprise normalizes its current operating state—absorbing accumulated variance into behavioral patterns that people treat as "how things work here" rather than as conditions requiring correction.

Cultural patterns exert disproportionate influence on normalization because they form the environment in which human interpretation stabilizes or loses common reference (Table 6.9). Six pattern types—behavioral norms, decision habits, conflict patterns, psychological safety[4], learning appetite, and openness under pressure—each govern a distinct dimension of how the enterprise processes and ultimately absorbs variance. What makes these patterns structurally consequential is not their individual condition but their collective normalization effect: As each pattern adjusts to accommodate variance, the enterprise's baseline shifts without the shift being registered.

Culture Under Pressure

Culture becomes most legible under pressure because pressure removes discretion and reveals which patterns are structural rather than situational. As deadlines compress, errors surface, customers respond, or market conditions shift, people rely on the patterns they have already learned to trust. Under pressure, interpretation narrows, and the enterprise defaults to its most stable human signals.

Where cultural patterns have normalized coherence, pressure reinforces capability rather than destabilizing it. Information surfaces without delay, reality is confronted directly, and coordination remains intact as conditions change. Shared meaning persists, decisions stay compatible, and action remains synchronized without additional oversight.

Where cultural patterns have normalized variance, pressure exposes the normalization itself. Teams retreat into functional or personal boundaries, communication contracts, and decision resolution slows precisely when convergence is required. Coordination increasingly depends on escalation, repeated clarification, and manual intervention—absorbing energy to maintain baseline operation without advancing it. What was invisible under normal conditions becomes structurally visible under load.

Cultural Decay

Cultural decay is an early structural signal of misfit within the People + Alignment domain, and it is the most advanced stage of normalization. It begins as a gradual softening of shared expectations, not as a visible breakdown. Norms lose definition, accountability disperses, hesitation replaces resolution, meetings shift from decision-making to performance, problems recur without closure, and truth circulates more slowly across the enterprise.

Initially, these changes appear behavioral or interpersonal. Over time, they reveal a structural condition. As shared norms diverge, coherence detaches from operating reality, and the enterprise relies on additional oversight, coordination, and control to sustain baseline performance.

Cultural decay functions as a systemic signal that the human domain no longer corresponds to the enterprise's current scale or demand—a structural condition, not a subjective one. Left unaddressed, it becomes a precursor to destructive polarity and enterprise divergence.

The cost of cultural decay is not the decay itself but the loss of the enterprise's capacity to detect and correct it—because normalization has made the decayed state indistinguishable from operation.

INCENTIVE ALIGNMENT AS ENERGY DIRECTIONALITY

What leaders declare as priorities does not govern behavior. People act on what is rewarded, what is measured, and what carries consequence. Incentives are the mechanism through which those reinforcements take form. They create directionality in human effort by shaping what draws attention, how tradeoffs resolve, where energy is invested, and which outcomes are treated as legitimate. Incentive alignment is therefore not an exercise in pay-structure design; it is a structural mechanism that directs enterprise energy within the People + Alignment domain.

Every enterprise emits incentive signals, whether intentionally designed or structurally implied. These signals condition how success is interpreted and how effort is allocated. As interpretive conditions shift elsewhere in the system, incentives increasingly determine whether effort converges or disperses. Incentives that reinforce shared priorities stabilize interpretation and make coordinated action sustainable without continual intervention. Incentives that point toward competing outcomes redirect energy to incompatible paths rather than coordinated motion.

Incentive alignment governs how enterprise energy moves: what accelerates, what is deferred, what absorbs attention, and what loses directionality entirely. Even well-designed processes and technologies cannot carry work when incentives pull behavior elsewhere. Under these conditions, incentives do not influence behavior at the margin; they redirect the enterprise's operating capacity. Incentive signals that reinforce the Natural Order—shared direction, compatible decision-making, and coordinated action—carry load through structure rather than through pressure or oversight.

By the time variance has normalized into cultural patterns, the enterprise's incentive signals determine whether energy continues to flow toward enterprise priorities or has already been redirected. Incentives do not create variance; they give it directionality. Where normalization has made variance invisible, incentive signals determine the direction in which the enterprise's remaining capacity is spent—and that direction may or may not serve the enterprise's stated priorities.

Incentive alignment operates through five structural elements—rewards, performance metrics, recognition patterns, career outcomes, and decision rights—each of which establishes directionality in a distinct dimension of human effort (Table 6.10). These elements do not describe reward-structure design or individual inducement. They describe the structural signals through which the enterprise's energy is either concentrated toward shared priorities or dispersed across competing aims.

What determines whether incentives redirect energy is not the design of any single element but the degree of fit between the full incentive structure and the enterprise's operating priorities.

When that fit remains intact, effort concentrates without compulsion: Decisions reinforce enterprise direction, accountability consolidates, and performance sustains itself across cycles. As fit erodes, the redirection is cumulative: Teams pursue local success because incentive signals reward it, behavior loses consistency because metrics contradict stated priorities, and leadership responds with oversight and intervention because structural correction has not occurred. The enterprise increases control without restoring directionality, and load rises without the additional effort producing proportional return.

Once incentives have redirected energy away from coordinated motion, the conditions under which downstream domains operate are altered. Processes carry work shaped by incentive logic instead of enterprise logic. Execution reflects what was rewarded, not what was intended. Customer experience registers the inconsistency before the enterprise does. The cost is not measured solely by incentive misalignment, but by the cumulative redirection of enterprise capacity away from the outcomes the enterprise requires.

Incentive Elements and Energy Redirection

Incentive Element	Structural Function	How Energy Redirects When Misfit
Rewards	Define the reference frame through which people interpret success—which outcomes are worth pursuing and which are incidental	Where rewards favor isolated results over enterprise-level performance, interpretive contradiction appears and effort redirects toward outcomes that do not reinforce the system
Performance Metrics	Translate incentive logic into daily behavior by indicating what is measured, what is ignored, and what carries consequence	Where metrics reward activity disconnected from enterprise priorities, effort disperses and people succeed in ways that weaken the system—destructive polarity accelerates
Recognition Patterns	Condition behavior over time by making certain actions visible and valued beyond compensation—what leadership acknowledges becomes cultural currency	Where recognition conflicts with formal incentive signals, behavior splits between what is rewarded and what is acknowledged—the enterprise emits contradictory directionality
Career Outcomes	Communicate which capabilities and behaviors are trusted with greater responsibility through promotion, advancement, and expanded scope	Where advancement rewards isolated results without regard for enterprise impact, interpretive variance increases at the enterprise's highest-leverage coordination points
Decision Rights and Autonomy	Signal trust and ownership by establishing where authority resides and how consistently it is applied	Where autonomy is granted ambiguously or inconsistently, hesitation replaces resolution, escalation substitutes for judgment, and behavior diverges across the enterprise

Table 6.10

INTERPRETIVE CONDITIONING AND SYSTEMIC INFLUENCE OF PEOPLE + ALIGNMENT

Enterprises do not collapse when interpretive conditions degrade. They compensate. Variance enters through leadership behavior, is amplified or absorbed through organizational design, degrades communication pathways, exceeds talent capacity, normalizes into cultural patterns, and acquires directionality through incentive signals. Through each stage, the enterprise continues producing work, resolving decisions, serving customers, and reporting results. Nothing appears broken because nothing has stopped. But the mechanism through which the enterprise sustains motion has shifted. Structure no longer carries the load. Substitution does.

Substitution is the enterprise's compensatory response to degraded interpretive conditions. It appears when the conditions that were supposed to precede work—shared meaning, common reference, compatible interpretation—have eroded to the point where work proceeds without them. The enterprise does not halt; it replaces structural fit with added effort, manual coordination, escalation, oversight, and corrective activity. These substitutions sustain motion, but they do so at compounding cost, because every substitution absorbs capacity that would otherwise convert into enterprise value.

People + Alignment as the Interpretive Conditioning Domain

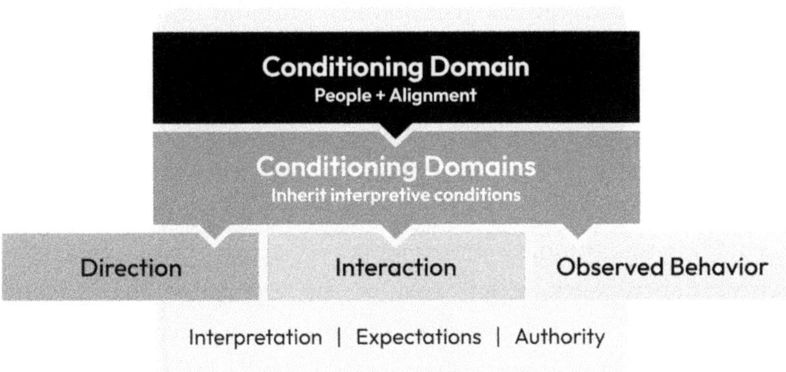

Figure 6.2

The behavior shift is systemic. It does not appear in a single domain or function. It appears everywhere the enterprise encounters the gap between what interpretive conditions were supposed to provide and what those conditions now deliver.

How Substitution Presents Across the Enterprise

Processes now carry interpretive debt. Where shared meaning once preceded structural design, processes now compensate for meaning that was never resolved. Exceptions accumulate not because conditions are exceptional but because the process was built on interpretive assumptions that no longer apply. Workarounds persist because removing them would expose the underlying unresolved variance. Process complexity becomes the visible cost of upstream interpretive failure—but the enterprise attributes it to operational scale or market demand rather than to degraded conditions in the human domain.

Execution now absorbs coordination cost directly. Where coordinated action once proceeded from compatible interpretation, execution now sustains itself through repeated meetings, escalation chains, and corrective cycles that substitute effort for coherence. Pacing becomes inconsistent, not because teams lack capability, but because the interpretive baseline from which they operate has fragmented. Reversals increase, rework compounds, and the enterprise experiences execution instability that it diagnoses as a performance problem rather than an interpretive one.

The substitution registers in customer experience before the enterprise detects it. Consistent behavior once stemmed from shared interpretation; customers now encounter variability that reflects the internal fragmentation. Commitments vary across interfaces, responsiveness depends on which part of the enterprise the customer encounters, and the coherence of the enterprise's external presence degrades. Customers do not diagnose interpretive failure—they experience it as unreliability, and their response reshapes the enterprise's relational position before internal metrics register the shift.

Financial signals absorb substitution cost without distinguishing it from productive work. Economic indicators that once tracked the conversion of enterprise energy into enterprise value now record compensatory effort as operating expense. Margins compress, not because pricing or demand has shifted, but because the enterprise is spending more energy to produce the same results. Forecasts lose accuracy because the assumptions beneath them are no longer grounded in shared interpretation. Financial systems become records of substitution cost disguised as operating expense.

Why Disruption Is Misdiagnosed

The most consequential effect of substitution is misdiagnosis. The enterprise experiences process complexity, execution instability, customer inconsistency, and financial compression—and attributes each to the domain where it appears. Process teams address process exceptions. Execution leaders increase oversight. Customer-facing teams adjust messaging. Finance tightens controls. Each response is locally rational and systemically insufficient, because the origin condition—degraded interpretive reference in the human domain—is never addressed.

These are not execution problems, process problems, customer problems, or financial problems. They are substitutive responses to interpretive breakdown upstream. As shared reference erodes at the source, the enterprise relies on added effort, tighter control, and increased oversight to preserve motion without restoring the conditions that would make motion self-sustaining. The cost of substitution is not the effort itself—it is the displacement of that effort away from enterprise value creation and toward the maintenance of operating continuity under degraded conditions.

THE WORK OF RENEWAL IN PEOPLE + ALIGNMENT

Interpretive conditions do not restore themselves. The degradation sequence described in the preceding sections does not reverse because leadership recognizes it. Recognition is necessary but does not produce reversal on its own. Renewal is the structural discipline through which interpretive conditions are deliberately restored after degradation has accumulated beyond what ongoing adjustment can absorb.

Renewal in this domain is not a communication initiative, a culture program, or an alignment workshop. Those interventions operate on the surface expressions of interpretive breakdown without addressing the structural conditions that produced them. An enterprise that responds to fragmented interpretation by increasing communication volume compounds distortion without restoring shared reference. One that responds to cultural decay by restating values addresses the symptom while leaving the structural sequence —variance, amplification, degradation, normalization—intact. Renewal restores the structural conditions themselves: the consistency of leadership signals, the fit between organizational design and the work being carried, the integrity of communication pathways, the correspondence between talent architecture and enterprise demand, and the alignment between incentive logic and enterprise direction.

When Renewal Becomes Necessary

Renewal becomes necessary when substitution has displaced coherence as the enterprise's operating mode. The signals are systemic, not isolated: Coordination cost rises across domains instead of within one, misdiagnosis becomes habitual where it was once occasional, and the enterprise's compensatory responses have themselves become sources of structural load. At this point, the interpretive conditions that preceded work have degraded enough that continuous adjustment—leadership attention, informal correction, localized realignment—no longer restores shared reference. The enterprise is operating on interpretive debt that compounds with each cycle it is not addressed.

An enterprise may continue operating under degraded interpretive conditions for extended periods, but it does so by absorbing escalating cost through substitution. Each cycle of deferred renewal narrows the margin between the enterprise's interpretive capacity and the demands its conditions impose, until modest changes in scale, complexity, or external pressure produce disproportionate coordination failure.

How Renewal Works

Renewal in People + Alignment follows the same structural logic as renewal in every domain: It restores fit between the domain's architecture and the work the enterprise must now carry. In this domain, the architecture is interpretive—the conditions through which people form shared meaning, resolve priorities, establish trust, and convert agreement into compatible action.

Renewal begins with observation of how interpretation actually occurs rather than how leadership assumes it occurs. The distance between declared alignment and operating reality becomes visible at the points where decisions require repeated reconciliation, where priorities produce competing action, where trust has been replaced by verification, and where coordination persists because shared reference has fragmented. These are the structural indicators that interpretive conditions have separated from enterprise demand.

Renewal proceeds by restoring the structural conditions in sequence. Renewal begins upstream. Leadership signals are recalibrated so that behavior under pressure reinforces the interpretation the enterprise requires rather than contradicting it. Once leadership consistency is restored, organizational design is reassessed for fit with the work now being carried, because structure that no longer matches demand compounds the variance that leadership is attempting to contain. The same discipline extends through communication pathways where signal degradation has severed the connection between leadership interpretation and operating reality, through talent architecture where capacity limits have hardened into structural ceilings, and through incentive logic where redirection has separated energy from enterprise priorities.

The sequence matters. Restoring incentive alignment without first restoring leadership signal consistency produces incentives that reinforce incoherent interpretation. The same principle operates at every level: Communication pathways rebuilt on top of misaligned organizational design carry variance more efficiently without reducing it. Renewal that addresses downstream components while leaving upstream conditions intact reproduces the degradation sequence it exists to interrupt.

Renewal as a Leadership Discipline

Renewal in this domain is a leadership responsibility that cannot be delegated. The interpretive conditions that require restoration originate in leadership behavior and propagate through structures that leadership governs. No process redesign, technology implementation, or organizational restructuring restores interpretive coherence if the leadership signals that destabilized it remain unchanged.

Renewal encounters structural resistance that is predictable. The positions most responsible for interpretive conditions—leadership roles, communication gatekeepers, incentive administrators—are the positions most embedded in the current arrangement. Information that would surface the need for renewal may be filtered through the same interpretive structures that renewal would recalibrate. The structural dynamics of this resistance are treated in the discussion of Structural Interests in Chapter 2.

Renewal that occurs only after substitution has become the enterprise's dominant operating mode restores interpretive conditions at far greater cost than renewal that occurs when the earliest variance signals appear. Continuous renewal maintains interpretive fit as conditions change, preventing the accumulation sequence from advancing beyond the point where ongoing adjustment can contain it.

CROSS-DOMAIN INFLUENCE OF PEOPLE + ALIGNMENT

The effects described in the preceding sections—variance introduction, amplification, signal degradation, capacity constraint, normalization, energy redirection, and substitution—do not remain contained within the domains where they appear. They interact. Each domain's compensatory response to degraded interpretive conditions reshapes the conditions under which adjacent domains operate, producing compounding effects that exceed the cost any single domain absorbs independently.

This is what distinguishes cross-domain influence from domain-specific consequence. A process exception caused by unresolved interpretive variance is a domain-specific cost. When that same exception delays execution timing, which alters customer experience, which distorts the financial signal the enterprise uses to evaluate performance, that is cross-domain compounding. The total systemic cost of degraded interpretive conditions compounds rather than accumulates: Each domain's compensatory response degrades the conditions under which the next domain must operate, producing a cost that exceeds the sum of what individual domains absorb.

Three cross-domain compounding patterns appear consistently across enterprises where interpretive conditions have degraded:

First, substitution cost migrates downstream and accumulates. The compensatory effort one domain introduces to sustain motion becomes an inherited condition for the next domain. Process workarounds become execution constraints. Execution instability becomes the customer's experience. Customer inconsistency becomes the financial signal leadership uses to allocate resources. Each domain inherits not only the original variance but the compensatory cost the prior domain added to absorb it. The enterprise pays for the same interpretive failure multiple times—once in each domain it passes through.

Second, diagnostic accuracy degrades as the distance from the origin increases. The further a symptom appears from the human domain where the interpretive condition originated, the less likely the enterprise is to diagnose it correctly. Process teams see process problems. Execution leaders see execution problems. Customer teams see market problems. Finance sees margin problems. Each diagnosis is accurate within its domain but insufficient at the system level because the origin condition—degraded interpretive reference—is invisible from the point where the symptom presents. This is why enterprises respond to systemic interpretive failure with domain-specific interventions that increase cost without restoring fit. The mechanism operates through a specific sequence. A leadership transition produces inconsistent priority signals in People + Alignment: The incoming leader emphasizes speed to market while the inherited team operates on a quality-first assumption. Processes + Integration compensates by creating parallel approval pathways—one expedited, one standard—doubling interface load without resolving the interpretive divergence that produced the demand. Execution + Intelligence absorbs the inconsistency as variable quality standards: Some work follows the expedited path, some follows the standard one, and teams cannot predict which standard applies to any given deliverable. Customer + Interaction experiences the variance as inconsistent delivery—the same enterprise producing different quality levels across engagements without explanation. Economics + Metrics registers margin compression as the cost of maintaining two parallel systems exceeds the cost of operating one. The enterprise diagnoses a margin problem and responds with cost reduction, increasing pressure on the already overloaded parallel pathways. The origin—an unresolved interpretive divergence in the human domain—remains unaddressed through three cycles of intervention.

Third, compensatory responses in one domain constrain the adaptive capacity of others. When processes add controls to manage exceptions, execution loses flexibility. When execution adds oversight to manage instability, leadership attention is consumed by correction rather than directed toward structural adjustment. When financial controls tighten in response to compressed margins, investment in the conditions that would restore interpretive coherence—talent development, communication structure, organizational redesign—is reduced precisely when it is most required. Each domain's rational response to its own symptoms reduces the system's capacity to address the condition producing those symptoms.

Cross-Domain Influence of People + Alignment

Affected Domain	When People + Alignment Is Coherent	When It Is Incoherent
Processes + Integration	Structure reflects shared priorities; decision authority is embedded correctly; interfaces reduce ambiguity	Processes absorb interpretive disagreement; escalation replaces resolution; structure compensates for unclear meaning
Execution + Intelligence	Work advances intentionally; decisions land predictably; effort converts into outcome and learning	Fragmentation appears immediately; execution becomes inconsistent; learning degrades as work responds to ambiguity
Customer + Interaction	Purpose is expressed consistently; commitments feel credible; customer confidence strengthens	Mixed signals emerge; commitments feel uncertain; customer trust weakens
Economics + Metrics	Economic signals are interpretable; incentives reinforce priorities; forecasting and judgment stabilize	Signals contradict; incentives misalign; financial results reflect unresolved meaning rather than coherent motion
Enterprise as a Whole	Meaning propagates cleanly; coordination holds; coherence is reinforced across domains	Fragmentation spreads; effort increases to maintain results; system-wide strain accumulates

Table 6.11

The systemic consequence is an enterprise that is structurally intact but operationally self-limiting. Every domain continues to function. Processes execute, decisions resolve, customers are served, and financial results are reported. But the enterprise's total capacity to convert enterprise energy into enterprise value diminishes with each cycle, because an increasing share of that energy is consumed by substitution, correction, and compensatory effort rather than by coordinated motion toward enterprise priorities. The enterprise does not fail. It becomes progressively more expensive to operate at the same level of performance—and the source of that expense is invisible to the domains absorbing it.

People + Alignment does not influence the other domains through a single causal pathway. It conditions them through the interpretive layer that precedes all structure, execution, exchange, and measurement. When that layer is coherent, the enterprise compounds capability across domains. As that layer degrades, each domain's response compounds cost instead, and the total cost is systemic, not additive.

PEOPLE + ALIGNMENT AND ENTERPRISE VALUE CREATION

Enterprise value does not begin as revenue, margin, or market position. It begins as potential—the enterprise's latent capacity to convert coordinated human motion into outcomes that compound. That potential is created in the People + Alignment domain, where shared interpretation, trust, and direction converge to establish the conditions for coordinated action.

Value creation in this domain takes a specific structural form: the stabilization of meaning before work is carried. Where purpose, priorities, and constraints are interpreted through a common reference, enterprise energy becomes directional instead of diffused. Decisions reinforce one another and cease to compete. Motion begins without immediate correction. The enterprise does not yet have results, though it has the capacity to produce them: The interpretive conditions required for coordinated action are in place before structure, execution, exchange, or measurement are asked to perform.

This creation of value as potential reduces cost before cost is incurred. Shared interpretation lowers the burden of coordination before coordination is required. Trust reduces reliance on oversight before control mechanisms are applied. Direction clarifies tradeoffs before they become conflicts. These conditions do not produce results on their own; they determine whether results can be produced without substitution of effort for structure as work moves downstream.

People + Alignment therefore carries the Create function of enterprise value in its most consequential form: It creates the conditions under which value becomes possible. The enterprise's capacity to amplify value through structure, realize it through execution, recognize it through customer interaction, and protect it through economic discipline all depend on what is established here—not as aspiration, but as interpretive precondition.

When those conditions degrade, the enterprise does not lose existing value—the value never forms.

The loss does not appear in results. It never reaches results at all. It exists as the difference between what the enterprise's people, structure, and resources could have produced under coherent interpretive conditions and what they produce under degraded ones.

This is the structural meaning of lost potential in the People + Alignment domain. The enterprise retains its people, its capital, its market access, and its operational infrastructure. Nothing has been removed. But the conditions under which those assets convert into enterprise value have eroded, and the conversion rate—the proportion of enterprise energy that reaches value creation rather than being absorbed by substitution, correction, and compensation—declines with each cycle of unaddressed degradation.

Lost potential presents in forms the enterprise can observe but routinely misattributes: margin compression attributed to market conditions, execution overhead attributed to scale, talent attrition attributed to compensation, customer erosion attributed to competition. In each case, the assigned cause is accurate at the domain level and insufficient at the system level. The actual cost is the value that was never created—the enterprise energy that was absorbed by correction instead of converted into capability, the coordinated motion that never formed because interpretation fragmented before action could begin, the compounding that never occurred because each domain spent its capacity maintaining baseline and never advanced.

The enterprise does not experience lost potential as a single failure. It experiences it as the progressive narrowing of what is achievable—a ceiling that lowers incrementally, absorbs resources to maintain, and remains invisible to the domains operating beneath it until performance can no longer be sustained at any level of effort.

THIS CHAPTER ESTABLISHED that coherence begins with people. Shared interpretation, trust, and direction are the first conditions that allow enterprise motion to form at all. But alignment alone cannot carry work. Agreement does not determine how decisions travel, how effort connects, or how meaning survives contact with scale.

Once interpretation converges, a different question emerges: Can the enterprise carry what people now understand and intend to do? That question is structural, not human. It is answered by how work is sequenced, how responsibilities connect, and how motion is sustained without constant clarification. Chapter 7 turns to that problem directly, introducing Processes + Integration—the domain that determines whether alignment becomes repeatable motion or dissolves into compensatory effort as work accumulates.

Endnotes

1. People + Alignment governs the full span of the enterprise's relational system because the interpretive conditions it governs travel wherever the enterprise's people go—into every customer interaction in the Customer Field and into every working relationship with partners, vendors, and suppliers in the Market Field. The argument that enterprises must manage relationships across their full stakeholder environment has a well-developed foundation in stakeholder theory. R. Edward Freeman established the stakeholder approach in *Strategic Management: A Stakeholder Approach* (Boston: Pitman, 1984), arguing that organizational perfor-

mance depends on the enterprise's relationships with all parties affected by or affecting its operations. The boundary spanning literature addresses a related mechanism: Howard Aldrich and Diane Herker examined individuals who manage information and relationships across organizational boundaries in "Boundary Spanning Roles and Organization Structure," *Academy of Management Review* 2, no. 2 (1977): 217–30, and Michael L. Tushman and Thomas J. Scanlan addressed the antecedents of boundary-spanning effectiveness in "Boundary Spanning Individuals: Their Role in Information Transfer and Their Antecedents," *Academy of Management Journal* 24, no. 2 (1981): 289–305. Stakeholder theory addresses which relationships the enterprise must manage; boundary spanning addresses individuals who cross organizational lines. People + Alignment as used here governs something distinct from either: the interpretive conditions—shared meaning, trust, and common operating reference—that the enterprise's people carry into the Customer Field and Market Field regardless of their formal role, and whether those conditions constitute genuine alignment or only its appearance. The domain does not govern the relational fields themselves; it governs what the enterprise's people bring into them.

2. Variance amplification is an established concept in supply chain management, where it describes the amplification of demand variability as orders move upstream through a logistics chain—a phenomenon widely known as the bullwhip effect. See Hau L. Lee, V. Padmanabhan, and Seungjin Whang, "Information Distortion in a Supply Chain: The Bullwhip Effect," *Management Science* 43, no. 4 (1997): 546–58. The supply chain usage describes the amplification of order and demand signals in logistics. As used here, variance amplification describes something fundamentally different: how leadership behavior amplifies interpretive variance within the People + Alignment domain. When leaders send inconsistent signals—differences in emphasis, timing, or resolution—those differences expand without coordination across multiple interpretive surfaces, producing locally rational action that becomes globally incompatible. The mechanism is human and organizational, not logistical.
3. Signal degradation is a well-known concept in telecommunications and information theory, where it refers to the loss of signal quality as information traverses physical channels—noise, attenuation, distortion. Claude Shannon and Warren Weaver's mathematical model of communication established the foundational framework for understanding how signals lose fidelity in transmission. The concept also appears in supply chain literature, where it describes the loss of information accuracy across organizational systems. As used here, signal degradation describes an organizational and interpretive phenomenon: the progressive loss of shared reference across the enterprise as meaning degrades across handoffs, direction loses context in transit, and feedback arrives too late or too distorted to correct the conditions it registers. The mechanism is human interpretation, not technical transmission.
4. Psychological safety as a concept was introduced by Carl Rogers in 1954 and adapted to organizational settings by Edgar Schein and Warren Bennis in 1965. Amy C. Edmondson popularized the concept in its current organizational form in "Psychological Safety and Learning Behavior in Work Teams," *Administrative Science Quarterly* 44, no. 2 (1999): 350–83. Google's Project Aristotle (2012–2016) further established psychological safety as a central condition of high-performing

teams. The term is used here in its established Edmondson sense: the condition in which people feel safe to surface concerns, admit errors, and challenge assumptions without fear of punishment. It is listed as one of six cultural pattern types that govern how the enterprise stabilizes or loses common reference. It is referenced, not redefined.

7

PROCESSES + INTEGRATION

WHY PROCESSES + INTEGRATION IS THE STRUCTURAL DOMAIN

Every enterprise depends on movement. Work advances from interpretation into action, from one role to the next, from decision to consequence, and from signal to response. Whether that movement converts effort into enterprise value or absorbs it through delay, rework, and coordination cost is determined by structure. Tools may accelerate motion, but they do not govern it. Work moves because the surrounding architecture carries it, not because documentation exists or software is present.

> **Processes + Integration** is the enterprise domain through which work, decisions, and information are sequenced, connected, and carried wherever the enterprise must coordinate their movement, translating shared alignment into repeatable and predictable motion.

Without this domain, coherence established in People + Alignment cannot persist as work accumulates and interdependence increases. People + Alignment establishes interpretive coherence;

Processes + Integration determines whether that coherence is retained as volume grows, dependencies multiply, and coordination demand extends beyond what human attention alone can sustain. It governs how tasks connect, how handoffs occur, how dependencies resolve, and how reliably the enterprise responds to demand.

Processes + Integration: Where Motion is Carried

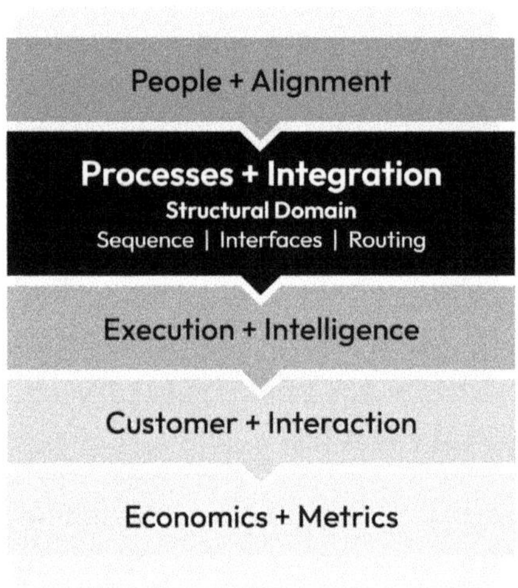

Figure 7.1

Processes + Integration is not an artifact layer. It is not documentation, tooling, or procedure in isolation. Processes are the operational sequences through which enterprise work is performed. Integration is the connective architecture through which work, decisions, and information advance without repeated clarification or manual intervention. Together, they define whether the enterprise carries its own motion or substitutes effort for structure as volume and variability rise.

This is the domain's foundational claim: Structure does what people cannot do at scale. People interpret, decide, and direct. Structure carries that interpretation across repeating cycles without requiring each cycle to be individually coordinated. Sufficient carrying capacity in this domain stabilizes movement and reduces resistance; strategy remains executable as conditions change because structure sustains the motion that alignment alone initiates. Insufficient carrying capacity forces the enterprise to absorb that deficit through delay, duplication, and coordination costs that increase with every additional unit of demand.

Across the enterprises I've supported, this constraint became visible only when I stopped evaluating plans, priorities, and stated intent and began examining how work actually advanced. Where decisions landed, how tasks moved between roles, how dependencies were resolved, and where coordination required repeated intervention revealed more about performance than any stated plan. Performance depended less on individual capability than on the architecture surrounding the work—how steps connected, how interfaces were designed, and how reliably the system carried load. Repeatedly, the limiting factor proved to be structural design rather than effort or capability. Processes + Integration revealed whether the enterprise had been built to carry the volume, variability, and pace it demanded. Architecture that matched the work stabilized downstream performance. Where it did not, even simple activity required disproportionate effort to sustain.

THE ROLE OF PROCESSES + INTEGRATION IN THE NATURAL ORDER

Processes + Integration is the structural domain of the enterprise. It governs how work moves, how information connects, and how decisions translate into coordinated action over time. People + Alignment establishes shared interpretation—purpose, intent, and expectation—and Processes + Integration provides the architecture through which that interpretation becomes durable motion.

In the Natural Order of the enterprise, this domain sits between human intention and executional consequence. It receives direction, priorities, and behavioral patterns from People + Alignment and gives them form. Alignment is rendered into sequence, roles into interfaces, and expectations into routines that can be carried repeatedly without continual clarification. Without this domain, even clear intent and capable leadership fail to produce consistent execution because nothing sustains meaning once work begins to move.

The Governing Role of Processes + Integration

Aspect	What This Domain Governs
Domain position	Second domain in the Natural Order
Primary function	Structural organization of enterprise motion
What it receives	Interpretive conditions
What it performs	Sequencing, interface definition, routing of work
Governing condition	Structural coherence

Table 7.1

Processes + Integration is where movement is constructed in practice. Not in diagrams or static workflows, but in the actual progression of work as it advances across roles, teams, systems, and decision points. This domain governs how steps follow one another, how responsibility transfers, how dependencies resolve, and whether clarification recurs or disappears because structure makes it unnecessary. Across the enterprises observed in this work, enterprise work advanced reliably only when structure could carry it without substitution of effort.

What This Domain Structures

Processes + Integration structures how work is sequenced, how information travels, how teams coordinate across boundaries, where responsibility begins and ends, how exceptions are absorbed or escalated, how routines stabilize, and how complexity is carried without collapse. These structural elements determine whether coordination is embedded in design or recreated manually through meetings, follow-ups, and escalation.

Structure that carries the work demanded of it stabilizes execution as demand increases. Work advances with fewer interruptions, issues surface earlier, handoffs require less interpretation, and teams coordinate without continual escalation. Strategic priorities translate into action with greater fidelity, and operational performance remains predictable as scale and interdependence grow.

Once structure no longer matches the work being carried, coordination shifts from predictable, patterned routines into manual activity. The enterprise absorbs that gap through manual reconciliation, escalation, and rework that increase in proportion to demand.

Structural Elements That Govern Enterprise Motion

Structural Element	What Is Structured	Effect on Enterprise Motion
Sequence	Order in which work advances	Predictable progression
Interfaces	Transfer of responsibility	Reduced coordination load
Routing rules	Where decisions and tasks resolve	Timely resolution
Synchronization points	Where teams align	Coordinated action
Flow pathways	End-to-end movement of work	Stable execution under load

Table 7.2

How This Domain Receives from the Enterprise System

Processes + Integration does not operate in isolation. While it governs structure, it is continuously shaped by conditions originating elsewhere in the enterprise system.

What appears as a process issue is often the structural imprint of conditions originating upstream. Each domain imposes its own form of demand on process architecture, and where that demand exceeds the structure's carrying capacity, the deficit registers as a property of Processes + Integration instead of its source.

Domain Inputs to Processes + Integration

Sending Domain	Shaping Mechanism	Consequence of Upstream Loss
People + Alignment	Interpretive clarity and decision authority define stable assumptions for sequence, ownership, and escalation	Structure absorbs uncertainty; workflows require clarification; process logic becomes conditional
Execution + Intelligence	Delay, overload, and repeated intervention expose where structure no longer carries work	Handoffs require manual coordination; exceptions multiply; pathways depend on intervention
Customer + Interaction	Experience signals press against existing interfaces at team, system, and authority boundaries	Inconsistency and confusion trace to process boundaries not designed for current expectations
Economics + Metrics	Cost, capacity, and scalability constraints bound process design	Processes consume excessive capacity, increase cost-to-serve, or limit scaling

Table 7.3

Processes + Integration as the Conversion Domain

In the Natural Order, Processes + Integration is the conversion domain. It converts human alignment into executable sequence and prepares the enterprise for what follows: the domain of Execution + Intelligence. Interpretation is rendered into structure at this boundary; what enters as shared intent exits as sequenced, routable motion.

Fit between structure and motion reduces the effort required to move work forward; without that fit, effort substitutes for structure, and coordination becomes explicit. The conversion either preserves the coherence established upstream or dissipates it into reconciliation before execution begins.

Fit is the relationship between what the enterprise is attempting to do and how it is built to operate. It describes whether the nature of the work, the scale at which it operates, the complexity it must carry, the capability available, the information required, and the decision patterns that coordinate activity are matched by the structure that carries them. Fit is not static. It changes as any of these conditions change—present fit reinforcing motion through structure, absent fit forcing the system to absorb the deficit through delay, duplication, and coordination cost.

This domain sits at the center of enterprise performance because it is the handoff point between people and execution. A structurally supported handoff produces system-level operation. Where it is not, fragmentation appears long before outcomes make the cost visible.

THE ARCHITECTURE OF FLOW: WHY STRUCTURE DETERMINES MOTION

Enterprise performance is governed by how work advances. The speed, quality, and reliability of execution are determined by the architecture that carries motion from initiation to completion. Processes + Integration is that architecture. It establishes whether work progresses predictably or whether the enterprise must substitute coordination and effort to sustain movement.

Enterprise motion is governed by structure. Effort, intent, and direction only convert into progress when the architecture surrounding the work can carry them. Without that fit, energy is absorbed before enterprise value appears, regardless of commitment, capability, or precision of purpose.

Structure determines the progression of work—from initiation through advancement, acceleration, and pause—along with the circulation of information, the absorption of exceptions, and the return of learning to the system. These properties are produced—not developmentally, but deliberately—by the way processes and integrations are arranged to carry work under real conditions.

Processes + Integration defines the paths that work follows. It shapes task sequence, interfaces between roles and teams, decision routing logic, synchronization points that preserve shared understanding, constraints that protect quality, and flexibility that permits adaptation. Together, these elements form the enterprise's flow architecture. Pathways fitted to the work being carried sustain stable motion. Where pathways are narrow, misaligned, or obstructed, capacity is consumed by corrective activity and coordination cost.

Structural Elements of Flow Architecture

Element	Function	Structural Fit	Structural Deficit
Flow Pathways	Route work from initiation to completion along the most direct path given current structure	Tasks advance without reinterpretation; dependencies visible; decision landing points clear; progression occurs without detour	Work circulates between teams, pauses for clarification, re-enters completed stages, or accumulates in waiting states; cycle time lengthens
Interfaces	Transfer responsibility, interpretation, and context across team and role boundaries	Work transfers predictably; priorities remain compatible; disagreement stays bounded by interface terms	Handoffs fail; responsibility deflects rather than transfers; conflict becomes positional; leadership intervention replaces structural coordination
Routing Rules	Determine where decisions land, who acts next, and how work progresses through the enterprise	Decisions resolve at appropriate levels and advance without escalation; ownership preserved within the originating cycle	Decisions defer, circulate, or remain unresolved; capacity absorbed; movement stalls without producing progress
Synchronization Points	Confirm shared interpretation across roles and teams before work advances past a boundary	Handoffs retain accuracy; shared understanding persists; interpretive distance between teams is reduced at each confirmation	Execution fragments; interpretation diverges; undetected divergence propagates into every downstream handoff, compounding correction cost

Table 7.4

Each element operates independently, but their effects compound. Pathways fitted to the work being carried reinforce interfaces, which reinforce routing, which reinforces synchronization. Degradation in any single element increases coordination demand at every subsequent boundary, and that demand accumulates faster than effort can absorb it. The mechanical function of interfaces in integration—how they transfer ownership, preserve context, and absorb exceptions—is addressed in the following section.

THE MECHANICS OF INTEGRATION

Integration is the connective structure of the enterprise. It is the structural condition under which work, information, and decisions move across roles, teams, and domains without losing coherence. People + Alignment establishes shared interpretation, Processes + Integration defines the paths work follows, and integration governs whether interpretation and structure remain intact as work advances across boundaries.

Integration is not a technical attribute. Tools, platforms, automations, and connectors implement integration, but they do not create it. Integration exists as a structural condition: whether context is preserved as work moves, whether learning circulates beyond its point of origin, and whether decisions retain coherence as they pass from one part of the enterprise to another. Structurally present integration transfers context with the work it describes; absent integration detaches context from movement, requiring reconstruction at each boundary even as activity continues.

Integration governs how shared intent is carried across teams, how workflows intersect, how information transfers with context intact, how decisions retain relevance, how exceptions are absorbed rather than propagated, and how learning becomes enterprise-wide rather than remaining local. Integration is not optional. Every enterprise integrates—either through design or through repeated manual reconciliation. The difference is whether coordination is embedded in structure or recreated through effort.

Interfaces Between Teams: Where Flow Fails First

Flow depends on continuity, but enterprise work does not move through a single unbroken channel. It crosses boundaries—between roles, between teams, between domains. The structural conditions at those boundaries determine whether motion continues or degrades.

> **Interface** is the structural boundary where work, decisions, or information transfer between roles, teams, domains, or relational fields. Because interfaces carry the highest coordination load, they are the first locations where incoherence becomes visible.

Teams rarely fail in isolation. Breakdown appears at transitions, where shared interpretation, timing, trust, and role boundaries must remain intact for work to advance. Structurally defined interfaces transfer work predictably: Ownership passes with definition, and disagreement remains bounded by the terms of the interface rather than expanding into positional conflict. Without that definition, handoffs require renegotiation, responsibility deflects without transferring, conflict becomes positional, and leadership intervention replaces the coordination that structure would otherwise carry. Interface failure is not a people issue; it is an architectural condition.

Cross-Functional Flow: How Work Actually Moves

Most enterprise outcomes require coordination across multiple teams. Work does not move within functions alone; it advances across them. Cross-functional flow reflects a basic system reality: the enterprise operates as a single, interconnected whole.

Structural support for cross-functional flow produces aligned priorities, anticipated dependencies, work that advances without repeated interpretation, and information that arrives before it is required. Coordination is carried by design and not enforced through escalation. Without that structural support, the enterprise absorbs the deficit through local priority narrowing, priority collision, and escalation that displaces collaboration. Work that depends on improvisation to cross boundaries is no longer being carried by the system. Cross-functional flow depends on shared interpretation, explicit integration, and well-defined interfaces.

System Integration: Technology as Amplifier, Not Solution

Technology does not substitute for integration. In existing operations, it amplifies the structural condition that already exists—extending coherent structure further and faster, or scaling incoherent structure at the speed of automation. Technology can also introduce structural conditions that did not previously exist: Platform architectures, algorithmic coordination, and automated decision systems create new forms of integration rather than merely amplifying prior ones. In both cases, whether the technology amplifies or introduces structure, the governing principle is the same: Coherence must be present in the design that technology implements. Technology that extends coherent design compounds enterprise value. Where technology implements incoherent design—or introduces new structural conditions without coherent structural design—the misfit it produces compounds at the same rate.

System integration functions as designed only when workflow logic is sound, roles and handoffs are defined, decision authority is established, required information is available in advance, and business rules remain stable. In the Natural Order, technology functions as a conduit for integration, not a substitute for structural design.

Knowledge Integration: Preventing Divergence Over Time

Knowledge integration ensures that experience circulates across the enterprise rather than remaining isolated within roles or teams. Without it, learning decays, divergence accelerates, and coherence erodes even as execution continues.

Knowledge integration governs the circulation of learning across enterprise structure. Present knowledge integration keeps learning in pace with change; absent knowledge integration recycles mistakes, dissipates institutional memory, and compounds resistance as scale grows.

What the enterprise learns must alter how it operates. Where knowledge integration is structurally present, that alteration occurs through updated routines and redesigned interfaces. Where it is absent, the enterprise repeats cycles it has already paid to understand. Knowledge integration operates through four structural mechanisms.

Knowledge Integration Mechanisms

Mechanism	Structural Function
After-action integration	Converts execution results into structural adjustments before the next cycle begins—redesign of the routines that carry the next cycle's work, not documentation
Cross-functional knowledge transfer	Carries insight generated in one domain to the domains whose structure that insight alters—customer feedback reaching process design, execution data informing capability investment, economic signals redirecting resource allocation
Structured exception analysis	Treats recurring exceptions as architectural evidence, not operational incidents—each repeated exception indicates structure that no longer fits the work being carried
Interface feedback circulation	Routes learning through the same interfaces that carry work—pathways governing motion also carry the adjustments that motion produces

Table 7.5

Where these mechanisms are absent, the enterprise generates learning it cannot structurally absorb. Knowledge remains local, exceptions recur without producing redesign, and the distance between what the enterprise has learned and how it operates widens with each cycle.

DESIGNING FOR FIT: PROCESSES AS STRUCTURAL CORRESPONDENCE

Processes are not documentation. In the Natural Order, a process is the structural correspondence between intent and motion. It establishes whether the work demanded of the enterprise can be carried reliably as volume, variability, and interdependence increase. Processes aligned to the work they must carry sustain stable movement; misaligned processes shift the burden onto people, and coordination is recreated through effort rather than carried by design.

Fit is the governing condition of this domain. It describes the relationship between what the enterprise is attempting to do and how it is built to operate—specifically, the relationship between the nature of the work being performed, the scale at which it operates, the complexity it must carry, the capability available, the information required, the technology in use, and the decision patterns that coordinate activity. Fit is not static. It changes as any of these conditions change. Present fit reinforces motion through structure. Where it does not exist, the system absorbs the deficit as a property of its own architecture—through delay, duplication, and coordination cost that compound as demand increases.

No process is neutral. Every sequence, interface, routing rule, and synchronization point either aligns with the work being carried or imposes a cost on it. A process built for one configuration of volume, variability, and decision frequency will resist another. Fit is therefore contextual: It depends on the operating conditions the enterprise actually faces, not the conditions it was built for. This dependency carries a corollary: Fit is only as reliable as the enterprise's reading of its own operating conditions. Structure built to correspond to misidentified conditions produces architectural precision aimed at a target that does not exist. The diagnostic consequence is that persistent misfit, even after deliberate redesign, may indicate not that the design is wrong but that the conditions it addresses have been misread.

Assessing fit requires examining the relationship between structure and conditions across five dimensions.

Fit Assessment Dimensions

Dimension	Assessment Criterion
Process sequence	Whether sequences correspond to the actual order in which work advances
Interface capacity	Whether capacity matches the coordination load passing through it
Decision routing	Whether routing reflects current authority and information distribution
Knowledge circulation	Whether knowledge circulates at a rate that keeps routines current
Architectural responsiveness	Whether the architecture responds to misfit signals with structural adjustment rather than compensatory effort

Table 7.6

Degradation in any single dimension produces friction; degradation across multiple dimensions produces the structural mismatch described in the following section. The assessment is relational in every dimension—each asks whether structure still corresponds to the conditions it must serve, not whether structure meets an abstract standard.

Fit does not resolve the strategic question of what the enterprise should attempt. That determination belongs to leadership judgment, informed by conditions across all five domains. Fit operates once direction has been established: It measures whether the enterprise's architecture can carry the work its direction demands. Two leaders who read the same enterprise conditions and select different strategic directions will produce different assessments of fit, and both assessments may be structurally valid. Fit is relational, not absolute—it describes the correspondence between architecture and chosen direction, not the correctness of the direction itself.

Fit and Flow

Sustained fit between structure and work keeps that movement stable; eroded fit—produced when conditions change while structure does not—makes movement sensitive to modest increases in load and variability. The distance between intention and action extends, and the enterprise substitutes urgency and control for the design it no longer has.

Friction is the first mechanical evidence that structural correspondence has been lost. As enterprises evolve while processes remain fixed, friction appears consistently and early. The specific forms friction takes—and how the enterprise can distinguish structural friction from normal operational variation—are addressed in the following section.

THE SIGNALS OF STRUCTURAL MISMATCH

Enterprises emit signals long before performance outcomes register change. Processes + Integration is the domain in which those signals surface first, because it is where the architecture of work either carries motion or begins absorbing it. As structural fit erodes, the enterprise does not collapse suddenly. Instead, enterprise value is reduced incrementally as rework increases, definitions blur, coordination becomes explicit, quality varies, and capacity is consumed by resistance.

Structural misfit is the underlying condition in which enterprise architecture is no longer fitted to the work it is required to carry. That condition becomes visible in operation through signals of structural mismatch. The two are related but not equivalent: misfit exists whether or not it is recognized; signals are how the enterprise reveals that misfit through behavior.

Conditions often interpreted as people problems, execution issues, or cultural breakdowns are frequently structural signals of mismatch. The architecture beneath the work no longer fits the work being asked of it, and the enterprise responds in consistent and observable ways.

Signals of Structural Mismatch

Signal	Observable Manifestation	Structural Origin
Rising Friction	Repeated follow-ups; recurring conversations; decision queues; local workarounds	Architecture no longer matches work being carried; effort substitutes for structure
Destructive Polarity	Priority conflicts; team-versus-team dynamics; contradictory decisions; escalation replacing collaboration	Structure forces competition where coordination is required
Structural Decay	Routines require exceptions; rework recurs in same locations; meetings substitute for structure	Design no longer corresponds to current scale or operating context
Distorted Learning	Insight remains local; errors repeat; lessons fail to update routines	Integration no longer returns experience to structure
Cross-Team Breakdown	Lengthening cycle times; expanding cross-team meetings; unclear dependencies	Interfaces cannot transfer work predictably across boundaries
Recurring Problems	Same issues re-emerge after apparent resolution	Integration gaps and misaligned routines leave structural causes unresolved
Customer + Financial Divergence	Inconsistent customer information; variable delivery; revenue unpredictability; rising cost-to-serve	Architecture no longer carries work with the consistency relationships and forecasts require

Table 7.7

These signals share a structural origin: architecture that no longer corresponds to the work being carried. What distinguishes them is where incoherence surfaces—in coordination demand, in team interaction, in routine reliability, in learning circulation, in interface performance, in recurrence patterns, or in customer and financial outcomes. Convergence across multiple signals is the condition that separates incremental aging from operating deficit. What friction requires is not additional effort but structural redesign, a distinction the enterprise often fails to make until coordination cost has already compounded.

THE WORK OF RENEWAL IN PROCESSES + INTEGRATION

Processes do not fail abruptly. They lose fit with the work as conditions change—through growth, product evolution, technology accumulation, shifts in customer demand, regulatory expansion, leadership transition, and talent movement. A process built to carry one scale or configuration does not automatically carry the next.

Decay is inherent in systems that evolve. Workflows that once carried work reliably and then begin producing delay, contradiction, or repeated reconciliation have not suffered execution failure—they have lost fit. Without renewal, the enterprise progressively relies on informal fixes, escalation, and manual coordination to sustain motion.

Processes + Integration operates under continual pressure. Even success introduces new structural demand. As the enterprise moves, the architecture that carries its work ages relative to current conditions.

Because enterprise conditions do not remain fixed, structural fit does not persist by default. Renewal is the mechanism through which process architecture is realigned with the work the enterprise must now carry. Without renewal, structure reflects a prior operating reality while work continues to change.

Renewal in this domain is not a one-time effort or a discrete program. It is frequently reduced to documentation updates, workflow audits, system changes, training refreshes, or short-term remediation efforts. These activities may accompany renewal, but they do not constitute it. Renewal restores structural fit between enterprise motion and the conditions under which that motion now occurs—it does not refine existing artifacts. It is the ongoing structural discipline through which fit between work and architecture is restored as conditions change, rather than after they have already compounded into visible failure.

A renewed process architecture is one in which work advances without persistent resistance, information arrives when and where it is required, decisions follow appropriate routes, roles match responsibility, handoffs transfer ownership cleanly, exceptions diminish, and structure carries coordination rather than displacing it into effort.

When Renewal Becomes Necessary

Renewal becomes necessary when the architecture of work no longer fits the reality of work. This condition surfaces through converging signals, not isolated incidents. The patterns described in the preceding section—friction, recurrence, polarity, decay, learning distortion, interface breakdown, and customer and financial divergence—establish the structural case. When these signals converge rather than appear in isolation, the architecture is no longer aging incrementally; it is operating in deficit.

An enterprise may continue operating with outdated process architecture for a period of time, but it does so by absorbing increasing cost through delay, lost capacity, reduced adaptability, and foregone opportunity. Renewal restores fit between structure and demand, reducing that cost before it compounds.

How Renewal Works

Renewal follows a consistent structural progression. It begins with observation of work as it occurs rather than how it is documented or assumed to occur. Abstract diagnosis causes renewal to miss the conditions that matter. Structural divergence becomes visible at the points where work slows, coordination accumulates, or interpretation must be repeatedly reconciled.

Renewal proceeds by restoring fit. This may require changes to sequence, interfaces, decision routing, role boundaries, system integration, or the tools and platforms that implement them. The objective is reestablishment of fit so that structure once again carries work without substitution—not change for its own sake. Because interfaces degrade faster than routines within teams, renewal must refresh the agreements through which work passes reliably between groups.

Renewal reconnects execution with learning. Experience must return to People + Alignment so that interpretation, behavior, and subsequent structural design reflect current conditions instead of outdated assumptions. In this way, renewal strengthens the enterprise's ability to sense change and adjust before mismatch accumulates.

Renewal as a Leadership Discipline

Renewal is a leadership responsibility, not a technical task. Processes + Integration does not remain coherent on its own. Structural fit must be monitored and restored as work, scale, and interdependence change. Leaders attend to this domain by observing where structure no longer carries work and by acting to restore fit before coordination is displaced into effort.

Renewal also encounters structural resistance that is predictable rather than incidental. The architecture that must be redesigned produces the positions from which redesign is governed—and those positions carry interests in the current arrangement. Information that would surface the need for renewal may be filtered or reinterpreted by the same decision pathways that renewal would restructure. The structural dynamics of this resistance—how positional interests form, how they operate through information gatekeeping and decision routing, and how renewal must account for them—are treated in the discussion of Structural Interests in Chapter 2.

Renewal that occurs only in response to disruption preserves function but forfeits adaptability. Each cycle of deferred renewal narrows the margin between operating conditions and structural limits, until modest increases in demand produce disproportionate coordination cost. Continuous renewal maintains fit as complexity increases; structure carries work without continual reconciliation.

The structural consequence is cumulative. An enterprise that renews in pace with changing conditions retains the carrying capacity its architecture exists to provide. An enterprise that defers renewal operates on borrowed structural margin—and that margin diminishes with each cycle it is not restored.

CROSS-DOMAIN INFLUENCE OF PROCESSES + INTEGRATION

Processes + Integration functions as the structural backbone of the enterprise. It is the domain where alignment becomes architecture, human intent takes the form of workflow, and consistency is made structurally possible. Positioned between People + Alignment and Execution + Intelligence, it translates interpretation into structure and structure into sustained enterprise motion.

Structural conditions established here propagate immediately across the enterprise, shaping how downstream domains behave and what forms of coordination they require. Fitted structure reinforces coordination through design; where fit has been lost, coordination displaces into effort, escalation, and manual reconciliation.

Lost structural fit disperses effort, localizes learning, fragments decisions, and severs strategy from execution because the architecture between intent and action no longer carries the translation; growth amplifies coordination demand but not capacity. Each of these effects compounds independently, but they also reinforce one another: Localized learning produces incompatible decisions, which fragment execution, which increases coordination demand, which absorbs the capacity that renewal would require. The system does not degrade in a single dimension. It degrades as a system.

Cross-Domain Influence of Processes + Integration

Receiving Domain	Structural Ft	Structural Deficit
Execution + Intelligence	Decisions resolve predictably; feedback returns in time; patterns visible early	Exceptions multiply; cycle times extend; improvisation replaces routing
Customer + Interaction	Consistent information; dependable timelines; stable customer-facing reference	Conflicting messages; shifting expectations; variable quality; degraded trust
Economics + Metrics	Reliable forecasting; stabilized margins; visible cost-to-serve; repeatable returns	Revenue unpredictability; rising cost-to-serve; weakening pricing discipline
People + Alignment	Accountability distributes; collaboration occurs; leadership credibility persists	Frustration accumulates; communication becomes defensive; authority erodes
Enterprise as a Whole	Learning circulates; decisions remain compatible; strategy converts to execution	Effort disperses; learning localizes; growth amplifies coordination demand

Table 7.8

PROCESSES + INTEGRATION AND ENTERPRISE VALUE AMPLIFICATION

Processes + Integration is the domain through which enterprise value is amplified. People + Alignment establishes the potential for coherent motion; this domain determines whether that potential accumulates or dissipates as work scales, interdependence increases, and repetition becomes unavoidable. Enterprise value created upstream either compounds here or is dispersed as activity increases.

Amplification occurs through the reduction of structural loss. When work, decisions, and information are sequenced and integrated in correspondence with the work being carried, effort does not need to be recreated with each cycle. Successful actions repeat without reinvention, learning embeds into the routines that carry the next cycle, and coordination proceeds from structure instead of recurring negotiation. Through these mechanisms, Processes + Integration converts isolated success into repeatable performance.

Structural amplification is produced by carry, not exertion. Interfaces that preserve context prevent meaning from being reconstructed at every transition, and under stable sequences, decisions reinforce one another rather than collide. Integrated pathways reduce the corrective effort required to maintain correspondence as volume increases—what worked once carries forward without a proportional increase in effort, and what was learned in one cycle enters the structure of the next. Coordination demand diminishes relative to volume because structure absorbs repetition rather than redistributing it into effort.

Once Processes + Integration no longer fits the work being carried, amplification reverses. Enterprise value that was created upstream is consumed by duplication, delay, and interface friction[1]. Work must be reinterpreted, decisions revisited, and exceptions addressed repeatedly—not because the enterprise lacks capability, but because the architecture cannot retain what prior cycles have already produced. Under these conditions, enterprise value does not compound. It resets.

This domain does not generate enterprise value on its own. It determines whether enterprise value that exists elsewhere in the system accumulates across cycles or dissipates with each increase in demand. That determination is structural: It is made by the architecture, not by intent.

THIS CHAPTER ESTABLISHED that coherence depends on structure. Alignment does not persist on intent alone; it requires sequences, interfaces, and integrations capable of carrying work, decisions, and information as volume, interdependence, and repetition increase. Processes + Integration determines whether enterprise motion scales through reinforcement or is displaced into rework, delay, and explicit coordination as conditions change.

Structure, however, remains untested until it encounters reality.

Its adequacy is demonstrated not in design, documentation, or intent, but in action. Work must advance under load. Decisions must resolve under consequence. Outcomes must form under variation. Only then does the enterprise learn whether its architecture carries motion or requires continual reconciliation to proceed.

That encounter occurs in execution. Chapter 8 turns to Execution + Intelligence—the domain in which structure is tested through behavior, where motion exposes fit or mismatch, and where learning determines whether enterprise value is reinforced or diminished over time.

Endnotes

1. The concept of friction in organizational and institutional contexts has been developed by several scholars. Frank R. Baumgartner and Bryan D. Jones introduced "institutional friction" as part of Punctuated Equilibrium Theory, describing how institutional structures create resistance to policy change. See Baumgartner and Jones, *Agendas and Instability in American Politics* (Chicago: University of Chicago Press, 1993). More recently, Robert I. Sutton and Huggy Rao developed a comprehensive framework of organizational friction in *The Friction Project: How Smart Leaders Make the Right Things Easier and the Wrong Things Harder* (New York: St. Martin's Press, 2024). Norman Long's Social Interface Theory (1989, 2001) addresses friction at points of social discontinuity. Interface friction, as used here, is narrower and more diagnostic than any of these: It describes resistance specifically at the points where work, decisions, or information must transfer across enterprise domain boundaries. It is a structural concept —a symptom of design that no longer carries the work—rather than a policy, workplace, or sociological concept.

8

EXECUTION + INTELLIGENCE

THE DOMAIN OF MOTION AND LEARNING

Every enterprise moves. Work advances, decisions form, tasks progress through defined paths, and commitments are acted on. What execution reveals is whether effort compounds into results under real conditions or is consumed before it reaches outcome. Motion exposes the enterprise's operating condition: how reliably structure carries the work, how consistently responsibility is placed, and how reliably information moves across interfaces. Every expression of enterprise behavior becomes visible in this domain long before outcomes are summarized elsewhere.

> **Execution + Intelligence** is the enterprise domain through which enterprise design is carried into action across all processes and converted into learning, insight, and adaptive response wherever that action encounters consequence. It governs how work advances under load and how feedback returns to sustain renewal.

Execution is not limited to production or delivery. It occurs wherever enterprise design is acted on—operationally, administratively, financially, and relationally. Because enterprise value is realized only through what the enterprise actually does, not what it intends, this domain functions as the primary visibility surface for value creation, amplification, and erosion. If something is acted on in the enterprise, it is execution, and its effects register here.

Execution + Intelligence: Where Reality is Revealed

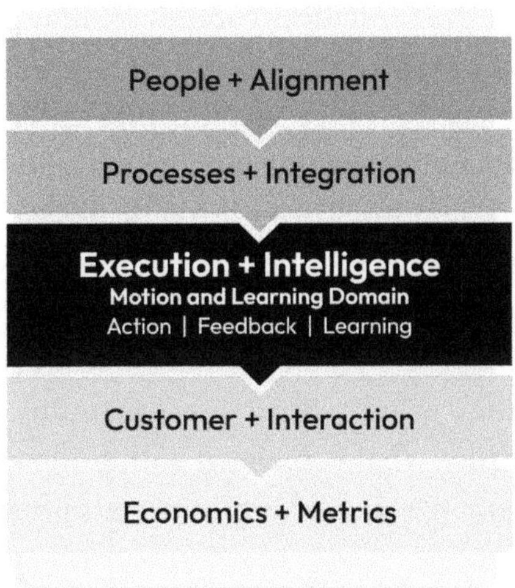

Figure 8.1

Organizational behavior has traditionally focused on the psychological and social dimensions of work—how individuals respond, how groups interact, how culture shapes attitudes, and how leadership influences behavior. That perspective is recognized within this system and is most appropriately situated in People + Alignment, the domain where interpretation, trust, and shared meaning first take form. Organizational behavior explains how intent is shaped, how expectations are internalized, and how human interpretation converges or diverges before work is released into motion. It accounts for how meaning is formed, but not how that meaning survives contact with structure and consequence.

This work addresses a different and more fundamental question:

how execution behaves as enterprise motion once intent encounters structure, load, and consequence. Enterprise behavior is not limited to individual action or choice; it is the observable pattern produced as work, decisions, information, and commitments move through people, systems, automation, customers, and markets over time. In this view, behavior is evidence of how the enterprise as a system is functioning, not a phenomenon to be corrected at the individual level. Execution as enterprise motion redirects attention from psychology toward the structural conditions that produce behavior, regardless of intent or skill.

Structure governs the range of outcomes enterprise motion can produce, but it does not determine outcomes alone. Leadership interacts with structure continuously—through design choices, priority decisions, renewal timing, and the quality of attention applied to the system. The same enterprise structure produces different outcomes under different leadership patterns because leaders shape the structural conditions they inherit. Structure constrains what is possible; leadership determines what is realized within those constraints. The relationship is interactive, not deterministic in either direction.

The Dual Motions of Execution + Intelligence

Motion	What Moves	What It Reveals
Execution	Work, decisions, commitments	Structural fit under real conditions
Intelligence	Feedback, insight, learning	Misfit, resistance, and renewal needs

Table 8.1

Execution + Intelligence is where structure becomes action, converting the alignment established in People + Alignment and the architecture formed in Processes + Integration into outcomes experienced by customers, markets, and stakeholders. This domain shows the enterprise as it operates, not as it is planned or described. Plans may be refined and processes documented, but execution exposes what the system can carry.

In modern enterprises, the constraint is not analysis or ideation; it is the capacity to convert intent into sustained motion. Most enterprises do not lack ideas, insight, or strategy. They struggle to carry decisions into coordinated action once work is distributed across roles, systems, and dependencies. Strategy artifacts multiply, meetings proliferate, and decisions are revisited—not because intent is absent, but because structure does not reliably carry decisions once execution begins.

Across my work with enterprises, execution registered pressure before any other domain surface—before reporting, before financial results, and before leadership recognized the pattern. What the enterprise could carry and what it could not appeared first in motion.

THE ROLE OF EXECUTION + INTELLIGENCE IN THE NATURAL ORDER

Execution + Intelligence is the domain in which enterprise intent encounters operating reality through action and consequence. It is where design, strategy, and the alignment established in People + Alignment are exposed to real conditions, and where assumptions are confirmed or contradicted through observable behavior. Every structural choice, leadership decision, and process design ultimately appears here—in how work advances, how decisions are made under load, and how outcomes take shape over time.

In the Natural Order of the enterprise, this domain sits between structure and relationship. It receives the architecture formed in Processes + Integration and carries that architecture into action, while simultaneously returning learning that conditions renewal upstream.

The Governing Role of Execution + Intelligence

Aspect	What This Domain Governs
Domain position	Third domain in the Natural Order
Primary function	Enterprise motion and learning from action
What it receives	Structure, constraints, priorities
What it performs	Action, feedback capture, learning formation
Governing condition	Operational coherence

Table 8.2

Execution + Intelligence governs two inseparable motions. Execution is the forward movement of work through the system, in which tasks, decisions, and commitments are carried into action under real conditions. Intelligence is the return movement of learning, insight, and feedback that interprets results, reveals misfit, and produces adjustment. These two motions form a continuous loop rather than a sequence. The enterprise corrects misfit before it compounds only when forward motion and returning insight remain connected. Once that connection degrades, activity persists, but correction does not.

What This Domain Governs

Execution + Intelligence governs how work progresses day to day, how reliably commitments are fulfilled, how consistently quality is produced, and how quickly issues surface.

It determines whether enterprise motion remains proportional to effort or begins to depend on escalation, intervention, and substitution of effort for structure. Execution that advances without substitution follows defined pathways—decisions are made where expected, and outcomes form without continual correction. Learning returns in time to inform adjustment before unresolved work, unanswered decisions, and recurring exceptions accumulate beyond the system's capacity to absorb them.

How This Domain Receives from the Enterprise System

Execution + Intelligence is shaped continuously by signals originating in the rest of the enterprise system.

People + Alignment shapes execution through priority interpretation and commitment credibility. Converging interpretation and credible commitment produce compatible timing across work. Unclear priorities or inconsistent commitment cause execution to hesitate—decisions linger and effort fragments into compensatory activity that substitutes for structural direction.

What Execution Tests and Reveals

What Is Tested in Execution	What Becomes Visible
Role clarity	Decision hesitation or confidence
Process fit	Delay, rework, or smooth flow
Integration	Handoff friction or continuity
Priority alignment	Competing demands or focus
Structural capacity	Overload or sustainability

Table 8.3

Processes + Integration shapes execution through structural routing and capacity. Structure that carries work through defined paths produces execution that advances without repeated reconciliation. Once structure no longer fits the work being carried, execution surfaces the condition immediately—through delay, overload, repeated clarification, and increased reliance on manual coordination. These signals do not originate in execution; they are exposed by it.

Customer + Interaction shapes execution through demand patterns and responsiveness expectations. Changes in customer behavior—volume, variability, urgency, or tolerance—alter the conditions under which execution must operate. Execution reveals whether the enterprise can respond proportionally or whether adaptation lags behind demand.

Economics + Metrics shapes execution through capacity limits and risk thresholds. Economic constraint defines how much work can be absorbed, how far commitments can extend, and where execution must adjust. Coherent economic signals keep execution operating within realistic bounds. Conflicting or lagging signals force execution to absorb pressure that structure was not designed to carry.

Increasing interdependence and accelerating change across markets, customers, and operating conditions shift the conditions under which execution operates. Execution now exposes misfit faster than planning cycles absorb it, and intelligence must return continuously if learning is to remain proportional to the rate of change the enterprise encounters.

What Execution + Intelligence Receives From Other Domains

Upstream Domain	What Registers in Motion and Learning
People + Alignment	Priority clarity and commitment strength
Processes + Integration	Structural fit, flow, and constraint
Customer + Interaction	Responsiveness expectations and demand patterns
Economics + Metrics	Capacity limits and risk thresholds

Table 8.4

Execution + Intelligence as the Governing Motion of Performance

Where execution and intelligence operate as a connected loop, the enterprise detects misfit, adjusts behavior, and sustains outcomes through coherence rather than substitution of effort for structure. Where one motion operates without the other, the loop breaks. Execution without intelligence repeats activity that never corrects itself. Intelligence without execution produces interpretation that never encounters consequence. The distinction between enterprises that compound performance and those that replace it with effort originates in whether this loop remains intact under load.

FLOW OF MOTION: HOW EXECUTION BEHAVES IN COHERENT SYSTEMS

Execution is motion—the coordinated advancement of work through the enterprise as structure, interpretation, and decision-making interact over time. It is where coherence and incoherence become observable.

In coherent systems, execution does not depend on continual intervention. Work advances in a predictable progression, teams anticipate dependency rather than react to disruption, decisions are made when they are required, and issues surface while they remain manageable. Learning returns quickly—adjustment occurs without destabilizing the system. Customers encounter consistency, leadership encounters stability, and results depend less on individual exertion and more on structural fit.

Execution immediately registers the loss of coherence. Work becomes harder to complete for reasons that are difficult to localize, delays accumulate, rework becomes expected, and teams increasingly spend time negotiating responsibility rather than advancing outcomes.

The behavior of execution can be read through four structural properties: velocity, variability, load, and quality. Together, these properties make visible how motion behaves inside the system.

These four properties are not independent metrics. They are expressions of a single underlying condition: the degree to which structure matches the work it carries. Velocity, variability, load, and quality move together. When coherence is present, all four stabilize. When coherence erodes, all four shift—and they do so in combination, each compounding the diagnostic signal the others produce. Of the four, quality registers most directly with customers, making it the point at which internal structural condition becomes external consequence.

The Structural Properties of Execution

Property	Definition	Coherent Expression	Consequence of Loss
Velocity	How quickly work moves from initiation to completion	Stable and forecastable; produced by structural fit, not pressure	Decision authority lacks definition, processes require repeated interpretation, teams operate at incompatible tempos, recurring delay and rework appear
Variability	Degree to which execution outcomes fluctuate over time	Contained; work follows defined paths with shared understanding	Workflows lose definition, responsibilities overlap, interfaces weaken, effort and coordination substitute for structure
Load	Amount of work the system can absorb while maintaining continuity	Carried by structure through defined routines, predictable advancement, clear escalation, balanced distribution	Delay, congestion at interfaces, bottlenecks, and reactive decision-making appear; people absorb what structure cannot carry
Quality	Structural outcome of coherent execution	Persists under pressure; work moves through defined pathways with consistent expectations and sequenced decisions	Fluctuates under ordinary conditions; undefined pathways, divergent interpretation, broken learning loops reduce reliability

Table 8.5

MODES OF ENTERPRISE MOTION

Enterprise motion does not express itself in a single way. Once alignment and structure encounter operating reality, motion takes on distinct forms based on how work, decisions, information, and commitments are being carried at that moment. These forms do not describe intent, effort, or outcome. They describe how motion is occurring as work advances and encounters consequence.

> **Modes of Enterprise Motion** are the distinct, active ways enterprise motion advances and encounters consequence—through propagation, action, or intervention—regardless of whether that motion is human-initiated, system-generated, or automated[1].

Modes of Enterprise Motion are conditions of motion, not roles, activities, or states of mind. At all times, more than one mode may be present.

Before examining each mode in detail, one additional distinction is crucial. Modes of enterprise motion may be enacted independently or in coordination, depending on the nature of the work and the structure carrying it. In some cases, motion advances through the actions of a single person or system operating within defined authority and clear interfaces. In others, motion requires synchronized activity across multiple people, teams, or systems acting together in time.

This distinction does not create additional modes. It describes how a given mode is expressed. Action, intervention, and propagation can each occur independently when structure carries work without requiring synchronization, or in coordinated form when dependencies require multiple actors to move together. What changes is not the mode itself, but the degree of dependency the structure must carry for motion to continue.

Weakening coherence shifts the balance. Independent motion gives way to coordinated motion, and coordination becomes more explicit, effortful, and persistent. This shift is diagnostic. It signals that structure is no longer carrying dependencies implicitly and that motion increasingly depends on synchronization rather than design.

1. Propagation

Propagation is the ambient motion of the enterprise. It is the execution that continues regardless of current intent, attention, or intervention, sustained by prior decisions, established structure, routines, incentives, and automation. Once released into the system, this motion persists on its own, advancing work, consuming capacity, and producing consequence without requiring anyone to actively "do" anything in the moment.

Modes of Enterprise Motion and Their Structural Signals

Mode	Description	Human Examples	System / Machine Examples	Diagnostic Signal
Propagation (Non-deliberate)	Ambient motion continuing without intent	Habitual reporting; recurring syncs; deferred decisions producing effects	Automated triggers; queued jobs; incentive-driven behavior	Invisible load growth; delayed consequence
Action (Deliberate)	Routine execution within coherent structure	Completing defined work; approving expected decisions; delivering services as planned	Automated workflows advancing correctly; systems routing work cleanly	Low coordination effort; stable timing
Intervention (Deliberate)	Corrective execution compensating for misfit	Escalations; firefighting; manual overrides; leader-mediated decisions	Emergency system patches; manual reprocessing; forced re-routing	Rising meetings; contextual expertise dependence

Table 8.6

In propagation, the enterprise is executing what it has already decided, built, or encoded. Automated workflows advance tasks, queues progress, standing routines repeat, and incentive structures continue shaping behavior. None of this motion is accidental, but neither is it deliberate in real time. It is the residual expression of past intent operating in the present.

Propagation is often invisible because it feels normal. Its effects are noticed only when capacity tightens, timing slips, or consequences surface far downstream from the decisions that set it in motion. In scaled or technology-dense enterprises, propagation can become the dominant mode of enterprise motion, carrying far more work and consequence than leaders realize. When propagation overwhelms attention, execution appears to accelerate even as coherence quietly weakens.

2. Action

Action is deliberate, forward-moving execution that advances work within coherent structure. It is the mode of enterprise motion that enterprises exist to sustain. In action, people and systems perform expected work, decisions are acted on as intended, and tasks progress without requiring repeated clarification, escalation, or manual intervention.

Action occurs when interpretation is shared and interfaces remain stable. Work can move independently because structure carries it. Roles are clear, decision authority is understood, and timing matches demand. In this mode, execution feels proportionate: Effort produces progress, and progress reinforces continuity.

Action is execution as progress. It reflects an enterprise whose alignment has successfully translated into structure and whose structure can carry motion under normal conditions. When action dominates, coordination remains light, intervention remains rare, and enterprise energy concentrates rather than disperses.

3. Intervention

Intervention is the deliberate execution applied to correct, override, or compensate for structural or interpretive misfit. It exists because the enterprise cannot carry work through design alone. In intervention, motion advances not because structure carries the work, but because people step in to make it function temporarily.

Intervention takes many forms—manual overrides, rerouting work, resolving ambiguity, firefighting, or direct leadership involvement—but its defining feature is that progress depends on personal attention rather than system capacity. In some circumstances, that attention draws on significant experience, specialized knowledge, or contextual judgment, particularly when situations are novel, high-consequence, or not anticipated by existing structure. Intervention is execution through substitution: It borrows from people to supply what structure no longer carries.

Occasional intervention is normal in any complex system. Persistent intervention is diagnostic. When intervention becomes routine, coherence has already weakened, even if results are still being produced. Enterprises often mistake high levels of intervention for strong execution, but intervention-heavy execution is inherently fragile. It consumes capacity, increases dependence on specific individuals, and accelerates fatigue without restoring structural fit.

COORDINATION AS THE SYNCHRONIZATION OF MOTION

In a coherent enterprise, coordination is embedded in structure. Shared timing assumptions, stable interfaces, and clear decision pathways produce coordination implicitly, with little conscious effort. In this state, coordination accompanies action without drawing attention to itself. Work advances because dependencies are already accounted for within the design.

> **Coordination** is the deliberate synchronization of motion across two or more people, teams, or systems. It is not a mode of enterprise motion but a mechanism that operates within and around the modes of enterprise motion, shaping how motion proceeds rather than whether motion exists. Its density and persistence signal whether execution is carried by design or held together by effort.

Coordination becomes explicit and effortful once coherence weakens. Work can no longer advance independently, and motion begins to depend on active synchronization—meetings, handoffs, clarification, sequencing discussions, and deliberate reconciliation across boundaries. In this condition, coordination no longer accompanies action; it compensates for the absence of structural support.

Coordination often intensifies alongside intervention. When structure cannot carry work, coordination is required to determine who acts next, when action may proceed, or how competing priorities are temporarily reconciled. Progress becomes dependent on alignment in the moment rather than coherence over time.

The diagnostic significance of coordination lies in its density and persistence. Rising coordination demand signals that action is no longer the dominant mode of enterprise motion. When coordination becomes continuous rather than occasional, execution is held together by effort rather than carried by design. Results may still appear, but they are produced through concentrated personal effort rather than structural capacity.

Coordination, in itself, is therefore not a sign of collaboration. Enterprises that design for coordination where dependencies require it carry work through structure. Enterprises that rely on coordination as a steady state are borrowing from future capacity.

NECESSARY, SYMBOLIC, AND COMPENSATORY COORDINATION

Coordination is not inherently beneficial or pathological. It is cost incurred when work contains dependencies that cannot be resolved by a single person, team, or system operating within defined authority. The diagnostic question is not how much coordination exists, how visible it is, or how long it persists, but why it is required and what it converts into motion.

Necessary Coordination

Some work requires coordination by nature. Interdependent delivery, tightly coupled systems, shared accountability, and complex execution demand synchronized action across people, teams, or technologies. When coordination exists because the work itself requires shared timing, shared interpretation, and concurrent action—and when enterprise structure is constructed to carry those dependencies

—coordination is performing necessary work. This is necessary coordination. It may be continuous or sustained, embedded in routines or formal forums, but it remains proportional to the work it resolves. Necessary coordination resolves real dependencies and advances execution without drawing on compensatory effort to hold work together.

Symbolic Coordination

Weakening coherence detaches coordination from necessity. Synchronization persists even when it no longer resolves dependencies or advances execution. Standing meetings continue, alignment forums remain in place, and coordination rituals multiply despite producing little change in outcomes. Participation becomes a proxy for governance rather than a mechanism for progress. This is symbolic coordination. Time is consumed, attention is fragmented, and enterprise energy is expended without conversion into forward motion. Symbolic coordination replaces structural design with discussion and accountability with presence, and capacity erodes even as work appears to be governed.

Compensatory Coordination

When coherence degrades further, coordination becomes inseparable from intervention. Work no longer advances unless people step in directly to reconcile conflict, resolve ambiguity, or override constraints in real time. Decisions wait for authority. Teams hesitate at boundaries. Leaders are pulled into daily execution, substituting personal attention for missing structure. In this condition, coordination is no longer a mechanism within execution. It *is the execution.* This is *compensatory coordination*. Motion advances through intervention rather than design, consuming capacity faster than it can be restored, and binding execution to specific individuals rather than to enterprise structure.

Modes of Coordination and Their Structural Meaning

Mode	What It Looks Like in Practice	Why It Exists	What It Signals Structurally
Necessary Coordination	Cross-functional teams coordinating release timing for a complex product launch; clinical staff coordinating care for a patient across specialties; engineers and operations synchronizing changes in a tightly coupled system	The work contains real, unavoidable dependencies that require shared timing, shared interpretation, and concurrent action	Structure is carrying work as designed; coordination is proportional to dependency and directly advances execution
Symbolic Coordination	Standing meetings with recurring agendas but few decisions; alignment forums that persist regardless of changes in work; review meetings focused on status updates rather than sequencing or resolution	Coordination has become a proxy for governance or oversight rather than a mechanism for resolving dependency	Structure is no longer sufficient, but intervention has not yet become dominant; capacity is being consumed without restoring coherence
Compensatory Coordination	Daily escalation calls to unblock routine work; leaders manually resolving priority conflicts; teams waiting for approval to proceed on otherwise standard tasks; crisis meetings to reconcile competing commitments	Structure can no longer carry dependencies, so motion advances only through personal attention and override	Coherence has weakened materially; execution depends on individuals rather than design; capacity and resilience are being depleted

Table 8.7

These forms of coordination are not sequential stages, nor do they appear uniformly across the enterprise. Different forms may exist simultaneously in different areas of work. What matters diagnostically is which form dominates and why. An enterprise characterized primarily by necessary coordination can sustain complexity and absorb pressure. An enterprise dominated by symbolic coordination is already losing capacity, even if results appear stable. An enterprise dependent on compensatory coordination is no longer executing through structure; it is substituting effort for design, and that substitution compounds with every cycle it persists.

READING THE DOMINANT MODE

Enterprises are always executing: Motion is continuous, consequence is unavoidable, and work is always advancing in some form. The question is not whether execution is occurring, but how it is occurring at any given moment.

When propagation dominates, consequence is accumulating beyond awareness. Motion continues without intent, automation advances work faster than it can be interpreted, routines persist regardless of fit, and deferred consequences begin shaping outcomes long before leaders recognize their source. Execution appears busy, but control over direction and impact is slipping.

When action is the dominant mode of enterprise motion, coherence is stable. Work advances as designed, decisions land where expected, and progress depends primarily on structure rather than on personal effort. Motion feels proportionate, and results reinforce credibility rather than consume attention.

When intervention becomes dominant, coherence is weakening. Progress still occurs, but it depends increasingly on corrective effort—overrides, escalation, manual alignment, and personal judgment substituting for structural support. Results may continue to be produced, but they depend increasingly on corrective effort and the sustained attention of a narrow group rather than on structural carry.

Execution problems are rarely problems of effort. They are problems of which mode of enterprise motion has become dominant. The dominant mode determines what execution reveals about the system—and by the time intervention dominates, structural misfit has already compounded beyond what effort alone restores.

Recognizing Dominant Modes of Enterprise Motion

Dominant Observation	Likely Mode	Likely Condition
Work advances without active attention or oversight	Propagation	Entropy increasing
Work advances cleanly with minimal effort	Action	Coherence holding
Meetings, syncs, and handoffs replace forward movement	Action displaced by coordination	Trust reinforced or eroded
Progress requires constant correction to continue	Intervention	Structural misfit

Table 8.8

THE ROLE OF INTELLIGENCE: FEEDBACK, SENSING, LEARNING

Intelligence is the backward motion of the enterprise—the return of insight, signals, and interpretation through which the system registers what execution has produced. Together, these two motions form a closed loop that sustains coherence only as long as both motions remain connected.

Intelligence is outcome interpretation—the enterprise's capacity to notice what is occurring in execution, read those signals accurately, and adjust structure to sustain coherence under changing conditions. It is distinct from data collection, reporting, analytics, or dashboards, all of which may inform intelligence, but none of which constitute it. Intelligence converts execution into insight and insight into structural reinforcement.

How effectively intelligence operates determines whether the enterprise adjusts before misfit compounds or repeats the same patterns at increasing cost.

Directional Flow of Action and Learning

In the Natural Order of the enterprise, execution and intelligence move in opposite but connected directions. Action advances through the domains as work, decisions, and commitments are carried into outcome. Learning returns from that movement as insight, signal, and interpretation, conditioning how future action is formed. Coherence depends on these two motions remaining connected.

The directional relationship is specific: Execution produces consequence; intelligence interprets that consequence and returns it to the structural and human domains where adjustment occurs. Execution + Intelligence is the domain where this directional relationship becomes visible, because it is where consequence is produced and where interpretation must respond.

A connected loop produces continuous adjustment through learning rather than delayed correction. Structure is refined before misfit accumulates, and decisions draw on lived execution rather than assumption. Once the connection weakens, action and learning separate. Execution continues, but correction lags. Learning arrives late, fragmented, or ignored. Coherence erodes when direction and response lose synchronization, not when effort itself diminishes.

Performance Signals: What Execution Reveals

Every act of execution generates information about structural fit. Some signals confirm coherence; others expose misalignment. They surface as delay, repeated questions, inconsistent handoffs, customer escalation, quality instability, overloaded teams, recurring bottlenecks, rework cycles, and decisions that fail to resolve. These are not problems to suppress; they are information to interpret.

Structural Signals First Revealed by Execution

Execution Signal	What It Indicates Structurally
Repeated delays	Process misfit
Recurring questions	Interpretive instability
Escalation becoming routine	Weak decision pathways
Unplanned work dominating	Load imbalance
Rework cycles	Broken learning loops

Table 8.9

Performance signals reveal the operating condition of structure, process fit, and alignment quality. Ignored signals cause the system to escalate the message through greater pressure and visible breakdown. Early interpretation reverses this sequence—leaders gain visibility into erosion before correction becomes costly. Performance signals are the first language of intelligence.

Learning Loops: How Insight Returns to Leadership

Learning loops determine how quickly the enterprise converts performance signals into structural adjustment. Intact learning loops surface issues early; patterns are interpreted rather than isolated events, correction remains proportional, continuity is maintained under pressure, and coherence persists through changing conditions. Degrading learning loops compound issues—problems remain isolated, recovery lengthens, defensiveness increases, and decision quality deteriorates.

Learning loops define the enterprise's capacity to recognize emerging patterns and adjust as conditions evolve. They determine whether experience strengthens structure or merely accumulates as unresolved pressure.

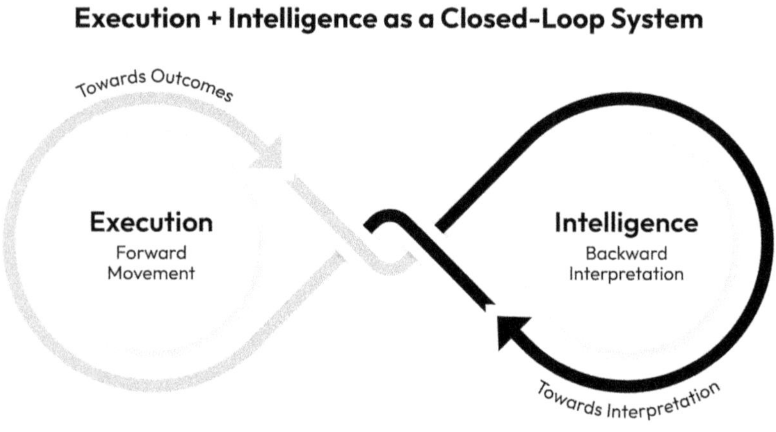

Figure 8.2

Sense-and-Respond Routines: Continuous Structural Sensing

Coherent enterprises do not wait for a crisis to force them to adapt. They operate through continuous sense-and-respond routines that convert execution data into actionable intelligence. Daily operational sensing, regular pattern interpretation, periodic strategic recalibration, and ongoing structural assessment function as structural mechanisms rather than meetings. These routines keep the enterprise aligned with reality rather than anchored to outdated assumptions.

Through these routines, the enterprise detects deviation early, recalibrates priorities, adjusts processes, refines decision pathways, renews interfaces, and maintains coherence in customer experience.

Operational Awareness: Seeing the System in Motion

Operational awareness is the ability to perceive execution as a system rather than as isolated tasks or outputs. It is the leadership capacity to recognize where decisions accumulate without resolution, where teams overload, where structural misfit emerges, where exceptions repeat, where resistance begins, and where quality destabilizes. This awareness gives leaders the capacity to diagnose coherence in real time.

Sustained operational awareness gives leadership visibility into structural erosion as it develops rather than after results have already degraded. Without it, intervention substitutes for interpretation, and correction is always late.

Execution supplies the truth of what is happening; intelligence supplies the meaning of what that truth implies. Together, they prevent motion from degenerating into disorder and produce the conditions under which the enterprise learns from what it experiences.

CONDITIONS OF ENTERPRISE MOTION

Modes of enterprise motion describe how work advances. Conditions of enterprise motion explain why that motion behaves the way it does once execution is underway. These conditions are not actions, decisions, or modes of execution. They are the system states that shape how motion is carried, resisted, or distorted as it encounters reality.

Enterprise motion never occurs in a vacuum. It always operates under conditions produced by prior alignment, structure, accumulated demand, and the system's ability to sustain coherence over time. These conditions are not static. They shift continuously as work advances, load accumulates, interfaces weaken, and consequences propagate. What leaders experience as "execution problems" are most often expressions of these underlying conditions rather than failures of effort or discipline.

These five conditions in Table 8.10 do not operate in isolation. Misfit, load, and entropy interact continuously, and their combined effect produces structural decay—the progressive loss of the system's capacity to carry motion cleanly. Coherence is the only condition that counteracts this progression, and it does so only through active maintenance. No enterprise remains coherent by default; coherence is sustained through renewal or lost through accumulation.

Conditions of Enterprise Motion

Condition	Definition	How It Manifests	Diagnostic Significance
Coherence	Structure supports motion; design, interpretation, and capacity remain aligned	Action dominates, coordination remains embedded, propagation produces predictable consequence	Determines whether complexity can be carried without constant correction
Misfit	Structure no longer matches the work it must carry	Action gives way to intervention, coordination becomes explicit, execution requires increasing personal attention	Accumulates gradually; visible in results only after it has already been shaping motion
Load	Demand placed on structure, people, and decision pathways relative to carrying capacity	Motion slows, intervention rises, coordination density increases	Often misdiagnosed as staffing or productivity; actually a structural condition of sequencing, decision release, and commitment accumulation
Entropy	Tendency of enterprise systems to lose order when coherence is not actively maintained	Motion becomes disorganized, interpretation diverges, effort yields diminishing return	Explains why execution feels heavier over time even when nothing obvious has changed
Structural Decay	Cumulative effect of misfit, load, and entropy acting together	Rising intervention, persistent coordination, delayed learning, increasing dependence on specific individuals	Not visible in any single moment; revealed only through patterns over time

Table 8.10

These conditions do not replace the modes of enterprise motion; they govern them. Growing misfit and accumulating entropy cause intervention to replace action, coordination to intensify, and propagation to carry more unintended consequence. Execution changes because the conditions under which motion operates have shifted, not because people choose to execute differently.

This is why execution functions as the truth surface of the enterprise: Motion makes conditions visible before any other domain registers the change. Intelligence—the capacity to interpret these conditions and transfer learning into the structural and human domains—determines whether the enterprise restores coherence or responds to deterioration by intensifying the effort that cannot resolve it.

EXECUTION AS OUTCOME INTERPRETATION: HOW MISALIGNMENT APPEARS

Execution is where the enterprise reveals itself. It is the point at which the Natural Order becomes visible and where every structural choice—effective or deficient—registers its consequence.

In the Natural Order, execution functions as the outcome-interpretation layer of the enterprise. Misalignment, resistance, and decay all originate upstream—in prior alignment, structural design, and accumulated misfit. Execution makes them visible. It is the surface on which their consequences register, often long before the originating condition is recognized elsewhere. Execution is therefore diagnostic, showing whether the architecture formed in Processes + Integration can carry the work and whether the alignment established in People + Alignment has converted into shared motion or fragmented into local interpretation.

Why Execution Reveals Misalignment First

Every enterprise operates with two concurrent realities: the designed reality, which reflects what leaders intend to happen, and the lived reality, which reflects what occurs in execution. Execution exists entirely in the latter. Work cannot disguise misfit. Timing exposes pressure, coordination reveals inconsistency, handoffs surface ambiguity, and exceptions accumulate naturally when structure no longer fits the work. Customers respond immediately, teams experience instability directly, and leaders observe effects well before strategic narratives change.

The Patterns of Misalignment

Misalignment rarely appears as a single dramatic failure. It emerges through repeatable patterns that grow more explicit over time. Execution-level signals include recurring delays in the same segments of work, questions that resurface after appearing resolved, inconsistent decisions across teams or leaders, handoffs that require repeated explanation, tasks delayed by unclear ownership, competing priorities forcing constant tradeoffs, irregular pacing that destabilizes workflows, escalation becoming routine, unplanned work displacing planned capacity, and reactive firefighting interrupting strategic activity.

These conditions are not execution failures. They are structural reflections of upstream misalignment.

How Structural Mismatch Shows Up in Execution

Structural mismatch in execution follows predictable forms once the architecture no longer fits the work. Execution begins requiring disproportionate effort and coordination, teams pull in opposing directions despite shared intent, and workflows that once held under load begin to degrade. Load concentrates in some areas while others remain underutilized, and quality fluctuates because the structure can no longer reliably carry the work. At the same time, learning erodes as issues repeat without being translated into structural change.

Execution does not produce these conditions. It surfaces them—and it does so with a specificity that no other domain provides at the same speed.

Why Firefighting Appears When Coherence Fails

Firefighting is not a leadership style; it is a compensatory response to structural misfit. When upstream domains lose coherence, execution absorbs the accumulated pressure, and leaders intervene through personal exertion instead of design. Firefighting temporarily restores motion but does so at increasing cost, producing exhaustion, dependency, bottlenecks, erosion of capability, reactive decision-making, and loss of strategic focus.

Enterprises respond to weakening coherence in predictable ways. Planning expands, coordination increases, and oversight intensifies. These responses add activity without restoring structural carry, increasing effort while leaving outcomes unchanged.

Persistent firefighting signals that renewal has been deferred beyond the point where effort alone restores structural carry.

Execution as the Enterprise's Earliest Sensing Surface

Execution surfaces signals long before dashboards display trends. Hesitation in a meeting, delay at a handoff, a surge of unplanned work, subtle inconsistency in customer experience, repeated clarification of the same decision, or outputs that no longer match inputs all indicate emerging misfit. These signals are neither random nor isolated. They form a coherent message when interpreted together.

Execution functions as the enterprise's earliest sensing surface, registering where structure no longer fits and where renewal is required. When these signals are interpreted as outcome data rather than as failure, correction occurs before breakdown forces it. When they are ignored, the distance between structural condition and leadership awareness widens—and the cost of restoration compounds with every cycle of delay.

CAPABILITY IN MOTION: HOW EXECUTION IS ACTUALLY POWERED

Execution is not sustained by effort alone. It is sustained by the interaction between capability, structure, and learning. In the Natural Order of the enterprise, capability is not static or abstract; it is expressed in motion, through how people work, coordinate, decide, and respond to new information.

Capabilities do not exist on paper. They exist in behavior. They become visible in how teams handle ambiguity, how issues escalate or resolve, how quality persists under pressure, and how direction is translated into action.

> **Execution Capability** is the enterprise's structural capacity to carry work into action under real conditions. It is not individual talent, effort, or intent. It is the combined effect of Technical Capability and Relational Effectiveness operating together as a system—expressed only in motion and visible only through behavior.

Execution Capability cannot be assessed in isolation. It emerges from the interaction of two categories of elements—Technical Capability and Relational Effectiveness—each of which conditions the other. Neither produces reliable execution on its own.

> **Technical Capability** encompasses the four structural elements that determine what the enterprise can do. *Skills* are the functional and technical abilities people bring to work—combining knowledge, judgment, experience, and interpretation. *Tools* are the workflow systems, communication platforms, automation, and analytics that extend and accelerate their effort. *Structure* is the architecture that channels their motion, governing where work begins, where decisions land, how information travels, and how exceptions are handled. *Capacity* is the system's ability to carry operational load without losing coherence. Sustained reinforcement among these four elements produces the enterprise's structural capacity to carry

work. As that reinforcement breaks down, execution degrades even under ordinary conditions[2].

Relational Effectiveness is the social dimension of Execution Capability—the enterprise's capacity to carry work through human interaction. It governs whether Technical Capability Creates and Amplifies enterprise value or Dilutes and Erodes it in transit. Relational Effectiveness operates at two levels simultaneously. At the individual level, each person's contribution to enterprise value is contingent on their own Relational Effectiveness—the degree to which they communicate clearly, collaborate across boundaries, and sense and respond to signals from those they work with and serve. At the enterprise level, the aggregate Relational Effectiveness of all people operating across teams, interfaces, and relational fields determines whether the enterprise's collective Technical Capability Creates and Amplifies enterprise value or Dilutes and Erodes it in transit. Relational Effectiveness is not a secondary condition of execution; it is the delivery mechanism through which Technical Capability either Creates and Amplifies enterprise value or Dilutes and Erodes it[3].

Relational Effectiveness operates across the full span of enterprise motion—from how individuals communicate within teams, to how teams coordinate across interfaces, to how the enterprise senses and responds across its relational fields with customers, partners, and markets.

The Execution Multiplier: Technical Capability × Relational Effectiveness = (+/−) Enterprise Value

The relationship between Technical Capability and Relational Effectiveness is multiplicative, not additive. If the two categories were summed, an enterprise with strong Technical Capability could compensate for weak Relational Effectiveness—the deficit in one dimension offset by strength in the other.

Elements of Execution Capability

Element	Function in Execution	Coherent Expression	Consequence of Weakness
Skills	Functional and technical abilities people bring to work; combines with judgment, experience, and interpretation	Composure under pressure, accurate triage, decisive action, cross-domain understanding, anticipation of downstream effects	Hesitation, slowed response to change, recurring mistakes, escalation substitutes for judgment, inconsistent interpretation of direction
Tools	Workflow systems, communication platforms, automation, and analytics that amplify effort	Accelerate motion, stabilize execution, support shared understanding, make intelligence easier to interpret	Scale misalignment, fragment information, hard-code poor workflows, amplify confusion faster than shared meaning
Structure	Architecture that channels motion; governs where work begins, decisions land, information travels, and exceptions are handled	Capable team inside strong structure sustains coherence; structure determines direction and sustainability of motion	Capable team inside weak structure underperforms; skills and tools cannot compensate for missing pathways
Capacity	System's ability to carry operational load without losing coherence	Load distributes proportionally, teams retain space to adjust, quality remains stable under pressure	Teams overwhelmed, work spills, errors increase, quality wavers, strategic work disappears, burnout accelerates
Relational Effective-ness	The social dimension of execution; the capacity of individuals and teams to communicate clearly, collaborate across boundaries, and sense and respond to signals from those they work with and serve	Work travels across interfaces without loss; signals reach the decisions they should inform; teams carry each other's execution needs without escalation; Technical Capability Creates and Amplifies enterprise value as designed	Technical Capability is present but Diluted in transit; execution degrades at interfaces and handoffs; signals fail to travel; coordination requires repeated escalation; enterprise value Erodes as the relational channel deteriorates independent of technical strength

Table 8.11

The product would remain positive. That is not how execution operates.

When factors multiply, weakness in either dimension discounts the entire product. An enterprise with highly developed skills, tools, structure, and capacity—operating through a deteriorating relational channel—does not produce reduced enterprise value. It produces enterprise value that approaches zero as Relational Effectiveness approaches zero, because Dilution and Erosion scale with the relational deficit. Technical Capability, no matter its strength, cannot recover a near-zero multiplier. The product collapses.

The Execution Multiplier:
Technical Capability × Relational Effectiveness =
(+/–) Enterprise Value[4]

The Execution Multiplier operates at two levels simultaneously.

At the individual level, each person's contribution to enterprise value is contingent on the product of their own Technical Capability and their own Relational Effectiveness. A technically excellent individual whose relational effectiveness is weak produces less enterprise value than their technical capability alone would suggest: The relational deficit discounts the individual contribution before it reaches the enterprise.

At the enterprise level, the aggregate Relational Effectiveness of all people operating across teams, interfaces, and relational fields determines whether the enterprise's collective Technical Capability Creates and Amplifies enterprise value or Dilutes and Erodes it in transit.

The distinction matters for two reasons. First, it reveals what a single-level reading cannot surface. A leader who reads Relational Effectiveness only at the enterprise level addresses structural or cultural conditions while the individual-level relational deficits producing the aggregate condition remain uncorrected. Reading it only at the individual level addresses performance management while systemic relational breakdown at interfaces and across domains compounds undetected.

Second, it describes how enterprise value accumulates—or does not. Enterprise value accumulates as the product of individual-level multipliers operating within an enterprise-level relational architecture—not as the sum of individual contributions. Weak individual relational effectiveness compounds across interfaces; strong individual relational effectiveness can be undermined by enterprise-level relational breakdown at coordination points.

This is why the enterprise cannot out-perform a relational deficit with technical excellence. The deficit does not subtract from the result: It scales the result down. Further investment in Technical Capability while Relational Effectiveness remains weak leaves the product unchanged. It increases the numerator of a fraction whose denominator is already determining the outcome.

The diagnostic question in any execution failure is not which element is weakest, but where the interaction between Technical Capability and Relational Effectiveness has broken down. The pattern of failure indicates the constraint.

When the same tasks fail regardless of who performs them, the constraint is structure or tools: The architecture carrying the work does not support it, or the systems extending effort compound the distortion rather than correcting it. Skills constraints present differently: tasks fail only in the absence of specific individuals, indicating that the enterprise depends on capability that has not been structurally distributed.

Tasks that succeed individually but fail under volume indicate a capacity constraint: The enterprise can execute at a certain scale, but not at the scale its conditions demand.

When Technical Capability is individually adequate across all four elements but execution degrades at interfaces, handoffs, or across the relational fields—when signals fail to travel, coordination requires repeated escalation, and teams cannot carry each other's work needs—the constraint is Relational Effectiveness. Technical Capability is present but Diluted in transit; enterprise value Erodes as the relational channel deteriorates. No structural investment in skills, tools, structure, or capacity addresses a relational constraint; the diagnostic must shift from Technical Capability assessment to Relational Effectiveness assessment.

The most common misdiagnosis treats a Relational Effectiveness failure as a Technical Capability weakness, producing investment in the wrong dimension: hiring to address a relational deficit, adding tools to address a coordination breakdown, restructuring to address a signal failure that originates in how people work together.

Responsible Autonomy: The Marker of Developed Execution

Responsible autonomy[5], as used in this system, is not a managerial approach to the labor process. It is a condition of enterprise execution that emerges from structure rather than supervision.

> **Responsible Autonomy** is the observable capacity of individuals and teams to act decisively and consistently within their scope without waiting for permission or compensating for missing structure. It is not a delegation preference or a management philosophy; it is a condition of enterprise execution that emerges from clear role definition, defined decision pathways, reliable information, stable interfaces, and learning mechanisms that close quickly enough to sustain judgment.

When responsible autonomy is present, execution remains coherent. Decisions propagate without distortion, escalation declines, trust strengthens, and leaders stop substituting personal intervention for structural support. Adaptability increases because action does not depend on oversight. Eroding responsible autonomy inverts the pattern: leaders become bottlenecks, people hesitate at boundaries, teams wait for permission, and execution slows to the speed of escalation.

The presence or absence of responsible autonomy is one of the most direct indicators of whether coherence is stable—and whether structure carries execution or personal intervention substitutes for it.

Performance Ritualization: Making Coherence Habitable

Execution capability stabilizes when the enterprise builds repeatable patterns that reinforce coherence. These are not meetings. They are structural practices that make performance predictable. Standardized handoffs, consistent review points, structured triage routines, standing check-ins, fast learning debriefs, coordinated planning cycles, and clear escalation paths reduce variability, reinforce reliable execution, and create space for insight to return to leadership.

Embedded practices make coherence structural rather than dependent on attention. Without them, execution reverts to intervention as the default mechanism for maintaining continuity.

THE CADENCE OF EXECUTION: LEADERSHIP ROUTINES AS FLOW REGULATORS

Execution does not remain coherent on its own. Even well-designed structures lose fit as conditions change, scale increases, and operational demand intensifies. To sustain coherence in motion, the enterprise requires cadence—a set of intentional leadership patterns that regulate flow, stabilize load, and keep execution continuously connected to learning.

Cadence is the structural pattern of execution—the deliberate tempo that ensures work advances at an appropriate pace, with coordinated handoffs and timely decision-making supported by relevant information. Without cadence, execution becomes reactive; with cadence, execution becomes reliable. Cadence prevents divergence without resorting to control because predictable connection points prevent small deviations from accumulating into systemic misalignment.

The cadence of execution operates across three interrelated

levels: daily and weekly patterns that govern near-term work, monthly learning cycles that convert experience into insight, and quarterly renewal cycles that restore structural fit.

Cadence Levels of Execution

Cadence Level	Function	Coherent Expression	Consequence of Degradation
Daily and Weekly	Synchronize near-term work; surface misfit before it hardens into delay	Teams aligned on immediate work, blockers surface early, handoffs improve, leaders spend less time chasing status	Teams diverge quickly, priorities conflict, work requires repeated explanation, issues compound, leaders pulled into reactive involvement
Monthly	Convert experience into insight; recognize patterns and begin structural adjustment	Patterns recognized earlier, corrective efforts targeted, operational pressure decreases, variability contained	Issues recur, misfit persists, learning fragments, decisions lose grounding, slippage normalized
Quarterly	Restore structural fit between Processes + Integration and current work	Structure evolves with the enterprise, renewal continuous, coherence preserved, complexity manageable	Structure decays quietly, processes fall out of date, integration weakens, execution compensates through added effort, performance becomes fragile

Table 8.12

The three levels operate as a single system: Each depends on the one below it for information and on the one above it for structural correction. When any level degrades, the enterprise loses that capacity—synchronization, learning, or renewal—and the remaining levels absorb pressure they are not structured to carry.

Cadence without intelligence hardens into ritualized activity—meetings that repeat without producing adjustment. Intelligence separated from cadence produces interpretation that arrives too late or lacks a structural mechanism through which to act. The enterprise sustains coherence only when cadence and intelligence operate together, because cadence determines when the enterprise attends to its own condition, and intelligence determines whether that attention produces renewal or repetition.

Three implementation failures appear consistently across enterprises that adopt cadence without structural discipline. Status substitution is the most common: Cadence sessions become status reporting rather than structural reading; the enterprise reviews what happened without interpreting what it means for system condition. A second failure, participation narrowing, contracts cadence attendance to operational leadership while excluding the people with direct structural visibility—front-line managers, interface coordinators, and customer-facing teams whose observations constitute the earliest signal set. Action disconnection completes the pattern: Cadence produces interpretation that does not reach the structural decisions it should inform; insights surface in weekly sessions and dissipate before monthly or quarterly decisions incorporate them. Each failure converts cadence from a structural sensing mechanism into ritualized repetition of the structural condition that prompted the cadence in the first place.

TECHNOLOGY AS MOTION AMPLIFIER, NOT SOLUTION

Technology does not substitute for execution capability, integration, or flow[6]. Within existing operations, it amplifies the structural condition that already exists. Technology can also create new structural conditions—new forms of coordination, new decision pathways, new modes of execution that did not exist before the technology was introduced. In either case, whether amplifying or creating, technology operates on the coherence present in its design. Coherent design is extended; incoherent design is accelerated.

Technology succeeds only when the enterprise has already established coherent workflows, defined decision rights, stable interfaces, structures that match the work, functioning learning loops, and predictable communication patterns. In such conditions, even modest tools perform well because they extend structural coherence rather than compensate for its absence. When these conditions are missing, even the most advanced tools underperform, not because the tools are deficient, but because they are amplifying an incoherent system.

Technology as a Mirror of the Enterprise

Technology reflects the enterprise's Natural Order. It makes visible whether alignment exists, whether integration remains intact, whether decisions have a clear path, whether expectations are shared, whether learning circulates, and whether the system can scale. Coherent enterprises adopt technology with relative ease; incoherent enterprises struggle with every implementation because structure is being asked to emerge from tools rather than be reinforced by them.

Technology introduced before coherence is established inherits the misfit it encounters. A platform migration illustrates the pattern. The new system arrives as a process architecture change—it reorganizes how work is sequenced, routed, and synchronized across Processes + Integration. That reorganization alters what execution must carry: new handoff structures, modified decision routing, and changed information dependencies propagate into Execution + Intelligence. If People + Alignment has not established shared interpretation of what the new architecture requires and how priorities shift under it, the platform inherits the interpretive variance it encounters. Customer + Interaction registers the outcome as inconsistent delivery, and Economics + Metrics records the cost as implementation overrun; in fact, the structural origin was upstream, in the gap between new process architecture and unchanged interpretive conditions.

What Technology Produces in Execution + Intelligence

When operating within coherent structure, technology strengthens clear routing, rapid visibility, shared knowledge, accurate sensing, timely feedback, expanded capacity, and predictable quality. Its function is to reinforce motion and learning, not to determine them.

In the Natural Order of the Five Enterprise Domains, people establish cadence, processes define pathways, execution animates motion, intelligence returns learning, and technology strengthens what already exists. Coherence is compounded by technology. Its absence is compounded equally—and technology does so at a speed and scale that only automation can produce.

THE WORK OF RENEWAL IN EXECUTION + INTELLIGENCE

Intelligence—the backward motion of the enterprise—provides continuous adaptation. Learning loops return insight, sense-and-respond routines detect deviation, and cadence structures convert experience into adjustment. These mechanisms sustain coherence under normal operating conditions. They do not restore coherence once structural misfit has accumulated beyond what continuous adaptation can absorb.

Renewal in this domain addresses the condition that appears when the gap between structure and reality exceeds the capacity of learning loops to close it. Firefighting has become persistent rather than occasional, intervention has replaced action as the dominant mode of enterprise motion, and coordination demand has intensified until synchronization consumes the capacity that execution requires. At this stage, the enterprise's intelligence mechanisms are registering misfit accurately but the structural conditions producing misfit are no longer within the range where incremental adjustment can correct. Renewal restores the structural conditions of execution—the architecture of motion, the balance of modes, the correspondence between capability and demand, and the integrity of the learning loop itself—so that continuous adaptation can operate within a structurally sound foundation.

When Renewal Becomes Necessary

Continuous adaptation and structural renewal address different conditions. Adaptation corrects within a stable architecture: A learning loop detects deviation, interprets the signal, and adjusts behavior or process within the existing structure. Renewal corrects the architecture itself when the modes of enterprise motion have shifted permanently toward intervention, when coordination has structurally displaced action, when capability no longer matches the work the enterprise must carry, or when the cadence that once regulated motion has hardened into ritual without producing adjustment.

Renewal becomes necessary when the conditions described earlier in this chapter converge. Misfit, entropy, and load interact to produce structural decay—the progressive loss of the system's capacity to carry its own work. When these conditions are present, learning loops continue to function but their outputs cannot reach the level of structural change required. The enterprise senses accurately and adjusts insufficiently, because the adjustments available within the current architecture are no longer proportional to the misfit the architecture has accumulated.

How Renewal Works

Renewal in Execution + Intelligence restores the structural conditions under which motion sustains itself through design rather than through compensatory effort.

Renewal begins with reading the dominant mode. The diagnostic structure this chapter established—propagation, action, and intervention as distinct expressions of enterprise motion—provides the structural baseline. Where intervention dominates, the enterprise identifies the specific conditions producing that dominance: whether capability has been outpaced by demand, whether interfaces have degraded to the point where coordination cannot carry work across them, whether cadence has separated from the learning it exists to produce, or whether accumulated entropy has eroded the predictability on which action depends.

Renewal proceeds by restoring the conditions that allow action to displace intervention as the dominant mode. This may require rebuilding capability where structural capacity has fallen below the threshold the work demands, redesigning interfaces where coordination cost has concentrated, recalibrating cadence where execution routines no longer produce structural adjustment, or rebalancing load where demand has exceeded what the current architecture can carry without compensatory effort. The objective is not the elimination of intervention—intervention is a normal response to complexity in any enterprise—but the restoration of structural conditions under which intervention is occasional rather than persistent.

Renewal in this domain is inseparable from renewal upstream. Execution architecture that has lost fit often reflects accumulated misfit in People + Alignment and Processes + Integration. Capability constraints may originate in talent architecture. Interface degradation may originate in process design. Cadence failure may originate in leadership signal inconsistency. Execution renewal that addresses downstream conditions without corresponding renewal upstream restores motion temporarily while leaving the structural sources of misfit intact. The enterprise regains execution coherence and then loses it again as upstream conditions reimpose the demand that produced the original degradation.

Renewal as a Leadership Discipline

Execution renewal is a leadership responsibility because it requires structural judgment that operating teams cannot exercise from within the architecture they occupy. Teams experiencing persistent intervention adapt to it—firefighting becomes competence, coordination becomes routine, and the distinction between compensatory effort and productive work becomes invisible from inside the operating condition. Leadership sees across the system, reads the dominant mode, and acts to restore structural carry before compensatory effort exhausts the enterprise's adaptive capacity.

Renewal encounters structural resistance. The patterns of intervention that renewal would displace have produced roles, routines, and recognition structures that depend on their continuation. Coordinators whose positions exist because structure cannot carry work across interfaces are invested in the current arrangement. The structural dynamics of this resistance are consistent with the discussion of Structural Interests in Chapter 2.

The structural consequence is cumulative. An enterprise that renews execution architecture as conditions change retains the capacity for action as its dominant mode; one that defers renewal operates on borrowed structural margin—sustained by effort, dependent on intervention, and increasingly unable to distinguish between execution that advances the enterprise and execution that merely sustains its compensatory patterns.

CROSS-DOMAIN INFLUENCE OF EXECUTION + INTELLIGENCE

Execution + Intelligence occupies the structural center of the enterprise's Natural Order. It sits downstream from People + Alignment and Processes + Integration and upstream from Customer + Interaction and Economics + Metrics. This position makes it uniquely influential because it is where structure is tested through action and where action is converted into learning. Execution exposes how the enterprise operates in practice, and intelligence interprets what that exposure means for renewal. Together, they determine how the system adjusts, sustains coherence, and evolves over time. Structure that carries work sustains the enterprise's own load without intervention or compensatory effort; diminishing capacity shifts load outward, and every other domain absorbs what execution can no longer carry.

Influence on People + Alignment

Execution is where people first experience the truth of alignment. Conversation can obscure divergence; execution makes it visible. Coherent People + Alignment produces execution that advances as coordinated motion. Without it, fragmentation appears immediately in how work develops. Execution shapes the human domain by building or eroding trust through delivery, reinforcing or disrupting orientation through the sequence of work, strengthening or weakening team cohesion through shared motion, and confirming or undermining leadership credibility through results. Misalignment becomes evident in execution long before it surfaces in dialogue, making execution the clearest signal of whether the connection established upstream is holding or deteriorating.

Influence on Processes + Integration

Execution is the proving ground for structure. No design remains intact once it encounters real conditions, and Execution + Intelligence reveals whether pathways are clear, interfaces are stable, decision rules function as intended, and processes fit the work being performed. It also exposes where decay is forming and where integration requires reinforcement. Execution does not damage structure; it tests it. Processes + Integration depends on this feedback to preserve fit and prevent silent decay.

Influence on Customer + Interaction

Customers do not experience strategy, culture, or process diagrams; they experience execution. Execution shapes Customer + Interaction through the consistency of delivery, accuracy of commitments, responsiveness to issues, stability of quality, coherence of communication, reliability of timelines, and continuity across contact points. Even minor misfit in execution surfaces immediately in customer experience. Wavering execution registers immediately as risk in customer perception. Execution is how the enterprise presents itself relationally—and customer perception registers the consequences.

Cross-Domain Influence of Execution + Intelligence

Affected Domain	When Execution + Intelligence Is Coherent	When It Is Incoherent
People + Alignment	Trust is reinforced through delivery; confidence strengthens as effort converts reliably into outcome	Credibility erodes; fragmentation appears as effort fails to produce consistent results
Processes + Integration	Structure is refined through feedback; interfaces remain stable and fit is preserved	Decay accelerates; pathways strain and integration weakens under real conditions
Customer + Interaction	Consistent experience builds confidence; commitments are reliable and responsiveness holds	Perceived risk increases; delivery variability undermines trust and continuity
Economics + Metrics	Stable, interpretable signals emerge; revenue, margin, and forecasts align with execution reality	Volatility and unpredictability increase; financial signals distort as execution degrades
Enterprise as a Whole	Strategic fit holds; predictability, trust, and learning reinforce one another	Reactivity rises; firefighting replaces learning and coherence becomes difficult to sustain

Table 8.13

Influence on Economics + Metrics

Financial outcomes are the most compressed expression of execution quality. Revenue stability, margins, cost-to-serve, cash-flow reliability, and forecast accuracy all trace back to how effectively execution converts intent into action. Predictable delivery stabilizes revenue, consistent quality reduces rework, efficient flow preserves margin integrity, controlled variability strengthens forecasting, disciplined use of capacity prevents exhaustion, and early detection avoids costly failure. Economics does not generate execution outcomes—it reveals them. When execution is coherent, financial signals stabilize. When execution degrades, financial signals distort.

Influence on the Enterprise as a Whole

Execution + Intelligence functions as the system's integrator—the point where structure meets reality, people experience the consequences of alignment, customers experience reliability, financial systems register consistency, and learning returns to renew the enterprise.

Coherent execution produces strategic fit, operational predictability, customer trust, financial stability, and consistent credibility across leadership. Weakening execution shifts the enterprise toward reactive intervention, recurring firefighting, unstable commitments, inconsistent customer experience, degraded financial predictability, and incomplete learning cycles.

The position Execution + Intelligence occupies in the Natural Order means that its condition registers across every other domain—forward through Customer + Interaction and Economics + Metrics as the predominant propagation path, and backward through the structural evidence returned to People + Alignment and Processes + Integration. Coherence here reduces the load on every other domain. Incoherence here increases it, and the cost of that increase compounds across the system with every cycle that passes without renewal.

EXECUTION + INTELLIGENCE AND ENTERPRISE VALUE AMPLIFICATION

Execution + Intelligence is the domain through which enterprise value is amplified through learning. Processes + Integration compounds value through structure and reuse; this domain determines whether value strengthens over time as conditions change.

This domain amplifies enterprise value by closing the learning loop. Enterprise design enacted across processes and encountering response under load produces outcomes that reveal fit, misfit, and variability. Intelligence converts those outcomes into insight—about capacity, timing, interfaces, and consequence—allowing the enterprise to adjust before corrective cost accumulates. When learning returns quickly and coherently, value is not merely repeated; it is compounded.

Amplification in this domain occurs because adaptation is cumulative. Effective responses become embedded while ineffective patterns are corrected before they harden, and decisions sharpen as evidence replaces assumptions. Over successive cycles, the enterprise increases the yield of its motion—not by exerting more effort, but by learning how to move with less loss. In this way, Execution + Intelligence multiplies the value already created and carried by upstream domains.

Coherence in this domain strengthens enterprise value through structural durability and responsiveness. Variability decreases as structural patterns stabilize, yet the system retains the capacity to respond to shifting conditions. Pressure does not consume capability because execution draws on architecture rather than effort, and change is absorbed through learning rather than disruption. The enterprise produces stronger results because it learns from what it encounters. Value compounds as performance strengthens relative to conditions, not merely in absolute output.

Weakening in this domain reverses amplification. Learning slows or fragments, errors recur without correction, and signals that should trigger adjustment are misread or ignored. Execution compensates through effort rather than adjustment, and value that could have been strengthened is consumed by rework, delay, and instability. In these conditions, motion continues, but value erodes because the enterprise fails to learn from its experiences.

Execution + Intelligence therefore carries the Amplify function through learning. It does not create value at origin, nor does it protect value across cycles. It determines whether value grows stronger with use, whether motion strengthens through experience, and whether the enterprise becomes more capable over time rather than merely busier.

THIS CHAPTER ESTABLISHED that execution is where enterprise coherence is tested and revealed. It showed how structure becomes behavior, how motion produces consequence, and how learning determines whether enterprise value strengthens or erodes over time. But execution alone does not complete the enterprise value cycle.

That determination occurs only when enterprise behavior encounters recognition beyond execution itself. Work can advance, decisions can land, and outcomes can form without enterprise value being realized. Enterprise value is created only when behavior is interpreted, adopted, and reinforced through customer and market response. Chapter 9 turns to that decisive threshold, introducing *Customer + Interaction*—the domain in which enterprise behavior is translated into perception, perception stabilizes as demand, and coherence is confirmed or rejected through sustained real-world response.

Endnotes

1. Organizational life-cycle models describe sequential developmental phases that organizations pass through over time. Larry E. Greiner's seminal "Evolution and Revolution as Organizations Grow," *Harvard Business Review* 50, no. 4 (1972): 37–46, describes five phases of organizational growth, each punctuated by a crisis. Ichak Adizes developed a ten-stage life-cycle model in *Corporate Lifecycles: How and Why Corporations Grow and Die and What to Do About It* (Englewood Cliffs, NJ: Prentice Hall, 1988). Both frameworks describe the stages an organization passes through sequentially. Modes of enterprise motion, as defined here, are fundamentally different. They describe three concurrent patterns of how execution advances at any given moment: propagation (ambient motion sustained by prior decisions), action (deliberate forward-moving execution), and intervention (corrective execution applied to compensate for misfit). These modes operate simultaneously, not sequentially. They describe how work is being carried right now, not what phase the organization has reached.

2. *Technical Capability* encompasses the four structural elements of Execution Capability—Skills, Tools, Structure, and Capacity—that determine what the enterprise can do. The concept of organizational capability has a well-developed foundation. Jay B. Barney's resource-based framework established the systematic analysis of firm resources and their contribution to sustained advantage in "Firm Resources and Sustained Competitive Advantage," *Journal of Management* 17, no. 1 (1991): 99–120. C. K. Prahalad and Gary Hamel addressed the strategic significance of core competencies—the collective learning embedded in how the enterprise coordinates production skills and integrates multiple technologies—in "The Core Competence of the Corporation," *Harvard Business Review* 68, no. 3 (1990): 79–91. David J. Teece, Gary Pisano, and Amy Shuen's dynamic capabilities framework addressed the firm's capacity to integrate, build, and reconfigure competences in response to changing environments in Teece, Pisano, and Shuen, "Dynamic Capabilities and Strategic Management," *Strategic Management Journal* 18, no. 7 (1997): 509–33. The resource-based view treats capability as a resource inventory; the competence framework treats it as embedded collective learning; dynamic capabilities treat it as a capacity for configuration and reconfiguration. Technical Capability as defined here is distinct from all three: it is not a resource stock, a competency portfolio, or a reconfiguration capacity—it is a structural sub-system of Execution Capability comprising four mutually reinforcing elements whose breakdown degrades execution even when each element is individually present. The diagnostic significance is structural rather than strategic: the question is not what the enterprise possesses but whether the four elements are reinforcing one another in motion.
3. *Relational Effectiveness* is the social dimension of Execution Capability—the enterprise's capacity to carry work through human interaction, governing whether Technical Capability Creates and Amplifies enterprise value or Dilutes and Erodes it in transit. The relational dimension of organizational performance is well-established in the literature. Jody Hoffer Gittell developed relational coordination theory, demonstrating that communication and relationship quality across functional boundaries governs the efficiency and quality of task performance: see Gittell, "Organizing Work to Support Relational Co-ordination," *International Journal of Human Resource Management* 11, no. 3 (2000): 517–34, and *High Performance Healthcare: Using the Power of Relationships to Achieve Quality, Efficiency and Resilience* (New York: McGraw-Hill, 2009). Janine Nahapiet and Sumantra Ghoshal addressed the relational dimension of organizational advantage through social capital theory in "Social Capital, Intellectual Capital, and the Organizational Advantage," *Academy of Management Review* 23, no. 2 (1998): 242–66. Relational coordination theory addresses task-level coordination through communication and relationship quality; social capital theory addresses how relational assets contribute to knowledge creation and organizational performance. Individual-level frameworks—including emotional intelligence research (Daniel Goleman, *Emotional Intelligence: Why It Can Matter More Than IQ* [New York: Bantam Books, 1995]) and interpersonal competence frameworks (Richard E. Boyatzis, *The Competent Manager: A Model for Effective Performance* [New York: Wiley, 1982])—address related capacities at the individual level. Relational Effectiveness as defined here is distinct from all of these: it operates at two levels simultaneously—at the individual level, where each person's contribution to enterprise value is contingent on

their own Relational Effectiveness; and at the enterprise level, where the aggregate Relational Effectiveness of all people operating across teams, interfaces, and relational fields determines whether the enterprise's collective Technical Capability Creates and Amplifies enterprise value or Dilutes and Erodes it in transit. It is not an individual attribute, a coordination mechanism, or a social capital stock; it is the delivery mechanism operating across both levels through which Technical Capability either produces enterprise value or loses it before it reaches those who depend on it.

4. The relationship between Technical Capability and Relational Effectiveness is multiplicative rather than additive: Technical Capability × Relational Effectiveness = (+/–) Enterprise Value. Human capital theory established the economic significance of skill investment for organizational performance—see Gary S. Becker, *Human Capital: A Theoretical and Empirical Analysis, with Special Reference to Education* (Chicago: University of Chicago Press, 1964), and Theodore W. Schultz, "Investment in Human Capital," *American Economic Review* 51, no. 1 (1961): 1–17. Human capital frameworks treat technical and relational dimensions as additive contributors to performance. Jody Hoffer Gittell, Rob Seidner, and Julian Wimbush examined the interaction between high-performance work practices and relational coordination in "A Relational Model of How High-Performance Work Systems Work," *Organization Science* 21, no. 2 (2010): 490–506, demonstrating that work system effectiveness depends on relational conditions—a finding directly adjacent to the multiplicative claim. Organizational research has also documented the pattern in which coordination and relational deficits defeat technically capable systems: Michael Beer and Russell A. Eisenstat identified relational and organizational dynamics as the primary mechanism of strategy implementation failure in "The Silent Killers of Strategy Implementation and Learning," *Sloan Management Review* 41, no. 4 (2000): 29–40. The Execution Multiplier as defined here is distinct from additive performance models and from empirical failure-pattern research: it expresses the multiplicative structural mechanism through which Relational Effectiveness governs the entire product—not subtracting from Technical Capability's contribution but scaling it. As Relational Effectiveness approaches zero, Dilution and Erosion scale with the relational deficit, and the product approaches zero regardless of the strength of Technical Capability. This is why the enterprise cannot out-perform a relational deficit with technical excellence.
5. The term *responsible autonomy* was introduced by Andrew Friedman in *Industry and Labour: Class Struggle at Work and Monopoly Capitalism* (London: Macmillan, 1977). Friedman, writing as a sociologist of labor, described responsible autonomy as a managerial strategy in which workers are granted latitude over how they organize their tasks as an alternative to direct supervisory control. Gerard Fairtlough later adopted the term in his triarchy framework. The book acknowledges this origin explicitly in the body text. The usage here is distinct: Responsible autonomy is not a managerial tactic or delegation preference, but a structural condition of enterprise execution that emerges from clear role definition, defined decision pathways, reliable information, stable interfaces, and learning mechanisms. It is a diagnostic marker—where responsible autonomy is present, execution capability is mature; where it is absent, compensatory coordination has displaced structural support.

6. Capability as an organizational concept is well-established. David J. Teece, Gary Pisano, and Amy Shuen introduced the dynamic capabilities framework in "Dynamic Capabilities and Strategic Management," *Strategic Management Journal* 18, no. 7 (1997): 509–33, describing the firm's ability to integrate, build, and reconfigure competences in response to changing environments. Business Capability Modeling in enterprise architecture (TOGAF) treats capability as a relatively static design artifact. Strategy execution frameworks broadly address the gap between intent and outcome. Execution capability, as defined here, is more specific than any of these. It is the enterprise's structural capacity to carry work into action under real conditions—expressed only in motion and visible only through system behavior, not through individual talent, effort, or intent. The "expressed only in motion" framing distinguishes this definition from frameworks that treat capability as something an organization possesses, independent of whether it is being exercised.

9

CUSTOMER + INTERACTION

THE RELATIONAL DOMAIN

Customer + Interaction is the relational domain of the enterprise: the field where enterprise behavior encounters customer interpretation and where that encounter determines whether enterprise value is realized, reinforced, or undermined. It does not correspond to marketing, sales, service, or positioning as discrete functions; it governs how enterprise priorities and customer priorities meet in practice, conditioning the enterprise's capacity to validate enterprise value through experience and sustain it over time.

> **Customer + Interaction** is the enterprise domain through which execution is interpreted as value, converting enterprise behavior into perception, perception into demand, and demand into relational signals that feed back into the enterprise and guide renewal wherever enterprise behavior is encountered.

Earlier enterprise models treated customers as separate from the system, assuming that enterprise value was produced internally and then delivered to customers. That framing fails to account for how enterprise value forms. Customers are participants in enterprise motion, not recipients of finished output. Their reactions, preferences, and expectations reflect how enterprise action integrates across domains, returning signals that reveal coherence or misfit long before enterprise value is confirmed economically. Coherence in this domain reinforces enterprise value through trust and continuity. Its loss erodes enterprise value through inconsistency and declining relevance—even if execution elsewhere remains strong.

Customers participate in the enterprise by interpreting value, shaping demand, and returning feedback that reveals whether the structure fits the work being carried. Their responses guide renewal and influence whether results stabilize or unravel over time.

Customer + Interaction: Where Value Is Interpreted

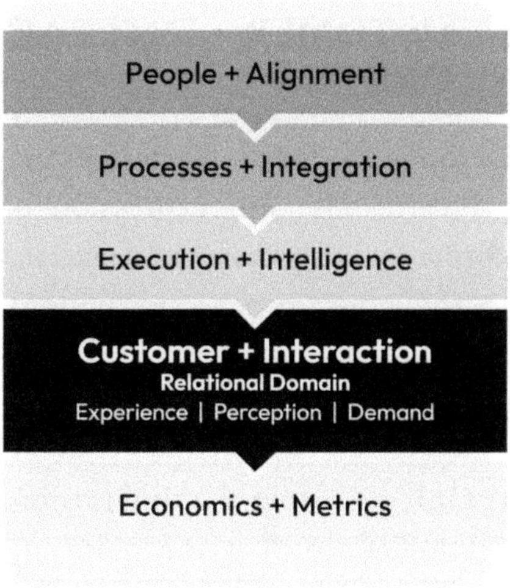

Figure 9.1

In an unwalled enterprise, the relationship between the enterprise and its customers is systemic rather than transactional. Customers respond to enterprise behavior, not enterprise intent. Their experience reflects how the enterprise is functioning across all five Enterprise Domains—the visible expression of enterprise coherence as it is encountered through relationships.

Customer + Interaction is where enterprise value is validated, because enterprise behavior is either confirmed or undermined through perception—often before any formal measure registers change.

The most revealing signals I've seen rarely emerged from reports or dashboards; they emerged from customers themselves. Sales cycles lengthened, adoption patterns shifted, renewal conversations changed in tone, and market response became variable for offerings that once performed reliably. Rather than marketing failures, these were relational signals indicating loss of coherence between the enterprise and the environments it served. Customer + Interaction consistently shows that markets interpret coherence quickly—and detect misfit even faster.

THE ROLE OF CUSTOMER + INTERACTION IN THE NATURAL ORDER

Customer + Interaction is the fourth domain in the Natural Order of the enterprise. It receives the full expression of everything that precedes it—interpretation, structure, and execution—and returns that expression to the enterprise as perception, experience, and demand. It is within this relational domain that enterprise behavior is interpreted by others, and where coherence becomes visible beyond intent.

In the Natural Order, Customer + Interaction sits downstream from Execution + Intelligence. It is the point at which enterprise motion encounters response. Execution may advance work and produce outcomes, but those outcomes remain structurally incomplete until they are interpreted and reinforced through relationships. Enterprise priorities and customer priorities interact continuously within this relational field—through behavior, meaning, and consequence.

The Governing Role of Customer + Interaction

Aspect	What This Domain Governs
Domain position	Fourth in the Natural Order
Primary function	Interpretation of enterprise behavior as value
What it receives	Alignment, structure, execution
What it returns	Perception, demand, relational signals
Governing condition	Relational coherence

Table 9.1

This domain resolves a small set of structural questions that determine whether enterprise effort becomes enterprise value. It reveals whether enterprise motion makes sense to the people the enterprise serves, whether experience reflects coherence or misalignment, and whether enterprise priorities remain aligned with what customers value. Sustained coherence in this domain means effort is recognized as value by the people the enterprise serves. Loss of coherence reverses that recognition—misalignment appears first in relationships, long before it becomes visible elsewhere.

What This Domain Governs

Customer + Interaction governs how enterprise behavior is experienced, interpreted, and reinforced across customer and market relationships. It determines whether interactions register as relevant or dissonant, whether commitments are received as reliable or conditional, whether value exchange is perceived as sustainable or pressured, and whether enterprise motion accumulates credibility or introduces hesitation over time.

Customers do not assess coherence directly—they experience it through consistency, tone, timing, and reliability. For this reason, Customer + Interaction is the enterprise's first interpretive surface beyond the enterprise itself. It is where coherence becomes relational coherence and where misfit becomes perceptible through experience.

How This Domain Receives From the Enterprise System

Customer + Interaction is shaped continuously by conditions originating elsewhere in the enterprise system. Each upstream domain conditions the relational field through a distinct mechanism, summarized in Table 9.2.

How Upstream Domains Condition Customer + Interaction

Upstream Domain	Conditions Through	Coherence State	Loss of Coherence
People + Alignment	Relevance and tone	Customers experience consistency and credibility in enterprise communication	Customers encounter mixed signals, inconsistent messaging, and uncertainty about what the enterprise represents
Processes + Integration	Interaction predictability	Customers experience continuity across interactions over time	Experience fragments as handoffs break down and interfaces lose definition
Execution + Intelligence	Reliability and responsiveness	Customers experience follow-through and timely response	Customers encounter delay, inconsistency, and loss of trust
Economics + Metrics	Value sustainability	Customers experience stable value exchange	Customers experience pressure through pricing inconsistency, reduced flexibility, or diminished perceived value

Table 9.2

Customer + Interaction therefore reflects the enterprise's overall coherence as it moves through its relational environment. Customer experience is coherence in motion—enterprise behavior perceived through relationships.

How This Domain Sends Signals Back Through the System

Customer + Interaction receives from the enterprise system and returns to it—experience feeds directly back into the enterprise as relational intelligence, not as passive data but as structural input that conditions subsequent motion.

Customer behavior carries structural information: Shifts in engagement indicate changes in relevance, inconsistency across experience signals structural misfit, changes in tone or trust reflect interpretive divergence, demand patterns expose execution limits, and economic pressure surfaces through value perception. These signals do not describe marketing performance; they describe system condition.

Because of directional dependence, this domain is often where misalignment becomes visible first. Customer + Interaction therefore functions as the enterprise's earliest relational warning system, revealing whether coherence is sustained across interpretation, structure, execution, and economics.

Customer + Interaction as the Value-Creator Domain

Value creation is completed through relationship, not through execution alone. Enterprise value emerges when enterprise motion aligns with what customers prioritize and are willing to sustain—when work is recognized, adopted, and reinforced through the relational field this domain governs.

Loss of coherence in this domain undermines enterprise value quietly—through relevance that narrows, continuity that breaks, or trust that withdraws.

VALUE CREATION VS. VALUE PERCEPTION

In the Natural Order of the enterprise, the realization of enterprise value depends on what customers recognize, prioritize, and act upon

—not solely on what the enterprise produces. Enterprise value also accumulates through forms that do not require direct customer recognition: intellectual property, institutional capability, regulatory compliance capacity, workforce depth, data assets, and strategic positioning all constitute enterprise value independent of customer perception. Customer + Interaction is the domain through which enterprise value is validated relationally—one structural source among several. Enterprises that attend only to customer-recognized value risk underinvesting in the structural and intellectual assets that sustain their capacity to create value over time. Within the relational domain, the distance between what the enterprise believes it is delivering and what customers actually perceive becomes a structural condition rather than a communication gap.

This distance is not resolved through messaging or intent. It is governed by how coherently enterprise motion registers across the dimensions through which customers actually interpret value—dimensions that operate simultaneously, whether or not the enterprise attends to them individually. The sections that follow name those dimensions and the structural gap they expose.

The Five Forms of Value Perceived by Customers

Value perception is not singular. Customers interpret enterprise coherence through five distinct dimensions that operate simultaneously, and misalignment in any one dimension weakens the overall relationship. The Five Forms of Value Perceived by Customers[1] in Table 9.3 names these dimensions and what they express.

Functional value is foundational to the other four. When functional reliability degrades, no other dimension compensates—economic, emotional, social, and strategic value all depend on the enterprise's capacity to perform the work customers require. The remaining dimensions interact continuously: economic value governs whether the relationship is sustainable, emotional value governs whether customers remain willing to engage, social value governs what the relationship signals beyond the immediate exchange, and strategic value governs whether the relationship carries consequence over time.

Five Forms of Value Perceived by Customers

Dimension	What Customers Interpret	Expressed Through
Functional Value	Whether the enterprise reliably allows customers to accomplish what they need	Reliability, usability, speed, convenience, accuracy, outcome quality
Economic Value	How customers judge cost relative to benefit	Pricing fairness, efficiency gains, time savings, return relative to constraint
Emotional Value	How the experience registers for the customer	Trust, ease, relief, perceived risk, reduction of frustration
Social Value	What association with the enterprise signals to others	Status, belonging, identity, credibility, professional validation
Strategic Value	How the enterprise supports the customer's longer-term direction	Alignment with customer ambition, trajectory, and opportunity

Table 9.3

The Perceived Customer Value Gap

The perceived value gap[2] is the distance between what the enterprise believes it is delivering and what customers actually perceive. This gap reveals coherence or incoherence faster than any formal measure. Enterprise motion that reinforces customer priorities strengthens value perception across dimensions; motion that separates from those priorities weakens it—and the deterioration registers through perception before it registers anywhere else.

The gap becomes visible as declining functional reliability, weakening economic integrity, loss of emotional resonance, erosion of social identity, or loss of strategic relevance. Customer + Interaction identifies where enterprise motion has separated from customer meaning and where recalibration is required.

The Perceived Customer Value Gap

Enterprise Belief	Customer Perception	Structural Implication
Value delivered	Value is interpreted through actual interaction, not intention. Customers assess whether what they encounter feels useful, appropriate, and worth sustaining based on lived experience rather than claims.	Coherence holds when perceived value aligns with enterprise intent; coherence weakens when customers encounter inconsistency or irrelevance despite internal confidence.
Capability strength	Capability is experienced in use, not inferred from reputation. Customers judge relevance based on whether enterprise capability solves real problems under real conditions.	Structural fit exists when capability matches customer demand; misalignment appears when capability is present but not experienced as relevant or usable.
Execution quality	Consistency is perceived across repeated interactions. Customers notice whether outcomes are reliable, timing is dependable, and behavior is predictable over time.	Trust is reinforced when execution holds across contexts; trust erodes when variability appears, even if isolated interactions succeed.
Strategic intent	Meaning is recognized through behavior, not messaging. Customers infer what the enterprise stands for by how it acts, responds, and prioritizes.	Renewal occurs when intent is reinforced through interaction; decay sets in when behavior contradicts stated direction or purpose.

Table 9.4

Experience as Coherence Made Visible

Customer experience expresses enterprise coherence through relationship, and every interaction, response, delay, handoff, and clarification reveals how well the enterprise is operating as a system—whether structure carries work cleanly, whether execution sustains under load, and whether interpretive convergence translates into consistent behavior.

In an unwalled enterprise, experience is formed directly by how the enterprise behaves in action. Experience is the point at which structural reality meets relational interpretation, making coherence perceptible and misalignment immediately apparent.

Experience as Flow, Interface, Signal, and System Health

Experience makes coherence visible through four dimensions, each of which surfaces enterprise condition at a different level of the system. Table 9.5 summarizes how each dimension expresses coherence and its loss.

Four Dimensions of Customer Experience

Dimension	What It Reveals	Coherence Expression	Loss of Coherence Expression
Flow	Structural continuity of work through the enterprise	Sequencing is consistent, handoffs remain intact, timing is predictable, exceptions resolve without distortion	Work requires re-explanation, steps repeat, decisions linger, transitions fail
Interface	Enterprise behavior at points of customer contact	Definition, competence, trust, reliability, shared understanding	Confusion, contradiction, inconsistency, uncertainty
Signal	Customer reactions as relational intelligence	Experience consistency confirms structural fit	Slow responses, missed commitments, confusing workflows, inconsistent policies, contradictory messages
System Health	Overall enterprise operating condition	Predictable responses, consistent quality, reliable follow-through, stable patterns	Execution becomes variable, messaging loses coherence, timelines become unpredictable, quality varies

Table 9.5

These dimensions do not operate independently. Flow expresses the structural continuity of work through the enterprise; interfaces expose that continuity—or its absence—at every point of customer contact. Customer reactions at those interfaces carry structural information back into the enterprise, and the consistency of that information across time is the most reliable indicator of overall enterprise condition. When experience is coherent across all four dimensions, customers encounter the enterprise as a single system. Weakened coherence in any single dimension propagates through customer behavior before it appears in any formal report.

Customer experience is a system outcome—the relational expression of how well the Five Enterprise Domains are operating together. It reflects whether interpretation, structure, execution, learning, and economics are reinforcing one another or quietly working at cross-purposes.

MARKET SENSING: READING THE RELATIONAL FIELD

Enterprises operate within a continuously shifting relational field shaped by customer expectations, partner capabilities, platform dynamics, competitive behavior, and regulatory conditions. These shifts are not pressures applied from outside the system; they are relational signals moving through the same system in which the enterprise itself operates.

Market sensing[3] is the enterprise's capacity to perceive these signals accurately, interpret their implications, and adjust before misfit hardens into failure. It functions as the learning mechanism of the Customer + Interaction domain—the means by which the enterprise sustains coherence with the people, platforms, and environments that determine relevance.

In the Unwalled Enterprise, sensing is continuous rather than event-driven. The enterprise is always embedded in its relational field, and signals are always in motion through customers, partners, platforms, markets, and operating conditions. There is no discrete moment when sensing begins or ends. Signals arrive whether the enterprise attends to them or not; market sensing does not create information, it disciplines attention by converting ongoing relational input into usable insight.

Signal Types

Relational signals arrive through five distinct channels, each of which surfaces enterprise condition from a different vantage point within the relational field. Table 9.6 classifies these signal types[4] and what they reveal.

Forms of Relational Signal

Signal Type	Source	What It Reveals	How It Appears
Direct Customer Signals	Customer communication and behavior in response to enterprise action	Where the enterprise is or is not coherent with what customers value	Feedback, usage patterns, service interactions, renewal decisions, buying behavior, abandonment
Behavioral Signals	Customer behavior patterns over time	Structural misfit before it is articulated	Declining engagement, reduced usage, slower adoption, increased support interaction, switching behavior, changes in decision criteria
Market Dynamics	Broader relational environment	Where enterprise relevance is shifting	Competitor behavior, technological change, platform rules, regulatory developments, macroeconomic conditions, industry innovation
Competitive Patterns	Competitor actions	How customer expectations and value perception are evolving	Pricing changes, product shifts, partnership formation, experience redesign, narrative shifts, distribution changes
Platform and Regulatory Signals	Platforms and regulators	Structural conditions within which coherence must be maintained	Policy change, new standards, distribution constraints, algorithm updates, compliance requirements, data expectations

Table 9.6

Direct and behavioral signals are the most immediate—they

carry customer-level interpretation of enterprise coherence. Customers rarely describe structural breakdowns directly, but their choices reliably reveal where the enterprise is coherent with what they value and where it is not. Individual customer actions may be ambiguous; sustained patterns are systemic. These patterns often surface structural misfit long before revenue, retention, or margin measures register change.

Market dynamics, competitive patterns, and platform and regulatory signals operate at a longer wavelength. They describe the relational environment within which coherence must be maintained rather than customer-level interpretation of enterprise behavior. Competitive signals reveal how customer expectations and value perception are evolving; platform and regulatory signals define the structural conditions the enterprise cannot avoid. Ignoring either introduces interface friction for customers and instability for the enterprise.

The Cadence of Sensing

The enterprise must read relational signals across multiple, nested time horizons, because different forms of meaning emerge at different speeds. Market sensing therefore operates through a disciplined cadence that spans daily and weekly observation, monthly interpretation, and quarterly recalibration. Together, these cycles prevent the enterprise from reacting too late or adjusting too slowly as conditions evolve.

Daily and weekly sensing captures immediate relational signals—customer interactions, behavioral shifts, experience patterns, and emerging points of resistance. At this cadence, the enterprise is not drawing conclusions; it is maintaining contact with reality. Small changes in tone, hesitation, inquiry volume, usage behavior, or response timing often appear here first, long before they register as trends. This cadence keeps the enterprise attentive to what is changing now, not what has already solidified.

Monthly sensing converts accumulated signals into relational intelligence. Patterns that are ambiguous day to day become legible over time. At this cadence, the enterprise interprets recurring customer behavior, shifting expectations, and emerging sources of interface friction. Monthly sensing distinguishes isolated deviations from systemic conditions and provides insight to leadership while adjustment is still possible.

Quarterly sensing operates at the level of structural recalibration. At this horizon, the enterprise steps back from individual signals and patterns to assess whether its structure, assumptions, and execution still fit the relational field in which it operates. This cadence ensures that learning alters structure before misfit compounds.

Sensing is a distributed capability of the Customer + Interaction domain that operates continuously across these time horizons. The enterprise adjusts before relevance erodes only when all three cadences are sustained; a breakdown at any level separates the enterprise from its relational field and weakens coherence with the people and environments it serves.

LEADERSHIP ATTENTION AS THE RELATIONAL GOVERNING SIGNAL

Market sensing produces intelligence. Whether the enterprise acts on that intelligence is determined by leadership attention. The Customer + Interaction domain generates relational signals continuously—through customer behavior, market shifts, competitive repositioning, partner dynamics, and platform changes—but the conversion of those signals into enterprise response depends on where leadership directs its interpretive capacity and how consistently it treats relational feedback as structural information rather than as background.

Leadership attention in this domain operates differently than it does in the upstream domains. The upstream domains each define a different structural role for leadership: synchronization in People +

Alignment, structural renewal in Processes + Integration, cadence regulation and mode reading in Execution + Intelligence. In Customer + Interaction, leadership determines whether the enterprise remains connected to the relational field it depends on—whether customer signals reach the structural level where they can reshape priorities, redirect investment, and trigger renewal before misalignment compounds.

The distinction matters because this domain does not produce its own motion. It receives the full expression of enterprise behavior and returns the relational response that determines whether enterprise value is realized. Leadership cannot synchronize this domain the way it synchronizes interpretation, nor can it design this domain the way it designs process architecture. Leadership interacts with Customer + Interaction by governing the enterprise's attentional capacity—what the enterprise notices, how seriously it treats what it notices, and how quickly relational signals convert into structural adjustment.

How Leadership Attention Shapes Relational Response

Leadership attention produces three structural effects in the Customer + Interaction domain, each governing a different stage of the enterprise's relational response.

Leadership attention determines signal priority. Relational signals arrive continuously across multiple channels and time horizons. Which signals reach leadership interpretation—and which are filtered, delayed, or dismissed—is governed by what leadership treats as important. Where leadership treats customer signals as structural intelligence, the enterprise maintains contact with its relational field and detects misalignment early. As that attention narrows—when customer signals are subordinated to financial or execution metrics—the enterprise gradually separates from its relational field, and the separation becomes visible only after customer behavior has already shifted.

The second effect operates on response speed. The interval between signal detection and enterprise response is a structural property of leadership interaction, not an operational metric. Enterprises whose leadership interprets relational signals as conditions requiring structural attention respond before misfit compounds. Once that interpretation is deferred—routed to quarterly reviews, customer satisfaction programs, or marketing functions—the enterprise responds after the relational field has already moved, and the cost of recalibration increases with each cycle of delay.

The third effect determines whether relational intelligence reaches the domains where structural adjustment occurs. Customer signals that remain within the Customer + Interaction domain produce local responses—service adjustments, communication refinements, experience modifications—without addressing the structural conditions that produced the misalignment. Leadership attention that connects relational intelligence to People + Alignment, Processes + Integration, Execution + Intelligence, and Economics + Metrics converts customer signals into enterprise-level structural recalibration. Without that connection, the enterprise adjusts its relational surface while leaving its structural interior unchanged.

The Consequences of Leadership Inattention

When leadership attention withdraws from the relational field, the enterprise does not stop receiving signals. Customers continue to respond to enterprise behavior, markets continue to shift, and competitive dynamics continue to reshape the relational environment. The enterprise stops interpreting those signals structurally, and the gap between enterprise motion and relational reality widens without producing a corrective response.

The consequences compound in sequence. The sensing cadence described in the preceding section degrades as daily observation narrows, monthly interpretation becomes superficial, and quarterly recalibration loses contact with actual relational conditions. Market sensing produces data without producing intelligence, because intelligence requires leadership attention to convert observation into structural meaning. The patterns of customer misalignment described in the following section accumulate faster than the enterprise can detect them, and by the time financial signals register the relational separation, the cost of restoration has already compounded beyond what surface-level adjustment can address.

Leadership inattention to the relational field is not a failure of effort. It is a structural condition in which the enterprise's interpretive capacity is directed elsewhere—toward execution pressure, financial constraint, internal coordination, or upstream domain renewal—while the relational field that determines whether enterprise value is realized continues to evolve without enterprise response.

PATTERNS OF CUSTOMER MISALIGNMENT

Customer misalignment is a relational signal that the enterprise has separated from the people it serves—not a marketing issue, a communication failure, or a service breakdown. When coherence between enterprise motion and customer priorities weakens, customers experience incoherence immediately, even when they cannot explain its source.

Because customers encounter the enterprise across multiple interfaces, misalignment anywhere within the Five Enterprise Domains is reflected back through customer behavior. Experience becomes inconsistent, expectations diverge, credibility weakens, decisions slow, and trust deteriorates. These are systemic reflections of structural misfit, not isolated incidents. The Customer + Interaction domain interprets these patterns as diagnostic insight into enterprise coherence rather than surface feedback. Table 9.7 identifies the seven most reliable patterns through which customer misalignment becomes visible, along with the structural conditions that produce them.

Each pattern names a different form of incoherence as it registers through customer behavior, and each traces to identifiable conditions within the enterprise system. Mismatched expectations and emotional disconnect typically originate in People + Alignment, where interpretive convergence has weakened. Inconsistent delivery and responsiveness gaps point to instability in Execution + Intelligence or to process architecture that no longer carries current demand. Channel friction reflects fit issues in Processes + Integration and Execution + Intelligence simultaneously. Strategic irrelevance and value narrative divergence signal that renewal has slowed—that enterprise assumptions, offerings, or positioning no longer track where customers are moving.

These patterns do not arrive independently. In practice, they compound. Inconsistent delivery introduces emotional disconnect, which accelerates strategic irrelevance, which, in turn, widens value narrative divergence. As incoherence propagates across patterns, the enterprise's capacity to detect the originating condition diminishes—because customers experience the accumulated effect, not the isolated cause.

A manufacturing enterprise that redesigned its production sequencing to reduce cost experienced the compounding in this order. Delivery timing became variable as the new process stabilized—an inconsistency customers registered immediately even though internal metrics showed increased throughput. Sales teams, unaware of the sequencing change, continued committing to the original delivery windows, widening the gap between expectation and experience. Customers interpreted the inconsistency as a decline in commitment rather than an operational transition, and an emotional disconnect formed in the absence of any relational failure. Within two quarters, three long-standing customers had initiated secondary sourcing, not because quality had declined but because predictability had. The enterprise diagnosed a customer retention problem and responded with account-level relational investment—a domain-specific intervention that addressed the symptom without reaching the structural origin in process redesign. The misalignment compounded across four of the seven patterns before the enterprise recognized that the originating condition was an unmanaged interface between process change and customer communication.

Seven Patterns of Customer Misalignment

Pattern	What Customers Experience	Structural Origin
Mismatched Expectations	Outcomes differ from what was anticipated, commitments feel inconsistent, timelines do not match assumptions, information arrives too early or too late	Interpretation gaps in People + Alignment; sequencing and fit issues in Processes + Integration
Inconsistent Delivery	Experience varies between interactions, quality depends on timing or on who the customer encounters, outcomes are not repeatable	Instability in Execution + Intelligence; process architecture that no longer supports current load or complexity
Emotional Disconnect	Interactions feel transactional, service appears indifferent or variable, communication becomes scripted or disjointed, enterprise behavior sends mixed signals	Misfit in People + Alignment (tone, shared understanding); weakness in Execution + Intelligence (responsiveness, follow-through)
Responsiveness Gaps	Delayed responses, slow resolution, inconsistent follow-through, missed anticipation of need	Resistance in Processes + Integration; breakdowns in Execution + Intelligence where learning does not return quickly enough
Strategic Irrelevance	Declining relevance, reduced adoption of new offerings, customers outgrowing the enterprise, competitors winning on meaning rather than features	Renewal cycles have slowed; adaptation no longer matches environmental motion
Channel Friction	Inconsistent messages across channels, disjointed workflows, resistance during transitions, different expectations depending on the interface	Fit issues in Processes + Integration and Execution + Intelligence
Value Narrative Divergence	Messaging contradicts experience, value propositions age without renewal, competitive narratives overtake enterprise position, customers lose definition of what the enterprise represents	Lagging renewal or misfit across People + Alignment, Processes + Integration, and evolving customer priorities

Table 9.7

Enterprise Value Loss in the Customer Domain

The destructive motions of enterprise value first become visible in this domain. Destruction produces customer defection at scale—the sudden collapse of trust through failed commitments, breaches, or breakdowns registers as irreversible separation. Dilution operates differently: Inconsistent experience disperses perceived value across interactions, weakening the relationship without a single identifiable failure. Erosion is the slowest and least visible, accumulating through gradual decline in adoption and relevance, often undetected until the loss is structural.

These are system conditions expressed through customer behavior, not customer problems. Customer + Interaction surfaces these signals and returns them upstream before enterprise value is destroyed through prolonged misfit.

RENEWAL THROUGH RELATIONAL FEEDBACK

Renewal begins where misalignment signals accumulate—when the enterprise recognizes that recalibration is structurally required. In an unwalled enterprise, customers participate directly in the system, and their behavior reveals where coherence is sustained, where interface friction begins to form, and where enterprise assumptions no longer match reality.

Renewal is the enterprise's capacity to interpret relational signals and recalibrate structure, interaction cadence, and motion before misfit compounds into permanent loss. As the relational field shifts, customers express—through behavior, perception, and preference—where the enterprise must recalibrate to remain relevant.

This domain functions as the enterprise's renewal mechanism, returning structural guidance to the rest of the system before decline becomes embedded.

Renewal Conditions

Renewal responds to five distinct conditions, each of which surfaces at a different level of the enterprise-customer relationship. Table 9.8 identifies these conditions, the signals through which they appear, and the structural dimensions renewal must address.

Five Customer + Interaction Conditions Requiring Renewal

Condition	What Triggers Renewal	How Signals Appear	What Renewal Addresses
Customer Priorities Change	Customer evolution outpaces enterprise adaptation	Shifting preferences, reordered priorities, altered constraints, rising expectations, new operating contexts	Value narrative, team interpretation of customer priorities, relational interfaces, interaction sequencing
Customer Percep-tions Shift	Value interpretation changes without a discrete event	Weakening credibility, increasing hesitation, multiplying questions, variable engagement, growing attention to alternatives	Relevance, relational gaps, experience consistency, communication quality, trust at interfaces
Market Conditions Reshape the Field	Relational environment shifts around the enterprise	New alternatives, changing business models, platform-driven adoption shifts, regulatory realignment, competitor repositioning	Workflow architecture, integration points, operational cadence, value logic, relational system partnerships
Experience Breaks Down	Coherence has weakened upstream	Repeated confusion, dropped handoffs, delayed responses, timing inconsistencies, fluctuating quality, contradictory messages	Interfaces, workflows, responsibility definition, decision pathways, shared interpretive norms
Value Interpre-tation Changes	Customers reassess how the enterprise fits their future	Evolving goals, changing norms, emerging alternatives gaining legitimacy, legacy offerings losing resonance, shifts in emotional or social meaning	Offering meaning, value narrative, strategic positioning, capability development, pricing logic

Table 9.8

The five conditions share a common structure: The enterprise's assumptions, offerings, or operating patterns no longer match what customers encounter, expect, or value. The difference between conditions is scope. When customer priorities shift, renewal addresses interpretation and relational interfaces. When perceptions shift without a discrete cause, renewal must restore credibility and experience consistency at the point of contact. When market conditions reshape the broader field, renewal extends to workflow architecture, integration points, and value logic. When experience breaks down, coherence has already weakened upstream, and renewal must address structural decay in process and execution. When value interpretation changes, the enterprise faces the most consequential form of misfit: Customers reassess whether it belongs in their future.

In each case, the structural requirement is the same. Signals arriving through Customer + Interaction convey where enterprise motion has separated from the relational field. Recalibration in response to these signals restores coherence and sustains the relationship. Without structural response, the separation widens—and each successive cycle compounds the cost of restoring coherence.

Renewal as a Structural Discipline

Renewal through Customer + Interaction is structural—it recalibrates enterprise cadence, customer meaning, relational fit, and market reality into a coherent whole. The enterprise compounds relational strength when renewal is sustained: Perception deepens, demand stabilizes, relationships consolidate, and relevance extends across cycles. Without sustained renewal, misalignment grows, erosion accelerates, trust declines, and the enterprise separates from its environment.

Customer + Interaction is the relational mechanism through which the enterprise detects the need to evolve—before loss of enterprise value becomes irreversible.

CROSS-DOMAIN INFLUENCE OF CUSTOMER + INTERACTION

Customer + Interaction operates within the same relational system as every other domain. Because it is where customers experience and respond to enterprise coherence, its signals do not remain confined to relationships—they propagate across the system, shaping how interpretation, structure, execution, and economics behave in practice.

Unlike the predominant propagation of consequences, customer influence does not follow the sequential path. Customer signals arrive simultaneously across domains, and each domain receives a different form of structural information from the same relational field. Table 9.9 identifies what Customer + Interaction reveals to each domain and how each domain is recalibrated in response.

What the table cannot show is how these influences interact. Customer signals that recalibrate People + Alignment—by exposing where interpretation has separated from customer meaning—simultaneously reveal where Processes + Integration no longer carries work in a form customers recognize. Execution + Intelligence receives the most immediate feedback: Customer behavior surfaces where motion slows, where quality does not sustain, and where the learning loop has broken. Economics + Metrics receives the most consequential feedback: revenue stability, margin behavior, and forecast reliability all respond directly to whether customers experience the enterprise as coherent.

These signals do not wait for formal measurement. Relational intelligence arrives through behavior, perception, and demand—and it arrives whether the enterprise attends to it or not. Structural interpretation of this intelligence strengthens coherence across domains, but when it is ignored or misread, misalignment propagates from the relational field inward, compounding through interpretation, structure, execution, and economics in sequence.

How Customer + Interaction Influences the Enterprise System

Domain Influenced	What C+I Signals Reveal	How the Domain Is Recalibrated
People + Alignment	Whether interpretation of purpose and priority corresponds to customer meaning	Relational feedback recalibrates shared understanding and decision-making around customer reality rather than enterprise assumption
Processes + Integration	Where processes introduce interface friction, where handoffs fail, where structural decay is forming	Process architecture adjusts to fit the customer relationship as it is actually encountered, not as it was designed
Execution + Intelligence	Where motion slows, where timing fails, where quality does not sustain under real conditions	Customer behavior completes the learning loop, returning performance information that execution cannot generate internally
Economics + Metrics	Revenue stability, margin behavior, pricing logic, portfolio relevance, cost-to-serve, forecast reliability	Financial signals recalibrate as relational fit strengthens or weakens—revenue, pricing, margins, and forecasting all respond to customer coherence
Enterprise as a Whole	Whether enterprise motion corresponds to customer meaning; whether the enterprise is operating as an integrated whole	Relational intelligence reveals relevance, initiates structural recalibration across all domains, and validates coherence by confirming or challenging whether experience is consistent

Table 9.9

Influence on the Enterprise as a Whole

Customer + Interaction integrates with the enterprise system through three structural functions. The first is relevance: The enterprise cannot determine its own relevance, and this domain surfaces whether enterprise motion meets customer meaning through the people who encounter it. The second is recalibration—customer signals carry the structural information that prompts adjustment across People + Alignment, Processes + Integration, Execution + Intelligence, and Economics + Metrics. The third is validation of coherence, where customer interpretation confirms or challenges whether the enterprise is operating as an integrated whole, strengthening coherence where experience is consistent and exposing it where misalignment appears.

Customer + Interaction sustains alignment between the enterprise and the people it serves.

CUSTOMER + INTERACTION AND ENTERPRISE VALUE CREATION

Enterprise value creation is completed in this domain—that condition is established by the Natural Order. What determines whether enterprise value endures is whether creation compounds or dissipates through the relational field over time.

When coherence in Customer + Interaction is sustained, enterprise value compounds. Customer understanding deepens across cycles, demand stabilizes as perception reinforces prior experience, and relational signals return to the enterprise with increasing precision—grounded in real response rather than assumption. Each cycle of coherent interaction strengthens the next: Customers commit more attention, more trust, and more consequential choice, and the enterprise receives more accurate structural information in return. This compounding is not automatic. It is the product of sustained fit between enterprise behavior and customer meaning across every dimension of value perception.

As coherence in this domain weakens, enterprise value dissipates. Enterprise motion continues, but it no longer converts into recognized value. Perception fragments across interactions, demand becomes volatile as customers lose a stable basis for commitment, and the relational signals returning to the enterprise degrade, carrying less structural information and more ambiguity. Upstream amplification produces activity without validation, and the distance between enterprise effort and customer recognition widens with each cycle. Enterprise value that could have compounded instead disperses through inconsistency, loss of relevance, and accumulating misfit.

Customer + Interaction therefore carries the Create function and determines whether that function compounds into durable enterprise value or dissipates before Economics + Metrics can sustain it. Without compounding here, the enterprise generates motion that never converts into lasting value.

THIS CHAPTER SHOWED that enterprise value that is created and compounded through customer and market response can still be quietly consumed—by overextension, misallocation, or delayed consequence accumulating faster than relational coherence can absorb them.

What remains unresolved is *whether the enterprise can carry what it has created.* That question is not answered through perception or demand, but economic reality—through trade-offs, constraints, capacity, and consequence accumulating over time. Chapter 10 turns to that final test, introducing *Economics + Metrics*—the domain that determines whether enterprise motion compounds into durable enterprise value or erodes under the weight of its own success.

Endnotes

1. The five forms of value perceived by customers—Functional, Economic, Emotional, Social, and Strategic—describe how customers interpret enterprise coherence through what the enterprise delivers. Customer value typologies have been extensively studied. Jagdish N. Sheth, Bruce I. Newman, and Barbara L. Gross proposed a theory of five consumption values—functional, social, emotional, epistemic, and conditional—that influence consumer choice behavior. See Sheth, Newman, and Gross, "Why We Buy What We Buy: A Theory of Consumption Values," Journal of Business Research 22, no. 2 (1991): 159–70. Their framework describes how individual consumers evaluate and select among competing alternatives based on five independent value types. The five forms of customer value as presented here translate this concept into enterprise-delivered value dimensions. "Strategic value"—organizational fit and capability alignment —replaces the epistemic and conditional categories, reflecting a relational enter-

prise perspective rather than individual consumption behavior. The Five Enterprise Domains System describes how customers perceive enterprise coherence, not how individuals make isolated purchase decisions.

2. The Perceived Customer Value Gap, as defined here, describes the distance between what the enterprise believes it is delivering and what customers actually perceive. This gap reveals coherence or incoherence faster than any formal measure. The concept of gaps between expected and perceived service quality was established by A. Parasuraman, Valarie A. Zeithaml, and Leonard L. Berry in "A Conceptual Model of Service Quality and Its Implications for Future Research," Journal of Marketing 49, no. 3 (1985): 41–50, and operationalized through the SERVQUAL measurement instrument in "SERVQUAL: A Multiple-Item Scale for Measuring Consumer Perceptions of Service Quality," Journal of Retailing 64, no. 1 (1988): 12–40. Their model identifies five gaps between expected service and perceived service, measured across dimensions of tangibles, reliability, responsiveness, assurance, and empathy. The usage here addresses a different asymmetry: It adds an organizational cognition dimension—the enterprise's own perception of its performance—that the SERVQUAL model does not address. It functions as a coherence indicator within the Five Enterprise Domains System rather than as a service quality measurement tool.
3. Market sensing, as used in this book, describes the enterprise's capacity to perceive relational signals within the Customer + Interaction domain, interpret their implications for enterprise coherence, and adjust before misfit hardens into failure. It functions as the learning mechanism of the domain and operates through a defined cadence—daily and weekly observation, monthly interpretation, and quarterly recalibration. The concept of organizational sensing has significant prior art in the strategic management literature. David J. Teece, Gary Pisano, and Amy Shuen introduced "sensing" as a core dynamic capability—the firm's capacity to identify, assess, and shape opportunities and threats in the external environment. See Teece, Pisano, and Shuen, "Dynamic Capabilities and Strategic Management," *Strategic Management Journal* 18, no. 7 (1997): 509–33. Teece further elaborated sensing as one of three dynamic capabilities (sensing, seizing, transforming) in "Explicating Dynamic Capabilities: The Nature and Microfoundations of (Sustainable) Enterprise Performance," *Strategic Management Journal* 28, no. 13 (2007): 1319–50. The dynamic capabilities framework treats sensing as a broad strategic capacity for opportunity and threat detection across the competitive landscape. The usage here is more specific: It ties sensing to relational signals within a single enterprise domain, with a disciplined cadence for detection and response, rather than treating it as a general strategic capacity.
4. The five signal types presented here—direct customer signals, behavioral signals, market dynamics signals, competitive pattern signals, and platform and regulatory signals—provide a structural taxonomy of the channels through which relational signals arrive within the Customer + Interaction domain. The concept of early-warning signals in organizations has significant prior art. H. Igor Ansoff introduced "weak signals" as subtle, incomplete early indicators of meaningful environmental change that precede clear trend emergence. See Ansoff, "Managing Strategic Surprise by Response to Weak Signals," *California Management Review* 18, no. 2 (1975): 21–33. Karl E. Weick developed sensemaking theory—how organizations interpret and act on ambiguous information—in *Sensemaking in Organiza-*

tions (Thousand Oaks, CA: SAGE Publications, 1995). Ansoff focuses on signal strength and the challenge of early detection; Weick addresses the interpretive processes through which signals become meaningful within organizational contexts. The contribution here is the classification of channels and their organizational pathways within a specific enterprise domain, rather than the nature of signal strength or the cognitive process of interpretation.

10

ECONOMICS + METRICS

THE ECONOMIC FOUNDATION BENEATH ENTERPRISE MOTION

Every enterprise creates enterprise value through motion: the coordinated work that advances across people, processes, execution systems, customer relationships, and market environments. Whether that motion produces durable enterprise value or dissipates through misfit is determined here. Enterprise value requires economic interpretation, disciplined protection, and sustained reinforcement over time; without these, motion produces activity rather than viability. Economics + Metrics is the economic foundation of the enterprise.

> **Economics + Metrics** is the enterprise domain through which motion is translated into economic meaning wherever enterprise motion encounters consequence, value is protected across cycles, and decisions are grounded in the enterprise's actual capacity to create, sustain, and renew value.

This domain governs the enterprise's economic logic, not merely its financial outcomes. Economics determines how trade-offs are decided under constraint, how opportunity cost is recognized, and how limited resources are distributed across competing priorities throughout the enterprise. These economic choices shape whether enterprise motion can be carried forward, repeated, and renewed, or whether it degrades under cumulative pressure. They occur at every level, from capital allocation and pricing to capacity commitments, customer agreements, and investment sequencing, and they condition the enterprise's ability to sustain enterprise value as conditions change.

Economics + Metrics: Where Constraint Is Enforced

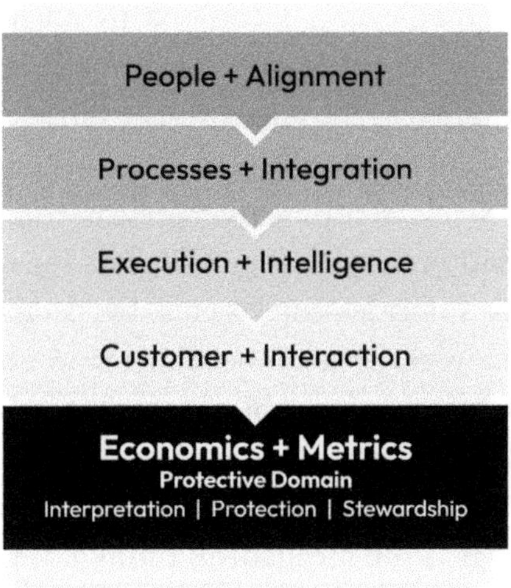

Figure 10.1

Economics + Metrics is not limited to accounting, finance, reporting, or forecasting. Through this logic, the enterprise interprets performance, decides what to invest in and what to forgo, sustains viability over time, and constrains destructive motions that emerge from overextension, misallocation, or unchecked coordination load. This domain determines whether the enterprise can scale, adapt, and remain coherent as conditions change—not by expanding effort, but by making economically grounded choices about where enterprise energy is best applied.

Financial strategy is one institutional expression of this economic logic. Metrics provide the interpretive discipline that makes economic consequence visible, comparable, and enforceable over time. Economics, financial strategy, and metrics form a single domain responsible for converting activity into viability—grounding enterprise decisions in what can be sustained rather than what is merely intended.

This domain sits last in the Natural Order because it clarifies what enterprise motion ultimately means. Performance is converted into economic understanding, revealing whether enterprise energy is compounding into enterprise value or being diluted or eroded through misfit and inefficiency. Decisions are anchored in economic reality, and enterprise value shaped in earlier domains is preserved rather than undermined as the enterprise advances.

Metrics in this domain are not confined to financial indicators. They constitute the enterprise's interpretive language—structured patterns of information through which leaders see what is happening across the system. Priorities interpreted by people, processes that carry or constrain work, execution behavior under load, customer response to enterprise motion, and the evolution of relevance over time all register through metrics. The enterprise makes sense of itself through this discipline rather than through intuition.

Financial strategy is the mechanism through which the enterprise protects the enterprise value it creates. By shaping capital allocation, economic models, pricing logic, resource deployment, and risk boundaries, financial strategy prevents enterprise value from being destroyed, diluted, or eroded by overreach or neglect. This domain carries the dominant Protect function. Its influence is structural, and it operates beneath visible performance. Coherent financial strategy produces grounded, stable, and directed enterprise behavior; weakened financial strategy surfaces as unstable performance, rising cost-to-serve, confused priorities, financial volatility, and declining relevance.

In an unwalled enterprise, where relationships, platforms, and markets interact continuously, the work of this domain becomes more consequential, not less. Economics + Metrics anchors the enterprise in reality, preventing coherence from being overwhelmed by speed, coordination demands, or relational variability. Decisions that do not match capability destabilize the system; investments that do not match priority dilute enterprise energy; performance interpretation that does not reflect the system's actual condition obscures economic truth.

Financial patterns revealed something in my work that no other domain could: whether an enterprise's decisions, structures, and relationships were actually sustainable. I learned this first as a CFO and later as a strategist. Financial performance never deteriorated randomly or in isolation; it responded directly to how well the enterprise was functioning as a system. Revenue stability, margin behavior, cost-to-serve patterns, and cash pressure consistently reflected the quality of reinforcement across the Domains. Coherent alignment, structure, execution, and customer relationships produced grounded, predictable financial behavior. Deterioration in those relationships registered in financial signals quickly and without ambiguity. Over time, Economics + Metrics became the clearest indicator of whether an enterprise was creating durable enterprise value or drawing down more than it could sustain.

THE ROLE OF ECONOMICS + METRICS IN THE NATURAL ORDER

Economics + Metrics is the final domain in the Natural Order of the enterprise because it performs the enterprise's most consequential interpretive and protective work. Enterprise motion formed in People + Alignment, Processes + Integration, Execution + Intelligence, and Customer + Interaction is interpreted here as a signal of enterprise value, viability, and long-term coherence. This domain does not operate in the background. It functions as the economic foundation that determines whether enterprise value is sustained, extended, or undermined over time.

The Governing Role of Economics + Metrics

Aspect	What This Domain Governs
Domain position	Final domain in the Natural Order
Primary function	Economic interpretation of enterprise motion
What it receives	Alignment, structure, execution, customer response
What it performs	Interpretation, protection, stewardship
Governing condition	Economic coherence

Table 10.1

In the Natural Order, Economics + Metrics closes the enterprise loop. The upstream domains generate motion, interaction, and experience; this domain interprets what those movements mean economically and constrains whether they can continue. Consequences accumulate here and become unavoidable. For this reason, Economics + Metrics answers a single governing question that no other domain can resolve: whether the enterprise is economically, structurally, and strategically sound given how it is operating.

What This Domain Governs

Economics + Metrics governs how enterprise performance is interpreted, how enterprise value is protected, and how decisions are grounded in economic reality rather than aspiration.

This domain performs three inseparable stewardship functions. It interprets performance by clarifying what results actually signify rather than what leaders hope they mean. It protects enterprise value by constraining destructive motions—Destroy, Dilute, and Erode—before they compound. And it shapes stewardship decisions that preserve structural and strategic coherence as conditions evolve.

Together, these functions make Economics + Metrics the final integrator of the system.

Stewardship Functions of Economics + Metrics

Stewardship Function	What It Does	What It Prevents
Interpret	Clarifies what performance signifies	Misreading results
Protect	Constrains destructive motions	Destroy, Dilute, Erode
Sustain	Preserves viability across cycles	Value loss over time

Table 10.2

How This Domain Receives From the Enterprise System

Economics + Metrics does not generate signals of its own. It receives and integrates the economic consequences of how the rest of the enterprise is functioning.

People + Alignment shapes this domain through the consistency of priorities and incentives. Convergent interpretation and reinforcing incentives stabilize economic signals because effort is applied coherently. Fragmented priorities or competing incentive structures register as wasted capacity, rising coordination burden, and inconsistent accountability. Each of these conditions carries economic consequence—the cost of interpretive divergence registering as lost capacity and fragmented accountability.

Processes + Integration shapes Economics + Metrics through cost-to-serve and scalability. Structure that fits the work carries volume and complexity without disproportionate cost; structure that loses fit produces rising cost-to-serve, limited scalability, and increasing expense required to maintain the same level of output. These signals reveal whether architecture is reinforcing enterprise value or consuming it.

Execution + Intelligence shapes this domain through variability, load, and stability. Patterns of delay, overload, inconsistency, and recovery register economically as execution encounters real conditions. Economics + Metrics reflects whether performance is strengthening, plateauing, or deteriorating, not in abstract terms, but through capacity pressure, volatility, and sustainability of results. From these signals, leaders can determine whether the enterprise can scale responsibly or is operating beyond its economic limits.

Customer + Interaction shapes Economics + Metrics through demand stability and pricing power. Customer behavior—adoption, continuity, sensitivity, and responsiveness—translates directly into an economic signal. Recognized and trusted value stabilizes demand and preserves pricing integrity. Weakening relevance surfaces as volatility, discounting, and reduced predictability. Each of these signals is an economic reflection of relational coherence, not a marketing indicator.

Through this integration, Economics + Metrics converts dispersed signals into a single economic interpretation of enterprise condition. It reveals whether enterprise motion is compounding into durable enterprise value or quietly drawing down future capacity.

What Economics + Metrics Receives From Other Domains

Upstream Domain	What Registers Economically
People + Alignment	Consistency of priorities and incentives
Processes + Integration	Cost-to-serve and scalability
Execution + Intelligence	Variability, load, and stability
Customer + Interaction	Demand stability and pricing power

Table 10.3

Economics + Metrics as the Value-Protection Domain

The first four domains determine how enterprise value is created, amplified, and experienced. Economics + Metrics determines whether that enterprise value can be protected and sustained. It constrains destructive motions before they accumulate into irreversible loss and informs renewal when structure, execution, or relevance no longer fit the enterprise's operating reality.

This domain receives the fullest expression of enterprise behavior. It does not initiate motion, but it determines whether motion can continue. Economics + Metrics is therefore the architecture of enterprise viability, the domain that anchors the enterprise in reality and preserves coherence over time.

PROTECTING ENTERPRISE VALUE: THE STEWARDSHIP FUNCTION OF THIS DOMAIN

Economics + Metrics carries the enterprise's dominant Protect value function. It preserves the enterprise value generated across the system over time.

Protection is structural stewardship—the discipline of converting enterprise energy into enduring enterprise value rather than allowing it to dissipate through poor judgment, unclear priorities, weak interpretation, or inconsistent investment logic. Without this domain operating coherently, even strong performance in the other four domains can be undone by decisions that exceed capability or by choices that ignore economic consequence.

Economics + Metrics grounds decisions in economic truth, maintains enterprise structures as conditions evolve, and constrains destructive motions before they compound.

What It Means to Protect Enterprise Value

To protect enterprise value is to prevent what has already been created and amplified from being undermined by misaligned investment, inconsistent pricing or cost logic, poor risk framing, ungrounded commitments, structural misfit, incoherent performance interpretation, or imbalanced resource deployment. Protection also encompasses preventing dilution of enterprise value in customer relationships and constraining gradual loss of relevance or trust.

Economics + Metrics functions as the enterprise's economic stabilizer, maintaining commitments as viable, credible, and sustainable over time. Protection is fundamentally the work of fit—economic fit, structural fit, relational fit, and strategic fit—maintained as conditions change. Enterprise value is preserved only when motion is translated into durable outcome rather than consuming more value than it creates.

Constraining the Destructive Motions

The destructive motions—Destroy, Dilute, and Erode—describe how enterprise value is lost.

Constraining the Destructive Motions

Destructive Motion	How It Appears	How Economics + Metrics Constrains It
Destroy	Catastrophic loss driven by decisions that exceed capability, violate coherence, or expose the enterprise to risk it cannot absorb.	Commitments that remain within capacity, economically sound investment logic, and strategy grounded in operational and financial reality rather than optimism.
Dilute	Dispersed enterprise value through inconsistency, inefficiency, unclear metrics, or misaligned objectives.	Coherent investment logic, incentives aligned with enterprise priorities, and unified measures that prevent fragmented decision-making.
Erode	Gradual decay caused by structural misfit, declining relevance, or accumulated inefficiency.	Early detection of misfit, visible declining performance patterns, and renewal initiated before decay becomes irreversible.

Table 10.4

Economics + Metrics constrains all three motions through the same mechanism: economic interpretation that translates signals into grounded decisions before consequences compound. Financial strategy is the institutional expression of that discipline.

Protection Through Stewardship

Financial strategy is the enterprise's stewardship mechanism for value protection. It shapes how resources are allocated, how risk is bounded, and how economic decisions are made across the system. Disciplined capital allocation, pricing logic that reflects value and cost-to-serve, economic model integrity aligned with the enterprise archetype, resource capacity planning that prevents overload, and risk orientation that limits overexposure—these keep enterprise value intact across cycles.

Stewardship prevents enterprise value from being compromised by short-term reaction, fragmented incentives, or poorly managed trade-offs. It aligns renewal with economic capacity rather than urgency.

Protection Through Fit

To protect enterprise value, the economic model must maintain fit with the enterprise's relational field, structural design, archetype (Physical Asset or Intangible Asset), customer expectations, market dynamics, operational capability, resource capacity, and strategic commitments. Economic misfit is one of the fastest paths to enterprise value loss.

Loss of fit registers as compressing margins, pricing that loses traction, declining trust, and escalating renewal cost. Economics + Metrics constrains this outcome by aligning economic structure with enterprise reality as it evolves.

Protection in an Unwalled Enterprise

In an unwalled environment, market signals arrive quickly, customer expectations shift continuously, partners shape operational outcomes, platforms influence visibility and demand, competitive pressure emerges from unexpected directions, and economic shocks travel rapidly through the system. Protection therefore becomes a continuous structural discipline rather than an activity performed at intervals.

Exposure in an unwalled enterprise is continuous and relational, not bounded by discrete events. Platform dependency, partner behavior, competitive repositioning, regulatory shifts, and market signal velocity all generate risk that enters the enterprise through its relational field rather than through discrete events. Conventional risk management treats exposure as identifiable and containable. In an unwalled environment, exposure is distributed across relationships the enterprise does not fully control and conditions it cannot fully predict. Risk therefore accumulates not only from internal misfit but from the evolving distance between enterprise architecture and the relational field surrounding it. Economics + Metrics must interpret this external accumulation alongside internal signals, or protection fails against precisely the conditions the unwalled enterprise faces most frequently.

The enterprise remains embedded in its relational field at all times. Exposure does not pause, and enterprise value is never insulated from surrounding conditions. Protection cannot be treated as a periodic task; it must be sustained through ongoing economic coherence[1]. Economics + Metrics performs this work by interpreting signals across relational fields, stabilizing decision-making under pressure, and linking renewal to economic capacity.

Without this domain functioning coherently, the enterprise becomes vulnerable regardless of the apparent strength of the other four domains.

FINANCIAL STRATEGY: DESIGNING THE ECONOMIC ARCHITECTURE

Financial Strategy is the design of the enterprise's economic architecture—the structure through which resources are allocated, commitments remain viable, and enterprise value is protected over time—not the management of money. This domain determines whether the enterprise can honor its obligations, adapt as conditions shift, and maintain coherence as demand, capacity, and priorities change.

At its core, Financial Strategy resolves three governing questions: how resources are allocated to reinforce coherence, how the economic model must be structured to sustain enterprise value, and how risk, optionality, and adaptive capacity are maintained across time horizons. These three determinations keep the enterprise economically sound, structurally viable, and capable of moving at an appropriate pace in relation to the people and markets it serves.

Capital Allocation as Strategic Design

The enterprise directs attention, builds capacity, and reinforces priorities through where it allocates resources. Capital allocation is strategic design in action. Every allocation decision strengthens or weakens the enterprise's architecture by signaling what is valued, which capabilities are prioritized, which constraints are relieved, which risks are accepted or avoided, and which opportunities are pursued or deferred. These choices shape structural capacity well before outcomes appear.

Coherent capital allocation strengthens enterprise structure; fragmented allocation dilutes enterprise value. Financial Strategy aligns investment with enterprise purpose, structural fit, customer relevance, market dynamics, renewal requirements, economic viability, and enterprise pacing relative to capacity. Capital allocation is therefore the most direct mechanism leaders possess for maintaining or restoring coherence.

The Enterprise Economic Model

The economic model is the logic governing how the enterprise creates, delivers, and sustains enterprise value. It expresses the enterprise archetype, capabilities, cost structure, revenue pattern, pricing logic, value narrative, strategic position, and relational environment. Financial Strategy maintains fit between this model and the conditions in which the enterprise must operate, rather than an idealized version of those conditions.

A model that fits its conditions strengthens relevance, preserves pricing integrity, keeps cost-to-serve predictable, stabilizes margins, and aligns customer meaning with enterprise motion; renewal under these conditions becomes proactive rather than corrective. Loss of fit produces unsustainable cost structures, pricing that loses traction, compressing margins, weakening customer meaning, faltering strategic commitments, and renewal that becomes expensive and disruptive. Misfit between the economic model and enterprise motion is among the fastest paths to enterprise value erosion.

Risk, Optionality, and Adaptive Capacity

Risk is the relationship between exposure and capability, not the presence of uncertainty. Financial Strategy defines how much exposure the enterprise can absorb, how that exposure is priced, and how adaptive capacity is designed into the system. Risk logic shapes commitments, growth pacing, contract structure, supply-demand variability management, and decisions to invest in or divest from capability.

> **Optionality** is the enterprise's preserved capacity to redirect resources, commitments, or structure without destabilizing coherence. It is not flexibility in general; it is the specific economic condition in which redirection remains affordable and structurally sound.

> **Adaptive Capacity** is the enterprise's structural ability to absorb change, reallocate resources, and maintain coherence without requiring compensatory effort or emergency intervention. It is not general preparedness; it is the specific economic and structural condition in which the enterprise can respond to shifting demands while preserving fit[2].

Optionality is a core component of adaptive capacity. It emerges when the enterprise preserves economic flexibility, maintains room to maneuver, avoids overcommitment, and embeds structural flexibility into its architecture. Adaptive capacity is the outcome of economic coherence, producing viability under stress and sustained relevance as conditions change.

Risk does not accumulate only through financial exposure or strategic overcommitment. It accumulates structurally, across domains, through misfit that persists without correction. A process that no longer fits its load generates compounding cost exposure. A customer relationship sustained through discounting rather than through value the customer recognizes erodes pricing integrity over time. An execution system operating above its capacity threshold produces variability that registers across every downstream commitment. These conditions do not announce themselves as risk events; they register as rising cost, declining predictability, and increasing compensatory effort. Because they originate in different domains and surface through different signals, they are frequently interpreted as separate operational problems rather than as compounding exposure. Economics + Metrics is the only domain positioned to interpret these dispersed signals as a single risk condition, because it receives the economic consequences of all four upstream domains simultaneously.

Renewal and Economic Adaptation

Renewal is the mechanism through which fit is restored. Financial Strategy determines whether renewal is affordable, sustainable, and paced appropriately.

> **Structural Renewal** is the ongoing recalibration of processes, interfaces, roles, and economic architecture required to restore fit as scale and relational conditions evolve. It is not an initiative; it is a necessary response to the natural decay of fit in living systems[3].

Financial Strategy funds renewal through capability development, rebalanced resource allocation, updated economic models, strengthened pricing and cost logic, process redesign, technology and integration investment, capacity realignment with demand, and incentives matched to renewed priorities. Renewal is an economic necessity, not a discretionary cost. Enterprises that defer renewal force other domains to compensate through inconsistency or improvisation, and both paths lead to erosion. Financial Strategy keeps renewal feasible before misfit becomes systemic.

Why Financial Strategy Determines Viability

The enterprise can move only as far and as sustainably as its economic architecture permits. Financial Strategy grounds decisions in economic truth, maintains structural viability across cycles, and preserves the economic conditions under which customer relationships, capabilities, and coherence can be sustained. It is formative rather than reactive, defining the boundaries within which the enterprise can operate coherently and protecting enterprise value through disciplined design rather than caution.

METRICS: THE ENTERPRISE'S INTERPRETIVE LAYER

Metrics are the structured means through which an enterprise interprets its own behavior—not the numbers themselves, but the patterns and relationships those numbers reveal. In an unwalled enterprise, where signals move continuously through relational fields, metrics become the most reliable indicator of coherence. They reveal what the enterprise is doing, how it is performing, and where fit is declining before consequence becomes unavoidable. Metrics expose not only outcomes, but system behavior: how motion persists, how consistency is maintained, and how enterprise behavior is experienced across relationships.

Metrics belong within the Economics + Metrics domain because they serve the same protective purpose as financial strategy itself.

They give the enterprise visibility into its own condition while adjustment remains possible. Metrics form the interpretive layer of the system by giving shape to execution, translating customer response into economic meaning, exposing structural misfit, and clarifying whether alignment, motion, and durability are sustained over time. Through metrics, leaders see reality with discipline rather than narrative.

Why Metrics Matter

Metrics matter for three structural reasons.

Metrics reveal coherence. Coherent signals across categories reinforce one another and move in compatible patterns; incoherent signals contradict one another and no longer describe the same system. Consistent performance signals, stable patterns, predictable outcomes, and legible cause-and-effect relationships characterize a coherent enterprise. Conflicting indicators, inconsistent interpretation, reactive decisions, and increasing difficulty sustaining results characterize an incoherent one. Metrics make visible whether the enterprise is functioning as an integrated system or beginning to diverge.

Metrics produce shared interpretation. Without metrics, teams interpret events through local lenses. A common interpretive language aligns meaning, expectations, decision logic, accountability, and pattern recognition across the system. This shared interpretive frame becomes essential as enterprises operate across distance, interfaces, and dense relational environments.

Metrics reveal the enterprise as a system rather than as a collection of functions. Individual measures do not tell the truth in isolation—patterns of metrics do, and system behavior becomes legible through the relationship among indicators rather than through any single measure examined alone.

The Major Categories of Enterprise Metrics

Because Economics + Metrics protects enterprise value across the entire system, it must integrate all categories of enterprise metrics, not only financial ones. An enterprise cannot protect enterprise value unless it can see enterprise value, recognize threats to it, and interpret the patterns that indicate where enterprise value is being strengthened or weakened.

The Five Major Categories of Enterprise Metrics

Metric Category	What It Measures	Domain Reflected	What It Reveals
Financial	Revenue behavior, margin integrity, cost-to-serve patterns, cash dynamics, pricing logic, and long-term viability.	Economics + Metrics (Protect function)	The enterprise's economic condition and its capacity to sustain enterprise value over time.
Operational	Consistency, stability of work progression, reliability under load, and responsiveness.	Processes + Integration, Execution + Intelligence	Whether enterprise motion is functioning as designed.
Customer	Experience consistency, perceived value, behavioral patterns, relationship strength, and engagement.	Customer + Interaction	How enterprise performance translates into market meaning.
Organizational	Consistency of interpretation, communication quality, decision timing, capability formation, and incentive alignment.	People + Alignment	Whether human coherence is sustaining enterprise motion.
Structural	Structural fit, interface quality, renewal effectiveness, process architecture consistency, and early signs of misfit or decay.	Cross-domain	Whether coherence is being maintained as conditions change.

Table 10.5

Enterprise metrics form a unified interpretive system that reveals coherence or misfit across domains. No single category is sufficient in isolation. The five major categories are financial, operational, customer, organizational, and structural.

The Dangers of Fragmented Metrics

Metrics do not fail on their own. Interpretation fails when metrics are fragmented, contradictory, or disconnected.

Structural Consequences of Fragmented Metrics

Condition	What Breaks Down	Enterprise Consequence
Isolated indicators	**Shared interpretation collapses.** Metrics are read locally rather than systemically. Example: Operations optimizes utilization while sales optimizes bookings, with no shared view of load.	**Conflicting decisions proliferate.** Actions reinforce local success while undermining system coherence. Example: Increased bookings trigger delivery overload.
Contradictory signals	**Decision logic becomes unstable.** Different metrics imply opposing actions at the same time. Example: Margin targets improve while customer retention declines.	**Reactive behavior replaces judgment.** Leaders chase the loudest signal. Example: Emergency discounts to fix churn worsen margin volatility.
Local optimization	**System understanding erodes.** Metrics reward parts without regard to interfaces. Example: Teams meet KPIs by pushing work downstream prematurely.	**Value erosion accelerates.** Gains in one area create losses elsewhere. Example: Faster cycle times increase rework and customer friction.
Narrative-driven selection	**Economic truth is filtered.** Metrics are chosen to support a story rather than reflect conditions. Example: Excluding cost-to-serve to sustain a growth narrative.	**Unchecked risk accumulates.** Decisions are justified until constraints surface abruptly. Example: Expansion continues past capacity limits.

Table 10.6

Fragmentation appears when teams rely on separate indicators, categories are isolated, signals conflict, or leaders select measures that reinforce existing narratives rather than reflect reality. Fragmented metrics are among the earliest indicators of enterprise incoherence, signaling that the enterprise is no longer interpreting itself as a single system.

Fragmented interpretation produces confused decision-making, inconsistent investment, misaligned priorities, unnoticed risk accumulation, distorted renewal, and eroding enterprise value. Metrics serve their purpose only when they are systemic rather than isolated. The systemic function of metrics becomes operational when categories are read in relationship rather than in isolation. A financial metric showing margin compression acquires structural meaning when read alongside an operational metric showing rising coordination overhead and a customer metric showing declining engagement consistency: Together, these indicate that process misfit is consuming enterprise value that was being created upstream. A single metric from any one category produces a number; the relationship among metrics across categories produces a diagnosis.

Risk Visibility Through Systemic Interpretation

Risk becomes visible through metrics only when metrics are systemic. Isolated indicators obscure risk because each appears manageable within its own category. Cost-to-serve rises while operational metrics show stable throughput. Customer retention declines even as financial metrics show revenue sustained through new acquisition. Execution variability increases, yet organizational metrics show alignment indicators intact. No single category reveals the compounding exposure underneath; each reports a partial condition that appears contained. Risk surfaces through the relationship among metrics, not through any single measure. Interpreting financial, operational, customer, organizational, and structural indicators together makes patterns of accumulating exposure legible before they become irreversible. Fragmented metrics leave risk to accumulate in the spaces between categories, invisible until the consequences have already compounded.

Unified Metrics as Structural Integrity

Coherence requires a unified interpretive frame, one shared way of understanding enterprise motion, customer response, operational behavior, and economic viability. Unified metrics establish shared meaning, interpretation, language, and decision logic across the enterprise. This domain is responsible for creating and maintaining that interpretive integrity.

Unified metrics reinforce decision coherence, strengthen structural investment, keep leadership grounded in reality, reduce the cost and delay of renewal, stabilize customer relationships, and increase economic durability. Unified metrics are a condition of structural integrity.

ECONOMIC COHERENCE: THE OUTCOME OF THE DOMAINS WORKING TOGETHER

Economic coherence is the condition that emerges when all five Enterprise Domains operate in reinforcing alignment. It is the state in which enterprise motion aligns with enterprise economics, where strategy, structural design, execution behavior, customer relevance, and economic stewardship reinforce one another rather than compete for influence. Economic coherence produces an enterprise that behaves as a single system; its absence makes enterprise value fragile even when individual domains appear strong.

> **Economic Coherence** describes the systemic condition in which enterprise motion, structural design, customer meaning, and economic logic reinforce one another, sustaining enterprise value without compensatory effort. It reflects whether the enterprise's architecture can reliably convert energy into durable enterprise value over time.

Economics + Metrics does not generate coherence directly; it reveals coherence, measures its strength, and protects it once established.

Economic coherence shows leaders whether the enterprise's architecture, behavior, and relational motion remain aligned with the economic model that must sustain them. It exposes whether commitments can be honored, capabilities can scale, and viability can be preserved as conditions evolve. In this sense, economic coherence represents the system's most reliable economic truth surface.

Economic Coherence and Enterprise Viability

When Economic Coherence Holds	When It Weakens
Metrics reinforce one another. Economic signals align across financial, operational, and customer measures. Example: Margin, delivery reliability, and retention trends move in compatible directions.	**Metrics contradict.** Different measures imply opposing conclusions. Example: Revenue growth coincides with rising cost-to-serve and declining retention.
Decisions are grounded in capacity. Commitments reflect what the enterprise can actually carry. Example: Growth targets are set with explicit visibility into execution load and capital constraints.	**Commitments exceed capability.** Decisions assume capacity that does not exist. Example: Sales commitments outpace delivery bandwidth, creating backlog and escalation.
Investment logic remains disciplined. Resources are allocated in proportion to structural fit and learning. Example: Capital is deployed to relieve bottlenecks rather than to amplify already-strained areas.	**Resource misallocation accumulates.** Investment follows narratives rather than conditions. Example: Additional headcount is added to compensate for structural misfit instead of redesigning flow.
Enterprise value is preserved. Economic interpretation supports continuity across cycles. Example: The enterprise sustains profitability while adapting to changing demand.	**Enterprise value erodes.** Economic incoherence compounds over time. Example: Short-term gains undermine long-term viability through cumulative strain.
Renewal occurs early. Economic signals prompt adjustment before erosion hardens. Example: Declining unit economics trigger structural redesign before margins collapse.	**Renewal becomes reactive.** Adjustment occurs only after economic pressure is acute. Example: Cost-cutting follows sustained losses rather than preventing them.

Table 10.7

The Condition of Economic Coherence

Strong economic coherence becomes visible when enterprise motion aligns with how enterprise value is earned, capabilities reinforce customer meaning, pricing reflects economic reality, and cost-to-serve remains predictable. Metrics across financial, operational, customer, organizational, and structural categories reinforce rather than contradict one another, producing a coherent picture of system behavior. The enterprise is able to scale without disproportionate cost or coordination burden because growth does not overwhelm structure, capacity remains stable, and workflows expand without distortion.

Customer relevance strengthens under these conditions because meaning remains aligned with enterprise motion and market signals confirm position rather than challenge it. Decisions consistently reinforce coherence rather than undermine it, as investment logic remains disciplined, resource choices align with priority, and risk remains within absorptive capacity. Renewal occurs proactively, with structure updated before decay hardens into misfit and renewal cycles aligned with economic conditions rather than reactive pressure.

The Consequences of Lost Economic Coherence

Consequences of Lost Economic Coherence

Economic coherence deteriorates when the enterprise's design, capabilities, and behaviors diverge from the economic model that sustains them. The problem is structural before it is financial—financial instability appears as a downstream consequence of architectural misfit.

Deteriorating coherence registers as costs rising faster than economic value creation, pricing logic losing traction, and margins compressing despite sustained effort. Metrics fragment across categories, producing patterns in which operational gains fail to translate into economic outcomes, customer perception gains appear while revenue stability declines, or alignment indicators remain positive while execution variability increases. Instead of reinforcing one another, signals begin to contradict each other.

Continued deterioration forces the enterprise to apply more effort for the same results. People work harder, processes overload, execution becomes inconsistent, and teams compensate manually for structural misfit. Customer meaning diverges from enterprise intention, producing inconsistent experience, slower adoption, declining trust, and reduced relevance. Market signals then expose deeper misalignment as competitive positioning shifts, platform conditions change, or relational environments evolve faster than the enterprise adapts.

Renewal in this state becomes reactive and costly. Adjustment occurs only after consequences accumulate, and structural decay compounds into structural misfit. Economic incoherence undermines viability long before formal financial data communicates the risk, making Economics + Metrics the earliest and clearest indicator of deteriorating system integrity.

Economic Renewal: Restoring Fit

Economic renewal is the discipline of restoring fit between enterprise motion and the economic model that must sustain it. It is a systemic recalibration that positions the enterprise's architecture to carry the work it must perform and the relational environment it must operate within. Economic renewal is a system-wide realignment, not a financial correction.

Renewal restores coherence by rebalancing resource allocation across domains, adjusting the economic model to reflect relational conditions, and correcting structural misfit before it compounds. It reconciles commitments with capability so the enterprise does not promise more than its architecture can deliver. Adaptive capacity is rebuilt by aligning exposure boundaries with enterprise capacity and environmental volatility.

Why Economic Coherence Matters

Economic coherence does not exist alongside other forms of coherence; it completes them. People + Alignment may function coherently, Processes + Integration may carry work effectively, Execution may remain disciplined, and customer experience may appear consistent. If the economic model does not fit the enterprise's architecture or relational field, the enterprise will not remain viable.

Economic coherence is the final expression of the Natural Order, the point at which alignment produces meaning, structure carries motion, execution converts into performance, customers interpret value, and the economic foundation sustains it all. Economics + Metrics protects enterprise value by maintaining the match between economic architecture and enterprise reality over time.

CROSS-DOMAIN INFLUENCE OF ECONOMICS + METRICS

Economics + Metrics interprets, stabilizes, and constrains the entire system without borrowing authority from any single upstream domain. The other four domains generate enterprise energy through alignment, structure, execution, and relationship; Economics + Metrics determines whether that energy compounds into durable enterprise value or dissipates through misfit and poor judgment. It performs this role by translating structural, relational, and operational behavior into economic consequence and by feeding that interpretation back into decision-making across the enterprise.

This domain does more than receive signals from the rest of the system. Its interpretations actively shape priorities, direct investment choices, and determine how work is paced and resourced across domains. Coherent economic interpretation gives the enterprise orientation and discipline because decisions are grounded in economic reality. Deterioration in this domain makes the enterprise reactive, with instability appearing across performance, coordination, and decision quality.

Cross-Domain Influence of Economics + Metrics

Affected Domain	When Economics + Metrics Is Coherent	When It Is Incoherent
People + Alignment	Priorities remain credible; incentives reinforce shared expectations; confidence propagates	Signals conflict; incentives pull in competing directions; confidence erodes
Processes + Integration	Investment preserves structural fit; interfaces remain supported; load is carried sustainably	Processes strain under load; interfaces decay; workarounds proliferate
Execution + Intelligence	Capacity aligns with demand; execution remains stable; learning loops continue	Variability increases; overload appears; performance becomes compensatory
Customer + Interaction	Pricing aligns with value; commitments are trusted; relevance strengthens	Pricing loses credibility; cost-to-serve misaligns with value; relevance declines
Enterprise as a Whole	Discipline holds; decisions are grounded in viability; strategic confidence strengthens	Reactivity increases; coordination weakens; enterprise becomes fragile

Table 10.8

Influence on People + Alignment

People + Alignment shapes the human engine of the enterprise—meaning, coordination, interpretation, and trust. Economics + Metrics influences this domain by shaping the economic signals that direct human energy, including how performance is measured, how incentives are designed, how priorities are communicated, and how leaders interpret viability and constraint. Through these mechanisms, teams form an understanding of what is possible, what is expected, and what can be sustained.

Coherent economic interpretation keeps expectations credible, commitments realistic, incentives reinforcing shared priorities, and leadership judgment grounded. People trust that effort will convert into outcome because economic signals are consistent and legible. Deterioration in economic interpretation fragments alignment:

Signals contradict one another, incentives pull in competing directions, and shared meaning becomes harder to maintain. Economics + Metrics establishes the economic conditions within which People + Alignment operates.

Influence on Processes + Integration

Processes + Integration defines how work advances through the enterprise. Economics + Metrics determines whether those processes can operate with the investment, capacity, and renewal required for coherence. This influence becomes visible in where structural investment is directed, which interfaces are strengthened or neglected, whether tools and platforms are adequately resourced, and how load is distributed across teams.

Structural fit is preserved, investment in interfaces reinforced, and process decay addressed before cost escalates when economic stewardship is coherent. Weakened stewardship produces processes that overload, integration that fractures under pressure, teams that resort to workarounds, and structural misfit that becomes increasingly expensive to correct. Processes + Integration rises or falls with the economic discipline applied through this domain.

Influence on Execution + Intelligence

Execution is where enterprise behavior becomes observable reality. Economics + Metrics influences execution more directly than many leaders recognize because it governs capacity, investment pacing, and the balance between demand and capability. Workforce distribution, tooling investment, operational funding, and tolerance for volatility are all shaped economically.

Coherent economic logic keeps execution stable, work predictable, teams below overload thresholds, and learning loops productive. Deteriorating economic discipline produces rising variability, less reliable quality, slower responsiveness, and teams compensating for structural gaps through effort rather than design.

Execution is therefore the clearest expression of economic discipline in motion.

Influence on Customer + Interaction

Customer + Interaction interprets enterprise behavior through relational perception. Economics + Metrics shapes this domain by defining the value logic customers sense and respond to, including pricing integrity, cost-to-serve boundaries, offering viability, commitment pacing, and sustained investment in experience.

Pricing aligns with perceived customer value, commitments remain credible, relevance strengthens, and relationships stabilize when economic foundations are coherent. Loss of economic coherence surfaces as pricing that loses credibility, cost-to-serve misaligned with customer value, customer expectations diverging from enterprise capability, intensifying competitive pressure, and declining relevance. The economic architecture beneath the enterprise directly shapes customer experience.

Influence on the Enterprise as a Whole

Economics + Metrics does not influence domains selectively; its economic interpretation conditions every domain simultaneously. Decisions remain grounded in economic reality, commitments stay aligned with capability and relational conditions, and leaders are able to act decisively because they understand what the enterprise can afford, where it can grow, what it must protect, and where renewal is required.

Economics + Metrics reflects the true condition of the system and directs attention toward the adjustments required to sustain coherence. The enterprise moves deliberately, adapts with discipline, and preserves enterprise value over time only when this domain is functioning coherently.

ECONOMICS + METRICS AND ENTERPRISE VALUE PROTECTION

Economics + Metrics is the domain through which enterprise value is protected across time. The other domains create enterprise value as potential, amplify it through structure and learning, and validate it through recognition; this domain determines whether enterprise value can be sustained without being consumed by overextension, misallocation, or delayed consequence. It is the structural limit of viability, translating motion and response into economic meaning that constrains what the enterprise can responsibly commit.

This domain protects enterprise value by making trade-offs explicit. Economics clarifies opportunity cost, constraint, and capacity, so that choices made throughout the enterprise reflect what can be carried rather than what is merely desired. Metrics provide the interpretive discipline that renders consequence visible, showing where effort compounds, where it dissipates, and at what point reinforcement gives way to loss. Together, they prevent enterprise value created elsewhere from being undermined by decisions that exceed structural or economic limits.

Protection occurs because consequence is cumulative. Decisions about pricing, capacity commitments, investment sequencing, risk exposure, and resource allocation do not register immediately in other domains. They register here. Coherent Economics + Metrics surfaces these consequences early enough to redirect renewal before deterioration accelerates. Enterprise value is conserved when aspiration and capacity remain aligned, not when restraint substitutes for structural correspondence.

Coherent economic stewardship produces enterprise value that endures through discipline and fit—growth paced by what the enterprise can sustain, amplification bounded by economic reality, and learning translated into adjusted commitments. Protection does not slow the enterprise; it prevents motion from consuming more enterprise value than it creates.

Deterioration in this domain removes protection altogether.

Trade-offs become obscured, opportunity cost is ignored, and metrics fragment or contradict one another. Motion continues without economic grounding, and enterprise value is quietly consumed by inefficiency, distorted pricing logic, and accumulated risk. By the time instability becomes visible elsewhere, protection has already been lost.

ENTERPRISE VALUE IS SUSTAINED through economic reality—through trade-offs, constraints, capacity, and consequence accumulating over time—not through intent, effort, or recognition alone. Economics + Metrics reveals whether coherence is durable, whether motion is viable, and whether the enterprise can carry what it has created without quietly consuming itself.

With that foundation in place, one structural question remains: What shift in perception does the enterprise require if coherence is to be stewarded deliberately rather than reactively? Understanding the domains, the archetypes, and the economic limits is necessary—but not sufficient if the enterprise is still interpreted as a collection of parts rather than as a system in motion. Chapter 11 turns to that shift, introducing Seeing the Enterprise as a System—the perception required to integrate everything that has come before and to sustain coherence as a structural condition rather than a managerial aspiration.

Endnotes

1. The concept of coherence in economic and strategic contexts has been explored by several scholars. David J. Teece, Richard Rumelt, Giovanni Dosi, and Sidney Winter examined corporate coherence in "Understanding Corporate Coherence: Theory and Evidence," *Journal of Economic Behavior & Organization* 23, no. 1 (1994): 1–30, addressing how firms maintain coherent diversification through learning and path dependencies. Paul Leinwand and Cesare Mainardi introduced the "coherence premium" in "The Coherence Premium," *Harvard Business Review* 88, no. 6 (2010): 70–76, describing the performance advantage of aligning capabilities, strategy, and product portfolio. The term also appears in macroeconomic and

trade policy contexts (OECD, UNCTAD). Economic coherence, as defined here, is distinct from all of these: It describes a systemic condition within the Five Enterprise Domains System in which enterprise motion, structural design, customer meaning, and economic logic reinforce one another, sustaining enterprise value without compensatory effort. It is diagnostic rather than prescriptive—reflecting whether the enterprise's architecture can reliably convert energy into durable enterprise value over time.

2. Adaptive capacity is an established concept in organizational theory and resilience literature. Udo Staber and Jörg Sydow provided a structuration-based treatment in "Organizational Adaptive Capacity: A Structuration Perspective," *Journal of Management Inquiry* 11, no. 4 (2002): 408–24, defining it as the ability to learn at a rate faster than the rate of environmental change, with structural dimensions including multiplexity, redundancy, and loose coupling. Juan Carlos Eichholz developed the concept further as a leadership framework in *Adaptive Capacity: How Organizations Can Thrive in a Changing World.* Adaptive capacity, as defined here, is tied specifically to the Five Enterprise Domains System and the Economics + Metrics domain: It is the enterprise's structural ability to absorb change, reallocate resources, and maintain coherence without requiring compensatory effort or emergency intervention. It is an economic and structural condition—the result of economic coherence—rather than a learning rate or leadership capability. The definition is intentionally narrow: It describes not general preparedness but the specific condition in which the enterprise can respond to shifting demands while preserving fit.
3. See chapter 2, note 4. Structural renewal is discussed in the Economics + Metrics domain as the ongoing recalibration required to restore fit as scale and relational conditions evolve. For the distinction between this usage and the strategic renewal literature (Agarwal and Helfat, 2009; Tushman and O'Reilly), see the earlier note.

PART III

LEADING THE COHERENT ENTERPRISE

11

SEEING THE ENTERPRISE AS A SYSTEM

WHY LEADERS MUST THINK IN SYSTEMS

The work of leadership has changed. Modern enterprises no longer operate as collections of roles and responsibilities bound by reporting lines. They behave as systems—interdependent fields of activity in which movement in one area reshapes conditions everywhere else. Most leaders are trained to think in functional terms: Marketing addresses marketing issues, operations addresses operational issues, and finance addresses financial issues. That thinking is valid as far as it reaches. What it cannot reach is the structural interaction between functions—the conditions that determine whether functional effort compounds or is consumed. The Five Enterprise Domains make that interaction visible.

In my work with enterprises across industries, the same pattern appeared repeatedly: Leaders were intervening at the wrong level of the problem. They attempted to correct outcomes inside a function when the cause lived in the relationships between functions. They treated events as explanations when structural information lived in recurring patterns; symptoms received attention while the signals those symptoms expressed went unread. Isolated performance absorbed leadership focus at the expense of coherence across the system. They searched for answers in parts when the truth was distributed across the system.

The Five Enterprise Domains make this shift structurally legible. They name the structure beneath enterprise behavior: how people interpret purpose, how work advances, how execution behaves under pressure, how customers respond, and how economic signals register system condition. But the Domains become visible only when leaders think systemically. Pattern recognition displaces incident response. The relationships between functions demand the same attention as individual roles, and coherence—rather than activity—becomes the governing measure.

Leading in system terms does not require becoming a systems theorist. It requires recognizing that the enterprise cannot be understood—or influenced—one component at a time. Performance is never the product of individual excellence alone; it is the outcome of how well the system reinforces itself through coordinated motion.

The Five Shifts of Systems Thinking

Leading through the Five Enterprise Domains requires a fundamental change in how leaders interpret what they observe. Most enterprise problems do not arise from insufficient effort or capability; they arise from how leaders frame and diagnose what they see. Functional thinking produces functional answers. System thinking exposes the enterprise in terms that traditional logic cannot reach.

Through years of fieldwork, I observed that leaders who operated effectively in complex environments shared five consistent shifts in perception[1]. They learned to see the enterprise not as a collection of parts, but as a structure in motion. These shifts are perceptual disciplines, not techniques—they change what leaders notice and how they interpret it.

Five Shifts of Systems Thinking

Shift	Functional Interpretation	What the System Reveals
1. Parts → **Patterns**	Isolates components—teams, departments, roles, or tasks—and diagnoses each independently. A delay is attributed to the team where it occurred.	Components interact over time, and recurring patterns reveal structural condition. Repeated delay at the same interface indicates emerging misfit, not isolated underperformance. The diagnostic question shifts from which part is failing to what pattern is forming and where it originates.
2. Events → **Signals**	Treats events—missed deadlines, customer escalations, cost overruns—as the primary unit of information. Response follows the event.	Events are late information. Signals appear earlier: hesitation in decision pathways, inconsistent handoffs, irregular pacing between teams, subtle changes in customer behavior. Leaders who interpret signals rather than react to events can see coherence weakening while adjustment is still possible.
3. Functions → **Relation-ships**	Evaluates each function on its own terms—whether marketing, operations, or finance is performing against its own targets.	Enterprises rarely destabilize because a single team underperforms. They destabilize because relationships between teams are not structurally supported. Interfaces carry the true load. When leaders examine how well a function connects to the functions it depends on, cross-functional dynamics become legible rather than opaque.
4. Activities → **Motion**	Measures volume of activity—tasks completed, meetings conducted, output produced—as evidence of progress.	Motion describes how work advances: its sequence, variability, and fit with structure. Reading motion means attending to where work hesitates, where decision pathways slow, where processes require repeated interpretation, and where load concentrates. Motion reveals coherence or misalignment more reliably than activity levels.
5. Structure → **Fit**	Treats structure as a permanent design—once built, assumed to remain adequate.	Structure creates value only when it fits the enterprise's actual demands. Fit determines whether processes carry the load they were designed for, whether roles align with actual demand, and whether decisions resolve at the pace the environment requires. Fit is where coherence either strengthens or erodes.

Table 11.1

Each shift replaces a bounded interpretation with a systemic one. Parts become patterns when leaders attend to interaction over time instead of isolating components. Events become signals when leaders read early indicators—hesitation in decision pathways, irregular pacing between teams, subtle changes in customer behavior—rather than reacting to late information. Interface load and cross-functional dependence, given the same diagnostic attention as individual team performance, turn functions into relationships. Activities become motion when leaders stop measuring volume and start reading how work advances, where it hesitates, and where load concentrates. Fit displaces structure as the governing concern when leaders treat architecture as something that must be renewed alongside the work it carries, not as a permanent design.

These five shifts do not operate as a sequence or a method. They constitute the perceptual discipline through which the Five Enterprise Domains become visible as a working system—and through which leadership interaction with that system becomes structurally informed.

READING ENTERPRISE SIGNALS

Every enterprise communicates before its metrics change. Coherence strengthens or weakens through observable shifts in motion, interaction, and load that precede any formal measurement. Many enterprises rely on dashboards, reports, and periodic reviews to understand performance, but those instruments register conditions only after the system has already moved. Signals appear earlier—in how work advances, how decisions resolve, how teams interact under pressure, and how customers respond—and they reveal structural condition long before metrics confirm it.

> **Enterprise Signal** describes an observable pattern in motion, load, interaction, or response that indicates a change in systemic coherence before performance metrics register its effects. Enterprise Signals are not measurements; they are early indicators of how the enterprise is behaving as a system. They show whether reinforcement continues or whether misfit is forming.

Enterprise Signal Categories

Signal Category	What Leaders Observe	What It Indicates
Motion	Whether teams advance with shared or irregular timing; where work hesitates or accelerates unexpectedly; where sequencing breaks down and requires reinterpretation; whether decision pathways carry load	Coherent systems exhibit steady advancement; incoherent systems show irregular progression well before visible failure appears
Variability	Output fluctuating without clear cause; inconsistent quality; teams compensating for unexpected conditions; processes behaving differently under similar circumstances	Fit has weakened and reinforcement is failing—variability is structural, not operational
Load	Escalation repeatedly landing with the same roles; teams becoming bottlenecks regardless of intent; decision-makers carrying disproportionate weight; processes requiring increasing effort for unchanged outcomes	Where load accumulates, structural misfit is present
Interpretation	Different teams interpreting the same objective differently; decision criteria diverging; shared priorities becoming inconsistent; communication requiring more explanation than before	Coherence is weakening at the interpretive level—often precedes structural consequences
Interface	Delays at handoffs; rework from mismatched assumptions; coordination breakdowns; confusion about ownership and sequence	Emerging misfit at crossing points—interfaces exhibit early signs long before breakdown becomes visible
Customer	How quickly the enterprise responds; how predictable experience feels; whether expectations are met consistently; whether value feels stable or variable	Customer behavior mirrors enterprise condition without interpretive buffering—among the earliest and most reliable indicators
Financial	Margin behavior, cost-to-serve patterns, revenue stability, forecasting consistency, cash pressure, divergence among indicators that should move together	Financial patterns do not originate misfit—they validate what earlier signals already indicated

Table 11.2

In my work with midmarket enterprises, the leaders who understood how their enterprises behaved were not those with the most data, but those who learned to recognize subtle changes in how the enterprise moved. They watched decision timing, the consistency of handoffs, team responsiveness under pressure, customer behavior as it engaged with the enterprise, and early irregularities in financial patterns. Taken together, these signals reliably indicated whether the system was reinforcing itself or beginning to fragment.

What distinguished effective signal reading from ordinary observation was the ability to connect individual observations to system condition.

A single late handoff is an isolated occurrence. Late handoffs that concentrate at specific interfaces—and that concentrate differently under volume pressure than under normal conditions—indicate structural misfit at those interfaces.

Customer complaints that shift from product to responsiveness to trust within the same account, however, indicate something beyond isolated feedback: cascading incoherence moving through the enterprise's relational field.

A financial variance is a number. Financial variances that appear in categories corresponding to domains where motion signals have already changed indicate that structural conditions are converting into economic consequence.

What constitutes the signal is the pattern the observation belongs to, not the isolated observation itself. Enterprise signals fall into several interrelated categories that, taken together, form a coherent picture of enterprise condition.

Enterprise signals function as diagnostic information rather than problems requiring solutions—they expose the conditions within which leadership judgment operates, providing the earliest view of enterprise condition before formal measures register it.

SIGNAL INTERPRETATION IN PRACTICE

What signals look like in practice is less orderly than the categories suggest. They arrive without labels. A leader notices that a decision that was previously resolved in one meeting now requires three. A customer renews but reduces scope without explanation. A financial pattern that tracked reliably for eighteen months shifts by a margin too small to trigger a report but too consistent to be a random variation. Each of these is an enterprise signal. None of them names its own origin.

Consider a midmarket professional services enterprise where project handoffs between sales and delivery begin requiring additional clarification calls. The sales team attributes the problem to the delivery team's unfamiliarity with new service offerings. Delivery attributes it to sales overpromising on scope. Both explanations locate the cause inside a function. The signal—rising coordination demand at a specific interface—points elsewhere. The handoff interface was designed when the enterprise offered four service lines; it now offers nine. The structure that carries work between sales and delivery no longer fits the volume and variability it handles. The originating domain is Processes + Integration, not the performance of either team. A leader who reads the signal structurally routes attention to the interface architecture rather than to the people on either side of it.

In another enterprise—a regional distributor—customer reorder frequency declined by 12 percent over two quarters. The sales team interpreted this as competitive pressure and proposed pricing adjustments. But the signal preceded the pricing conversation: Delivery times had become inconsistent, not slower on average but less predictable. Customers whose operations depended on reliable timing shifted volume to a competitor whose consistency they could plan around. The financial signal—declining reorder frequency—registered in Economics + Metrics, but the structural origin was Execution + Intelligence, where load distribution had shifted without corresponding adjustment to routing and scheduling. The pricing response would have treated a symptom that the system had already explained through an earlier signal.

A third pattern emerged across several enterprises simultaneously: Leadership teams reported that quarterly planning sessions were producing agreement but not follow-through. Priorities were declared, acknowledged, and then displaced within weeks by operational demands. The visible symptom was execution inconsistency—commitments made but not sustained. The signal, however, was interpretive: The planning process appeared to produce alignment, but the participants interpreted priorities differently once they returned to their domains. What appeared as an execution failure originated in People + Alignment, where shared interpretation had not been established with sufficient depth to withstand contact with competing operational pressures.

In each case, the signal was available before the consequence matured. The discipline is not in seeing more data but in reading what the enterprise is already communicating—and in resisting the instinct to locate the cause inside the function where the symptom appears. Signals route to domains. The leader's work is to follow the signal to its structural origin rather than resolving it where it surfaces.

DIAGNOSING COHERENCE THROUGH MOTION

Most enterprises do not lack information about performance; they lack a reliable way to interpret what that information says about system condition. Leaders are generally comfortable discussing alignment—shared intent, stated priorities, and declared agreement. What they struggle with is coherence: whether the enterprise's actual behavior reinforces itself once work is in motion.

Alignment is declared, but coherence can only be observed—it appears in what the system does once motion begins, not in what leaders state before it. For this reason, alignment functions as a hypothesis about how the enterprise will behave, and coherence is the evidence that confirms or refutes it. Diagnosing enterprise condition, therefore, does not begin with statements of intent. It begins with reading how the system actually moves.

Coherence as Diagnostic Evidence

Domain of Observation	When Coherence Is Present	When Coherence Weakens
Motion	Teams advance with compatible timing; decisions resolve without repeated reinterpretation; handoffs remain proportional to the work being carried. Motion reinforces itself.	Pacing diverges, decisions accumulate without resolution, and processes require increasing manual support. Alignment is no longer converting into reinforcing motion.
Interpretation	A common understanding of priority, scope, and meaning persists across the system. Direction does not require constant restatement.	Teams begin interpreting the same direction differently. Priorities become conditional, decision logic varies by context, and apparent disagreement masks interpretive divergence.
Interfaces	Interfaces remain stable and proportional to the work passing through them. Crossing points carry load without accumulating rework.	Handoffs slow, responsibilities blur, rework increases, and coordination requires additional interaction cycles—conditions often mislabeled as process issues rather than evidence of weakening coherence.
Advancement	Work progression remains predictable even as coordination demand rises. Teams understand where decisions resolve.	Progression loses consistency, load shifts unpredictably, and effort rises faster than outcome. The system relies on compensatory effort rather than carrying work through structure.
Customer	Customers detect coherence through response timing, experience quality, reliability, and perceived value. Behavior remains consistent with enterprise intent.	Customers encounter inconsistency even when leaders assert alignment internally. Customer behavior is among the earliest indicators that alignment is no longer translating into coherent motion.
Economic	Revenue stabilizes, margins are sustained, cost-to-serve remains predictable, and metrics reinforce one another.	Economic patterns contradict each other or move unpredictably, confirming what motion, interface, and customer signals revealed earlier. Economic evidence appears last, not first.

Table 11.3

Coherence is a systemic condition that becomes visible only through interaction over time. It is present when enterprise motion is mutually reinforcing, when interpretation remains consistent across teams, and when interfaces carry work without repeated negotiation or compensatory effort. Incoherence appears when declared alignment no longer produces reinforcing behavior—when motion fragments, interpretations diverge, and work that once advanced begins to require additional explanation, coordination, or manual intervention. These shifts surface well before results decline, and leaders who learn to recognize them early prevent far more disruption than they later attempt to repair.

The diagnostic question is therefore not whether the enterprise is aligned, but whether the enterprise reinforces itself once alignment is assumed. Everything else follows from that distinction.

Diagnosing coherence begins with observing motion—whether it reinforces or fragments. It requires reading whether interpretations converge or diverge, whether interfaces carry work or absorb the consequences of misfit. Advancement, customer response, and economic patterns each confirm or contradict the same structural condition: whether the enterprise is reinforcing itself. These observations provide evidence of what the enterprise is actually doing, not what it intends to do. Coherence is a condition that must be sensed continuously—alignment is not proof of it, but a claim that must be tested through motion.

SEEING FLOW, FIT, AND INTERFACES

Long before results deteriorate, the system reveals whether its structure fits the work, whether its pathways can carry load, and whether its connections reinforce or impede advancement. Leaders who attend to flow, fit, and interfaces gain a reliable picture of enterprise condition without waiting for formal measures. These three concepts translate enterprise behavior into observable structure.

Flow: How Work Actually Moves

Flow shows leaders what the enterprise is doing, not what it intends to do. Every enterprise has a designed workflow, but the operative workflow is expressed in motion: the pace of advancement, the consistency of sequencing, the interruptions that arise, and the points where progress hesitates. Flow makes emerging interface resistance visible as it forms—decisions accumulate, responsibilities blur, and work requires reinterpretation instead of advancing cleanly.

In coherent enterprises, advancement remains proportionate to demand; in incoherent ones, even simple work begins to require disproportionate effort. Flow therefore indicates whether the system is reinforcing itself or substituting effort for structure.

Fit: Whether Structure Matches the Work

Structure creates enterprise value only when it fits the enterprise's actual demands. Workflows that once carried volume become constraints as conditions change. Roles shift from proportionate to limiting as load redistributes, and systems that previously scaled begin requiring manual intervention. Misfit precedes breakdown; it appears in processes that no longer carry current volume or variability, in decisions that land inconsistently because underlying structure is dated, and in customer expectations that outpace the enterprise's response.

Attending to fit means treating structure as an architecture that must evolve alongside the enterprise—not as a permanent design. Misfit becomes visible before breakdown occurs, but only when leaders treat structural correspondence as a condition to be monitored rather than assumed.

Interfaces: Where Enterprise Condition Is Revealed

Interfaces are the crossing points where work moves from one role, team, or domain to another. They carry the greatest structural load and reveal condition earliest. Capable teams can struggle when interfaces are weak; strong interfaces can stabilize performance even under pressure.

As coherence weakens, interfaces show it first: handoffs slow, assumptions diverge, coordination requires more explanation, rework increases, and responsibility becomes less defined. These patterns indicate structural condition rather than interpersonal failure. Interfaces indicate whether the Five Enterprise Domains are reinforcing one another or beginning to pull apart, making them the most reliable source of evidence for identifying where coherence requires restoration.

Flow, Fit, and Interfaces as Diagnostic Lenses

Lens	What This Lens Examines	What It Reveals When It Holds	What Becomes Visible When It Weakens
Flow	How work actually moves through the enterprise in practice	Advancement proportional to demand; consistent pacing; minimal interruption	Hesitation, accumulation, repeated reinterpretation, compensatory effort
Fit	Whether structure matches current work, volume, and variability	Structure carries load without friction; roles and processes remain enabling	Outdated workflows; structural constraints; manual workarounds; inconsistent decisions
Interfaces	Where work crosses roles, teams, or domains	Clean handoffs; aligned assumptions; clear responsibility	Slowing handoffs; divergent assumptions; rework; ambiguous ownership

Table 11.4

Once flow, fit, and interfaces are legible, patterns become recognizable and early signals gain meaning. Leadership attention shifts from symptom response to condition diagnosis—reading how work advances, identifying where structural correspondence is weakening, and interpreting what interface behavior reveals about the system's state.

EARLY WARNING SIGNS IN AN UNWALLED ENTERPRISE

In an unwalled enterprise, change rarely announces itself through formal measures. It first becomes visible through subtle shifts in how the enterprise moves, connects, and responds. Leaders who learn to recognize these early signals can restore fit while adjustment is still modest, before incoherence accumulates into structural decay. These early signs are seldom dramatic. They surface as small but persistent deviations in behavior, pacing, interpretation, and customer response. Once recognized, these signals convey more about enterprise condition than any report produced after the fact.

In examining enterprises over time, I found these indicators appeared in consistent patterns. They did not reflect isolated performance problems; they reflected emerging coherence issues, evidence that the system was beginning to work against itself rather than reinforcing its own motion.

These signals do not indicate failure. They indicate that fit is shifting and coherence is beginning to weaken—conditions that remain structurally addressable when recognized early. In an unwalled enterprise, the difference between proportional adjustment and compounding misfit is often determined by when the signal is read, not by the severity of the underlying condition.

THE LEADERSHIP WORK OF COHERENCE

Coherence does not emerge from slogans, alignment sessions, or formal structures alone. It is produced—and sustained—through how leaders interpret the enterprise as a system and through the decisions they make about design, interfaces, and motion. Leadership in a coherent enterprise is therefore not the direction of activity, but the stewardship of conditions. It is the ongoing work of keeping the Five Enterprise Domains mutually reinforcing as the enterprise moves through growth, pressure, and change.

Early Warning Patterns in Enterprise Coherence

Early Warning Pattern	What Leaders Observe	Common Misattribution	Structural Condition Revealed
Irregular Pacing Across Teams	Some groups accelerate while others slow. Handoffs lose sequence.	Attributed to team-level execution problems or resource constraints	Coordination that once occurred through design now requires explicit reconciliation
Processes Requiring Repeated Interpretation	Workflows require more discussion, judgment, and checks to advance.	Attributed to procedural defect or insufficient training	Structure no longer matches the work being carried; coherence is weakening at the design level
Load Concentrating in Specific Roles	Decision-makers and roles at major interfaces become bottlenecks.	Attributed to individual capacity limitations or delegation failure	Specific roles are compensating for misfit elsewhere — load concentration is diagnostic of structural imbalance
Decision Latency Increasing	More back-and-forth, extended context-setting, frequent escalation.	Attributed to hesitation or communication failure	Insufficient shared interpretation for decisions to resolve on the first pass
Interfaces Becoming Less Predictable	Handoffs slow, ownership becomes less defined, rework increases.	Attributed to interpersonal friction or poor process design	Relationships between domains are no longer structurally supported
Customer Behavior Shifting	Slower buying progression, reduced engagement, hesitation in renewals, attention to alternatives.	Attributed to market conditions or competitive pressure	Behavioral shifts reflect enterprise condition, not market conditions
Metrics Contradicting One Another	Revenue grows while experience weakens; margins move favorably while cost-to-serve destabilizes.	Attributed to mixed performance or measurement error	Compensatory effort is substituting for structural fit
Leaders Compelled to Stabilize Directly	More involvement in routine decisions, constant sense-making across teams.	Attributed to leadership diligence or commitment	The system no longer carries its own work — last early signal before misfit reaches results

Table 11.5

In my work with enterprises, the leaders who operated effectively within complex environments were not defined by charisma, tenure, or technical mastery. They were distinguished by their consistent movement between domains—treating interpretation, execution, customer response, and economic signals as expressions of a single system rather than as separate reporting categories. Their decisions accounted for how adjustment in one domain reshaped conditions in others, and they recognized when the relationships between domains had begun to weaken before any single domain showed visible decline.

Sustaining coherence also requires recognizing forces within the enterprise that resist the structural renewal required by coherence. Structural interests—the positions, access arrangements, and decision rights that the current architecture favors—produce predictable resistance when renewal would redistribute authority or reshape information pathways. The leaders I observed who sustained coherence across cycles did not treat this resistance as an obstruction to be overcome through force of personality. They accounted for it structurally: identifying where positional interests and system requirements had diverged, where information gatekeeping was filtering what leadership could see, and where coalition dynamics were slowing the decision routing that renewal required. Renewal that ignores structural interests is absorbed or blocked. Renewal that accounts for the redistribution renewal produces—realigning interests and architecture simultaneously—creates change that persists because the system and the positions within it have been restructured together.

Leadership in a coherent enterprise does not depend on personality, charisma, or positional authority. It depends on how leaders interpret motion, fit, and signals—how they understand system behavior and how they shape conditions under which the enterprise operates as one. The work is to sustain the conditions under which coherence persists instead of forcing alignment, and to renew structure as the enterprise evolves instead of treating it as fixed. That work is enterprise stewardship—continuous, structural, and governed by the system itself.

WHERE RENEWAL BEGINS

Enterprises that lose coherence rarely do so in a single domain. By the time leadership recognizes the condition, misfit has typically propagated across several domains simultaneously—execution is absorbing compensatory effort, customer response has shifted, and economic signals have begun to contradict one another. The question leaders face is not whether renewal is necessary, but where to begin when the system is weakening in multiple places at once.

The answer is structural, and it follows from directional dependence. Because consequences propagate from interpretation through structure, through execution, through customer response, and into economic signal, the upstream domains govern the conditions that downstream domains inherit. Renewal applied downstream—restructuring execution without addressing the process architecture that shapes it, or redesigning customer interaction without restoring the interpretive alignment that execution carries into every customer encounter—produces adjustment that does not persist. The downstream domain absorbs the intervention, but the upstream conditions that produced the misfit remain operative and reassert themselves through the next cycle.

In the enterprises I observed, the sequencing pattern was consistent. People + Alignment deficits had to be addressed before Processes + Integration redesign could become operative, because process architecture depends on shared interpretation of what the work requires and how priorities are ordered. Process correspondence had to be restored before execution discipline became sustainable, because execution inherits whatever structure (or lack thereof) processes provide. Enterprises that reversed this sequence—investing in execution systems while interpretive alignment remained fractured, or redesigning customer-facing operations while internal process architecture carried unresolved misfit—spent resources on renewal that the system could not retain.

This does not mean downstream domains are ignored while upstream renewal proceeds. It means the sequencing of structural investment follows the direction in which conditions propagate. A leadership team that recognizes execution inconsistency, traces the signal upstream to process misfit, and traces process misfit further upstream to diverging interpretation across the leadership team has identified a renewal sequence: restore interpretive convergence first, restructure the process architecture that interpretation governs second, so that execution inherits the renewed conditions rather than requiring direct correction. Each domain receives attention; the sequence determines where structural investment produces durable change versus where it produces temporary relief.

Renewal sequencing is among the most consequential leadership decisions the Five Enterprise Domains System surfaces. Enterprises that begin upstream—where renewed conditions propagate forward through the system—compound their investment across domains. Enterprises that begin where symptoms are most visible—which is almost always downstream—consume renewal capacity on corrections the system cannot sustain.

CLOSING REFLECTION: LEADING THE COHERENT ENTERPRISE

Coherence is a perceptual shift before it is an operational condition. It changes how leaders interpret what they observe, how they diagnose what they experience, and how they design the conditions under which the enterprise moves. Once leaders begin to see the enterprise as a system, what was previously attributed to isolated causes becomes recognizable as structural behavior. Motion reveals condition; fit determines what the enterprise can sustain. Interfaces expose misfit before formal measures register it, customers respond to what the enterprise actually does, and economic patterns confirm what earlier signals already indicated.

Leadership Interaction With Enterprise Coherence

Leadership Discipline	Interaction Pattern	System Consequence
Seeing the System	Resists diagnosing problems functionally; examines interpretation gaps, misaligned workflows, execution pacing, customer signals, and economic dynamics as connected patterns	Intervention operates at the level where the system has stopped reinforcing itself, not where symptoms appear
Strengthening Interfaces First	Refines handoffs, clarifies responsibility boundaries, aligns decision pathways, reduces unnecessary dependency	Interfaces carry the system's true burden—addressing them often produces greater systemic effect than optimizing functions on either side
Structural Adjustment Before Behavioral Demand	Examines how work is designed, whether roles and processes fit current demand, and where the system requires manual compensation	Removes conditions that generate recurring behavioral problems rather than asking people to absorb those conditions
Regulating Value Forces	Evaluates whether decisions strengthen or weaken Create, Amplify, or Protect—or accelerate destructive counterparts	Coherence is shaped continuously through structural decisions about fit, capability, and system preservation
Sensing Misfit Early	Detects early signs of misfit and adjusts interfaces, workflows, responsibilities, or processes before consequences compound	Renewal becomes a continuous discipline rather than a response to visible decline
Sustaining Shared Interpretation	Creates conditions in which meaning travels as effectively as information across teams	Motion reinforces itself instead of fragmenting into competing interpretations of priority, timing, and risk
Reading Customers Without Filters	Attends to hesitation, inconsistency, and shifts in customer expectation as primary signals of system condition	Customer behavior reveals structural issues before they are visible elsewhere—signals guide renewal across Domains
Leading Through Connection	Ensures information moves, meaning travels, and decisions reinforce shared purpose across relational fields	Coherence strengthens through connection rather than compliance; interdependence is sustained, not enforced

Table 11.6

What I discovered through fieldwork is not that coherence is rare, but that it is rarely recognized. It appears whenever purpose, structure, and motion reinforce one another, and it weakens whenever those elements begin operating on different assumptions. Some enterprises experience coherence briefly; a smaller number learn how to sustain it through cycles of growth, pressure, and change. The distinguishing factor is not intelligence, charisma, or strategy—it is whether leaders perceive the enterprise as a system whose structure must be continuously renewed.

The Five Enterprise Domains give language to that system. They make visible what leaders often sense but struggle to articulate: why performance rises or falls, why teams move together or fall apart, why customer response shifts over time, and why economic patterns change before the underlying causes are recognized. The Domains direct attention rather than prescribing action—showing where to look and how to interpret what becomes visible.

Stewardship in this context means attending to relationships, interfaces, and patterns that sustain the enterprise as one system. It involves sensing misfit early, interpreting signals accurately, adjusting structure with intention, and renewing fit before incoherence becomes costly. This is ongoing work, particularly in environments where conditions shift faster than most enterprises can describe them.

The pattern I first noticed years ago has repeated itself across every enterprise I have worked with since. Once coherence becomes visible—once leaders understand how the enterprise behaves as a system—they do not return to earlier modes of explanation. They stop searching for isolated causes and treating symptoms as problems; the assumption that effort alone can overcome misfit no longer survives contact with what they observe. They begin to see the architecture beneath performance and the signals that reveal whether the system is reinforcing itself or drawing down its own capacity.

This book offers a way of seeing the enterprise as it actually behaves—and a way of leading that respects interdependence and structural truth. Leaders who develop that discipline build enterprises capable of consistent results and renewal, because they understand the system rather than attempting to override it.

THE ENTERPRISE YOU CAN NOW SEE

The purpose of this book has been to make the enterprise visible—its structure, its motion, its relationships, and the forces that strengthen or weaken it. Enterprises do not behave randomly. They behave according to patterns that recurred consistently across the industries, business models, and stages of growth observed in this work. Once those patterns become visible, the enterprise becomes legible in ways that traditional leadership logic cannot make clear.

The Five Enterprise Domains reveal that structure—five interdependent systems of activity that determine how people interpret purpose, how work advances, how decisions form, how customers respond, and how economic outcomes emerge. These systems operate as fields of motion, not as functions or departments, and their interactions govern enterprise behavior, whether or not those interactions are recognized.

What distinguishes the operating environment is the concept of the Unwalled Enterprise. Modern enterprises function within fluid relational fields where customers, partners, platforms, data systems, and distributed teams shape performance as directly as any internal arrangement. Coherence must be created and sustained within this context, not despite it.

Enterprises do not require a uniform structure, as the Two Enterprise Archetypes make explicit. Physical Asset Enterprises and Intangible Asset Enterprises experience motion, load, variability, and customer meaning differently. Recognizing the archetype explains why similar symptoms behave differently across enterprises and why coherence must be grounded in context rather than standardization.

The Enterprise Value Functions explain how enterprise value is created, amplified, and protected—and how destructive forces emerge when coherence weakens. Value creation operates through reinforcement among the Five Enterprise Domains; when those relationships weaken, value is diluted or eroded well before decline becomes obvious.

Coherence is the condition that binds all of this together—the structural state in which purpose, structure, motion, customer meaning, and economic logic reinforce one another rather than competing. Where coherence exists, the enterprise responds to change with consistency. Loss of coherence reverses that condition—even simple work requires disproportionate effort, and customers sense inconsistency long before the enterprise identifies its cause.

READING THE ENTERPRISE AFTER THE LAST PAGE

This book has offered a way of seeing enterprise condition—not a method to implement but a structure for interpreting how the enterprise behaves. This chapter completes that view by developing the perceptual discipline required to lead through what becomes visible.

These ideas operate as elements of a single system—the Natural Order of enterprise behavior. Once that order becomes visible, the enterprise stops feeling unpredictable. Patterns emerge, signals make sense, misfit appears early, motion becomes legible, and leadership decisions become structural, not reactive. The enterprise becomes something to steward, not merely to direct.

By the time you reach this point, the enterprise should no longer appear accidental.

What once looked like isolated issues—slow decisions, inconsistent execution, persistent coordination, customer inconsistency, or unexplained financial pressure—should now register as expressions of structure rather than coincidence. The purpose of this book has not been to prescribe action, but to make the operating conditions of the enterprise visible so they can be interpreted correctly.

The book functions as a reference rather than a narrative read once and set aside. Chapters and sections can be returned to independently. A chapter on execution may become relevant months after first reading; a distinction between coordination and intervention may clarify a moment that previously felt ambiguous. Terms are used consistently so they retain meaning across contexts. The intent is not to produce uniform behavior, but to provide a stable structure for interpretation as conditions change.

After reading this book, certain patterns become harder to ignore. Persistent coordination registers as diagnostic information rather than reassurance, and repeated intervention appears as a structural signal rather than evidence of commitment. Results become less mysterious, even when they are not favorable. And restoring fit and coherence—rather than increasing pressure or activity—becomes the recognizable path toward structural reinforcement.

The enterprise does not change because it has been named. It changes because structure has been recognized—and once recognized, it governs how leaders interpret what they observe, where they direct attention, and what conditions they choose to sustain. Leaders who develop that discipline build enterprises capable of sustained motion, enduring coherence, and compounding enterprise value. The structural practices in the appendix that follows provide the entry point: cadenced leadership disciplines that convert structural recognition into sustained attention across the five domains.

Endnotes

1. The five shifts presented here—Parts to Patterns, Events to Signals, Functions to Relationships, Activities to Motion, Structure to Fit—describe specific cognitive transformations that change what enterprise leaders notice and how they interpret what they see. Systems thinking as an organizational discipline was established by Peter M. Senge in *The Fifth Discipline: The Art and Practice of the Learning Organization* (New York: Currency Doubleday, 1990). Senge presented systems thinking as the integrating fifth discipline for learning organizations, emphasizing the shift from event-based to pattern-based perception and from linear cause-effect chains to systemic interrelationships. Donella H. Meadows further developed accessible systems thinking principles in *Thinking in Systems: A Primer*

(White River Junction, VT: Chelsea Green Publishing, 2008). The five shifts presented here operationalize these general principles into enterprise-specific perceptual transformations. The Structure to Fit shift is a novel contribution specific to the Five Enterprise Domains System, reflecting the enterprise-specific concern with whether architectural design matches the work being carried. These are prescriptive leadership shifts tied to enterprise architecture and value flow, whereas Senge's framework addresses broader organizational learning principles.

APPENDIX

FIRST ACTIONS: STRUCTURAL PRACTICES FOR SUSTAINED COHERENCE

The structural understanding established in the preceding chapters produces a specific form of operational discipline: practices that make coherence observable and renewable as conditions change. What follows are entry points—repeatable, structured practices grounded in the Five Enterprise Domains, the relational fields, and the coordination taxonomy this book has described.

The Activity Blueprints (Appendix 1) establish where to look—the intersections where domains cross business functions. The Weekly Signal Scan and Observation Log (Appendix 2) provides the discipline of recording what you see and tracking how conditions change over time. The Monthly Interface Review (Appendix 3), Quarterly Coherence Conversation (Appendix 4), and Coordination Audit (Appendix 5) provide progressively deeper diagnostic instruments operating at longer structural intervals. Leadership Pattern and Enterprise Value Consequence (Appendix 6) presents ten recurring configurations of leadership behavior and their consequences for enterprise value. The Enterprise Signal Tables (Appendix 7) identify what to look for. The Glossary (Appendix 8) collects governing terms and definitions. Digital resources extending these instruments are available at entersci.com.

Each practice builds on the one before it. None replaces the others.

Appendix / Practice		Purpose	Answers
1	Activity Blueprints	Perception	Where do I look?
2	Weekly Observation Log	Discipline	What do I see, and has it changed?
3	Monthly Interface Review	Diagnosis	Where are interfaces under pressure?
4	Quarterly Coherence Conversation	Interpretation	What does the pattern mean for the system?
5	Coordination Audit	Assessment	How is coordination actually operating?
6	Leadership Pattern and Enterprise Value Consequence	Context	What patterns produce or consume enterprise value?
7	Enterprise Signal Tables	Reference	What should I look for?
8	Glossary of Terms and Definitions	Definitions	What do these terms mean?

APPENDIX 1: ACTIVITY BLUEPRINTS

THE STRUCTURAL POINT

Leaders encountering the Five Enterprise Domains for the first time will reach for familiar equivalences: People + Alignment must be Human Resources. Processes + Integration must be Operations. Customer + Interaction must be Sales. Economics + Metrics must be Finance. The mapping feels intuitive because each domain name shares surface vocabulary with a business function.

That mapping is wrong—and the error is structural, not semantic.

A *business function* is an organizational unit that performs a defined scope of work. A *domain* is a system of activity that governs how the enterprise behaves. Functions are contained within org charts. Domains cut across them. Every business function operates within all five domains simultaneously. Human Resources does not occupy People + Alignment—it occupies a row that crosses all five columns. Sales does not occupy Customer + Interaction—it occupies a different row that crosses the same five columns.

The blueprints that follow make this visible. Each blueprint presents a specific enterprise—defined by archetype, industry, and revenue range—with its business functions listed as rows and the five domains as columns. The cells are intentionally empty. Consider what is happening at each intersection: What signals does this function emit within this domain? Where is coherence stable? Where is it deficient? Where is it unstable?

A leader who can read each intersection has stopped thinking in functions and begun thinking in systems.

HOW TO READ ACTIVITY BLUEPRINTS

Each row represents a business function—a recognized organizational unit within the enterprise. Each column represents a domain—a system of activity that governs enterprise behavior across all functions simultaneously.

Every cell is an intersection where a business function participates in a domain. No cell is empty by nature. Production participates in Economics + Metrics. Finance participates in People + Alignment. Human Resources participates in Execution + Intelligence. The question is not whether the intersection exists—it always does—but what structural condition it reveals.

The Activity Blueprint establishes where to look within each domain. The Enterprise Signal Tables (Appendix 7) identify what to look for. The Weekly Signal Scan and Observation Log (Appendix 2) records what you see—one signal per domain, assessed across every business function, directly on the blueprint grid.

TAILORING THE ACTIVITY BLUEPRINT TO YOUR ENTERPRISE

The sample Activity Blueprints presented in the following sections use business functions drawn from observed enterprises. Refer to them to see how organizational charts translate into blueprint rows across different enterprise types and scales. The instrument becomes operational when the functions are yours.

Construct a blank Activity Blueprint using any application that produces a grid—a spreadsheet, document editor, or project management tool. The format is the same regardless of platform.

Step 1: List your business functions

In the first column, list every business function through which your enterprise carries its work. Each row is one function. Next to each function, record the name of the person accountable for that function —the leader whose decisions govern how work moves within it. This is not an organizational chart. It is a structural inventory: the units through which your enterprise operates, and the people who are accountable for what those units produce.

List functions at the level represented on your organizational chart—the named functional units that report to senior leadership. Most enterprises operate through four to ten business functions at this level. That range produces a grid that can be assessed in fifteen minutes and discussed in a leadership meeting. Functions below this level—teams, departments, groups within a function—belong inside a function's row, not in their own row. If the blueprint exceeds ten rows, the functions are probably listed at too fine a level of granularity. If it contains fewer than four, structural conditions that differ across major areas of the enterprise will be invisible within a single row.

Step 2: Add the Five Enterprise Domain columns

Create five columns to the right of the business function list, one for each domain in sequence: People + Alignment, Processes + Integration, Execution + Intelligence, Customer + Interaction, Economics + Metrics. Every cell in the grid—every intersection of business function and domain—is structurally active. No cell is empty by nature.

Step 3: Add the observation rows

Above the business function rows, add a "Signal under observation" row. This is where the selected signal for each domain is recorded each week when the blueprint is used as the Weekly Signal Scan instrument (Appendix 2).

Below the business function rows, add a "Domain reading" row. This captures the leader's overall structural assessment of each domain's condition across the enterprise—not an average of the cells above, but a judgment about the domain as a whole.

Step 4: Test for completeness

Trace how a piece of work moves through your enterprise from origin to completion. Every business function that work touches should appear as a row. If work crosses a boundary that is not represented on the blueprint, a function is missing. If a listed function never appears in observation notes after several weeks of use, it may not be operating at a level of structural consequence that warrants its own row.

COMMON ACTIVITY BLUEPRINT CONSTRUCTION ERRORS

Listing projects or initiatives instead of business functions

"ERP Implementation" and "Market Expansion" are temporary activities, not persistent structural units. The blueprint tracks how the enterprise carries work through its standing architecture, not what the enterprise is working on at the moment. Projects end. Functions persist. The rows must persist with them.

Listing domains as business functions

This is the mapping error the preceding section described—People + Alignment assigned to HR, Customer + Interaction assigned to Sales. Business functions have identifiable, accountable leaders. Domains do not. A domain is a system of activity that cuts across every business function simultaneously—no single person governs it, and no organizational boundary contains it. A leader who constructs the blueprint this way produces a grid where each function appears to own one domain, which is incorrect. The blueprint makes structural simultaneity visible; collapsing domains into functions defeats it.

Listing by person rather than by business function

In smaller enterprises, a single leader may govern multiple functions. If that leader occupies one row covering Sales, Marketing, and Customer Success, the blueprint is incorrectly constructed. Three structurally distinct functions have collapsed into a single row and their different domain conditions are invisible. The row represents the business function, not the person. Where one leader governs multiple functions, each function receives its own row. The leader's name appears in every row they govern.

Listing external entities as business functions

Vendors, customers, partners, and outsourced providers are not business functions. They belong in the relational field—the environment of continuous interaction within which the enterprise operates. The blueprint maps the enterprise's internal structural architecture. External entities influence what signals appear at the intersections; they do not occupy rows on the grid.

Omitting business functions that do not produce revenue

Finance, HR, Legal, and Operations Support disappear when a leader assumes only customer-facing or revenue-generating business functions carry structural consequence. Every function participates in every domain. The six enterprise value functions—Create, Amplify, Protect, Destroy, Dilute, and Erode—operate within every domain and therefore within every business function. Each cell intersection on the blueprint is a location where enterprise value is being created, amplified, or protected—or destroyed, diluted, or eroded. Omitting internal functions removes the intersections where structural pressure frequently originates—compensation decisions that compress margins, process boundaries that absorb coordination effort, reporting that produces intelligence no one receives.

Updating the business function list between observation periods

The blueprint is a persistent instrument. Changing the rows between observations destroys the ability to track directional change over time. The business function list changes when the enterprise's organizational structure changes—not when the leader's attention shifts or when a function produces an uncomfortable reading. Stability of structure is what makes the delta between observations legible.

The completed blank blueprint is the persistent instrument that supports the Weekly Signal Scan (Appendix 2), Monthly Interface Review (Appendix 3), Quarterly Coherence Conversation (Appendix 4), and Coordination Audit (Appendix 5). Construct it once. Refine it as your understanding of how your enterprise carries work deepens over time.

ACTIVITY BLUEPRINT SAMPLES

Blueprint Sample 1: Intangible Asset Enterprise—B2B Professional Services (USD 10–50 million)

Table A1.1 presents the Activity Blueprint example for enterprises in management consulting, IT services, engineering services, and specialized advisory. Typical headcount of 50–250.

Activity Blueprint™ Domain and Business Function
Intangible Asset Enterprise / B2B Professional Services / USD 10–50 million

Business Function	People + Alignment	Processes + Integration	Execution + Intelligence	Customer + Interaction	Economics + Metrics
Service Delivery					
Sales					
Marketing					
Human Resources					
Finance					
Administration					

Table A1.1

What each intersection reveals. Service Delivery—the billable professionals doing the work—crosses all five columns. Within People + Alignment, it is where shared interpretation of quality, scope, and client commitment either stabilizes or fragments across engagement teams. Within Processes + Integration, it is where methodology meets the actual sequence of client work. Within Execution + Intelligence, it is where the enterprise's work is produced and delivered—where the operating model is tested against real engagement conditions, and where the enterprise learns whether its structure converts effort into outcomes or absorbs it without return. Within Customer + Interaction, it is where the client relationship is sustained or lost—not in Sales, but in the daily experience of receiving the work. Within Economics + Metrics, it is where utilization, realization, and margin are determined by how engagement teams pace and scope their effort. One function. Five structural conditions. Every cell active.

Blueprint Sample 2: Intangible Asset Enterprise—B2B Professional Services (USD 50–100 million)

Table A1.2 presents the Activity Blueprint example for enterprises in regional or national consulting, managed services, professional services with multiple practice areas. Typical headcount of 250–600.

Activity Blueprint™ Domain and Business Function
Intangible Asset Enterprise / B2B Professional Services / USD 50–100 million

Business Function	People + Alignment	Processes + Integration	Execution + Intelligence	Customer + Interaction	Economics + Metrics
Service Delivery					
Sales					
Business Development					
Marketing					
Human Resources					
Talent Development					
Knowledge Management					
Finance					
Administration					

Table A1.2

What scale reveals. Three new functions appear: Business Development, Talent Development, and Knowledge Management. Each one existed inside another function at smaller scale—embedded in Sales, Service Delivery, or the leadership team itself. Separating them creates new rows, and every new row crosses all five columns. The enterprise does not simply have more functions. It has more interfaces—more points where interpretation, process, execution, experience, and economics must remain coherent across organizational boundaries that did not previously exist. At USD 10–50 million, the blueprint has thirty active intersections. At USD 50–100 million, it has fifty. The structural demand on coherence has not grown incrementally. It has changed in kind.

Blueprint Sample 3: Physical Asset Enterprise—Specialty Manufacturer (USD 10–50 million)

Table A1.3 presents the Activity Blueprint example for enterprises in contract manufacturing, precision components, specialty food or beverage, and building materials. Typical headcount of 75–300.

Activity Blueprint™ Domain and Business Function
Physical Asset Enterprise / Specialty Manufacturer / USD 10–50 million

Business Function	People + Alignment	Processes + Integration	Execution + Intelligence	Customer + Interaction	Economics + Metrics
Production					
Sales					
Marketing					
Human Resources					
Finance					
Administration					

Table A1.3

What each intersection reveals. Administration × People + Alignment: How the enterprise organizes its support functions shapes how production workers, sales staff, and managers experience their work. Scheduling, facilities, safety, and workplace conditions are People + Alignment conditions carried inside an administrative function. Marketing × Execution + Intelligence: In a specialty manufacturer, marketing produces the demand signal that determines production scheduling, lot sizing, and inventory positioning—connecting market-facing activity directly to execution behavior. Finance × Customer + Interaction: Credit terms, payment policies, and invoicing accuracy shape the customer's experience of the relationship as directly as product quality does. None of these intersections are obvious. All of them are structurally active.

BLUEPRINT SAMPLE 4: PHYSICAL ASSET ENTERPRISE—SPECIALTY MANUFACTURER (USD 50–100 MILLION)

Table A1.4 presents the Activity Blueprint example for enterprises in multi-facility manufacturing, branded products, and industrial equipment production. Typical headcount of 300–700.

What scale reveals. Quality Assurance did not exist as a separate function at USD 10–50 million. Quality was carried inside Production—one person's judgment, one team's discipline. At USD 50–100 million, Quality Assurance separates and immediately crosses all five columns. Within People + Alignment, it governs how the enterprise's interpretation of acceptable output is shared across shifts, lines, and facilities. Within Processes + Integration, it determines whether inspection, testing, and release are embedded in the production architecture or bolted on after the fact. Within Execution + Intelligence, it reveals whether the enterprise learns from its own defects or repeats them. Within Customer + Interaction, it is where the customer's experience of product reliability is structurally determined. Within Economics + Metrics, it is where the cost of quality—prevention, detection, failure—shapes whether the margin model holds. One function's separation exposes five structural conditions that were previously invisible inside another function's row.

Activity Blueprint™ Domain and Business Function
Physical Asset Enterprise / Specialty Manufacturer / USD 50–100 million

Business Function	People + Alignment	Processes + Integration	Execution + Intelligence	Customer + Interaction	Economics + Metrics
Production					
Sales					
Marketing					
Distribution					
Procurement/ Supply Chain					
Engineering/ R&D					
Quality Assurance					
Human Resources					
Finance					
Administration					

Table A1.4

The Structural Lesson

These four blueprints demonstrate the same principle at different scales and across both enterprise archetypes: Domains are not functions. Functions are organizational containers. Domains are systems of activity that cut across every container. The enterprise behaves as a system regardless of how it is organized. The cells are empty on the page. In the operating enterprise, every one of them is occupied.

APPENDIX 2: WEEKLY SIGNAL SCAN AND OBSERVATION LOG

The Activity Blueprint (Appendix 1) becomes the enterprise's weekly observation instrument when you select one signal per domain and assess its current state across every business function.

THE WEEKLY SIGNAL SCAN

Once per week, fifteen minutes. Review the five signal categories: motion, load, interaction, response, and financial signals. The purpose is contact—maintaining structural awareness of how the enterprise is moving. One question per domain:

- Is interpretive alignment converging or beginning to diverge?
- Are processes carrying work or requiring workarounds to proceed?
- Is execution proportionate to demand, or has intervention become the dominant mode?
- Are customers experiencing consistency, or has variation become detectable?
- Are financial patterns reinforcing one another or beginning to contradict?

The scan does not produce decisions. It surfaces where structural conditions are changing before those changes register as financial consequence. Scanning at weekly intervals captures directional change; less frequent observation misses the transitions between stable and deficient states.

OBSERVED CONDITION STATES

Three structural states describe the observed condition of each intersection.

State	Label	Definition
Coherent	**Stable**	Coherence is intact. Action is the dominant mode of enterprise motion. Work advances as designed. Progress depends on structure rather than personal effort.
Transitional	**Deficient**	Coherence is under pressure. The balance between action and intervention is shifting. Structure still functions, but coordination has become more explicit, effortful, and persistent—signaling that structure is no longer carrying dependencies implicitly. Results are still produced, but they depend increasingly on effort rather than design.
Incoherent	**Unstable**	Coherence has degraded. Intervention has become the dominant mode. Progress depends on corrective effort, override, and personal judgment substituting for structural support. Learning has separated from execution. Signals surface but the enterprise cannot convert them into structural adjustment.

Table A2.1

ACTIVITY BLUEPRINT: DOMAIN AND BUSINESS FUNCTION—WEEKLY SIGNAL SCAN AND OBSERVATION LOG SAMPLE ILLUSTRATION

For each intersection, assess the selected signal's current state within that business function and write a single letter in the cell:

- S (Stable)—Coherence is intact. Work advances as designed.

- **D** (Deficient)—Structure lacks what the work requires. Coherence is present but insufficient.
- **U** (Unstable)—Coherence is no longer reliable. Progress depends on corrective effort rather than structural support.

Leave no cell blank. Every business function participates in every domain. If you cannot assess an intersection, record that difficulty—limited visibility is itself structural information.

Before completing the log, select one signal per domain from the Enterprise Signal Tables (Appendix 7) and record it in the "Signal under observation" row. Select a different signal for each domain—the five signals observed in a given week should span all five domains, not concentrate in one.

Activity Blueprint™ Domain and Business Function Weekly Observation Log

Intangible Asset Enterprise / Software Development Services / USD 11 million annual revenue

Week: 12 Observer: CEO

Business Function	People + Alignment	Processes + Integration	Execution + Intelligence	Customer + Interaction	Economics + Metrics
Signal Under Observation	Decision timing	Friction at process boundaries	Variability	Behavioral signals	Cross-category reinforcement
Service Delivery	D	D	U	D	D
Sales	D	D	D	D	S
Marketing	S	S	S	S	S
Human Resources	D	U	S	S	U
Finance	S	D	D	S	D
Domain Reading	D	D	D	D	D

Table A2.2

A completed sample Weekly Signal Scan and Observation Log is presented in Table A2.2.

Cell Readings

Sales × People + Alignment (D):

Compensation decisions and discounting authority are resolving without shared reference to margin requirements. Decisions are forming from incompatible interpretive positions.

Sales × Processes + Integration (D):

Contracts are arriving at Service Delivery with pricing terms that delivery teams cannot execute profitably, requiring renegotiation or scope adjustment after engagement begins.

Sales × Execution + Intelligence (D):

Different contract terms are producing different margin outcomes depending on which terms were negotiated. The information is not returning to inform future negotiation.

Sales × Customer + Interaction (D):

Customers are exerting pricing pressure that Sales absorbs through discounting rather than addressing structurally. Deal cycles are being pushed.

Sales × Economics + Metrics (S):

Revenue continues to grow. Sales activity is producing results, though the economic consequence of discounting is registering in other functions rather than in Sales itself.

Marketing × all domains (S):

No structural pressure detected in this function across any domain during this observation period.

Service Delivery × People + Alignment (D):

Teams are beginning to interpret scope differently across engagement teams as new hires enter without consistent onboarding into the firm's value proposition.

Service Delivery × Processes + Integration (D):

The handoff from Sales is absorbing effort. Renegotiation or scope adjustment is required after engagement begins.

Service Delivery × Execution + Intelligence (U):

Outcomes are becoming less predictable. The same engagement type produces different margin results depending on which team executes, which contract terms were negotiated, and which compensation commitments were made.

Service Delivery × Customer + Interaction (D):

Customer relationships remain functional, but the gap between what was promised and what can be delivered profitably is widening.

Service Delivery × Economics + Metrics (D):

Margin results vary by team and engagement. The information exists in Finance but does not circulate to where it would inform structural adjustment.

Human Resources × People + Alignment (D):

Compensation decisions are being made without shared reference to margin requirements. HR is making decisions at normal pace from an incompatible interpretive position.

Human Resources × Processes + Integration (U):

HR's compensation process has no interface with Finance's pricing models. Raises are granted without visibility into the economic structure they affect. The structural absence is complete.

Human Resources × Economics + Metrics (U):

Compensation costs are rising disconnected from role economics or pricing models. The economic consequence compounds invisibly inside agreements no one is reexamining.

Finance × Processes + Integration (D):

No interface exists between Finance's pricing models and HR's compensation process. The structural gap is present on both sides of the boundary.

Finance × Execution + Intelligence (D):

Reporting is accurate, but the information does not circulate to the functions where it would inform structural adjustment. Intelligence is produced and does not return.

Finance × Economics + Metrics (D):

No immediate breach in unit economics, but revenue, margin, and compensation signals are contradicting each other. The cross-category pattern is one of progressive erosion.

System Reading

Finding	Reading	Notes
Overall system condition	U	Interpretive divergence between Sales, HR, and Finance is producing economic erosion that no single function can see from its own row. The enterprise is operating, but the interaction between the domain governing how decisions form (P+A) and the domain governing how value is protected (E+M) is producing a cross-domain condition that is Unstable—visible only at the system level, not within either domain's reading alone.
Intersection requiring most immediate attention	Sales × People + Alignment	No shared interpretation of margin requirements exists. Every contract negotiation proceeds from a different reference point. This intersection is generating the conditions that propagate into Economics + Metrics across multiple functions.
Condition to watch next week	Service Delivery × Economics + Metrics	Delivery costs are rising as compensation increases take effect. If this intersection moves from U to sustained U over consecutive weeks, the margin compression becomes structural rather than cyclical.

Table A2.3

HOW TO SELECT THE SIGNAL UNDER OBSERVATION

Select one signal per domain each week from the Enterprise Signal Tables (Appendix 7). The signal may remain the same across consecutive weeks—tracking a single signal over time reveals directional change. Or it may rotate—scanning a different signal each week builds structural awareness across the domain's full signal architecture.

Two selection approaches:

1. Sustained observation. Select the same signal for four consecutive weeks. This reveals whether a condition is stable, deficient, or unstable across the enterprise's business functions. Sustained observation is the default selection approach. Use it when a prior week's observation surfaced a Deficient or Unstable reading in one or more functions.

2. Rotating scan. Select a different signal each week, cycling through the domain's signal categories over time.

Observing every signal every week is not required. The signal tables contain 120 signals across twenty-eight categories. The Activity Blueprint carries five—one per domain—read across the enterprise's business functions. Over time, the full signal architecture is covered.

Example

Table A2.2 presents a completed Weekly Observation Log for the USD 11 million software development services company introduced in Chapter 1. It illustrates how five signals—one per domain—read across every business function, and how the same signal in different states across functions produces structural information about where in the enterprise the condition is concentrated.

Format Notes

This is a sample layout for the printed book appendix. Replicate this structure in Google Sheets, Excel, Ninety.io, Asana, Monday.com, or equivalent. Each row is one business function. Each column is one domain. The "Signal under observation" row identifies which signal the leader is tracking within each domain that week. The log is completed weekly in approximately fifteen minutes—one signal per domain, read across every business function.

The current state assessment records Stable, Deficient, or Unstable for each intersection. The observation notes record what the leader sees. The system reading records the leader's overall structural assessment.

Guidance Notes

1. How to complete the log

Fifteen minutes, once per week. Select one signal per domain from the Enterprise Signal Tables (Appendix 7), or carry forward last week's selection. For each business function, assess the selected signal's current state within that domain. Record what you observe. Complete the system reading.

2. What the log does not do

It does not produce decisions. It does not prescribe action. It surfaces where structural conditions are shifting before those shifts register as financial consequence.

3. What to watch for

Directional change matters more than absolute state. An enterprise that has been Stable for eight consecutive weeks and shifts to Deficient at one intersection has received structural information. An enterprise that has been Unstable and shifts to Deficient has begun renewal. The log makes both transitions visible.

4. The observation notes

Record what you see, not what you conclude. "Decision timing has slowed in the sales-to-implementation handoff" is an observation. "Our process is broken" is a conclusion. The log captures the first; the Quarterly Coherence Conversation (Appendix 4) addresses the second.

5. Domain reading vs. function reading

The domain reading is not an average of the function rows above it. It is the leader's overall structural assessment of that domain's condition across the enterprise. A domain may show Stable in five functions and Unstable in one—and the domain reading may still be Deficient, because the unstable function governs a critical interface.

6. Reading across rows vs. reading down columns

The blueprint reveals two kinds of structural patterns. Reading down a column shows how one signal behaves across every function—this reveals domain-level conditions. Reading across a row shows how one function is assessed across every domain—this reveals function-level conditions. Both patterns carry structural meaning. A column of Unstable signals points to a systemic domain condition. A row of Unstable signals points to a function under structural pressure from multiple directions.

Tips for Implementation

1. Start with one domain

Begin by selecting a signal in one domain and assessing it across all business functions. Add a second domain the following week. By week five, the full blueprint is active.

2. Use the same signal for at least four weeks before rotating

A single week's observation is a snapshot. Four consecutive weeks reveal trajectory. Establish a baseline before rotating.

3. Keep observations short and specific

The observation notes are a structural journal, not a narrative. One sentence per intersection that changed is sufficient. "Sales × People + Alignment: two new hires interpreting pricing authority differently from established team" is a complete observation.

4. Compare this week's blueprint to last week's side by side

The diagnostic value is in the delta. Print both or display them adjacent in your spreadsheet. Changed cells are the cells that matter.

5. Discuss the blueprint, not the conclusions

Bring the completed blueprint to leadership meetings. The blueprint is a shared observation instrument. When multiple leaders read the same grid and identify different patterns, the disagreement is itself structural information.

6. Watch for the cell you want to skip

The intersection that resists assessment is frequently the intersection under the most structural pressure. Difficulty assessing a cell indicates limited visibility into that function within that domain—a condition worth recording.

7. Customize the business functions to your enterprise

The function rows in this sample match the book's blueprint examples. Your enterprise may have different functions, additional functions, or functions named differently. The instrument works when the rows represent the organizational units through which your enterprise carries its work—not a generic template.

APPENDIX 3: MONTHLY INTERFACE REVIEW

Each month, one critical interface. An interface is any point where work, decisions, or information transfer between roles, teams, or domains—the handoff between sales and implementation, the boundary between strategy and execution, the connection between product and customer support, the interface between finance and operations during planning cycles.

SELECTING THE INTERFACE

The Weekly Signal Scan and Observation Log (Appendix 2) identifies where to focus. Intersections that showed Deficient or Unstable during the prior four weeks point to the interfaces under the most structural pressure. The monthly review examines one of these interfaces in depth. Two selection patterns surface from the weekly log:

1. Domain-concentrated pressure
When a single domain column shows Deficient or Unstable across multiple functions, the interfaces *within* that domain—between the business functions that share it—are the priority. The condition is domain-level, and the interface review asks where the domain's structural architecture is losing fit.

2. Function-concentrated pressure
When a single function row shows Deficient or Unstable across multiple domains, the interfaces *around* that function—between it and the functions it depends on or serves—are the priority. The

condition is function-level, and the interface review asks where the function's connections to the rest of the enterprise are under strain.

DIAGNOSTIC QUESTIONS

For each interface, four diagnostic questions:

1. Does context transfer with the work, or does the receiving side reconstruct meaning independently?
2. Is ownership clear on both sides of the transfer, or does accountability dissolve at the boundary?
3. Are exceptions absorbed by the interface structure, or do they require escalation?
4. Is coordination demand at this interface rising, stable, or declining compared to the prior quarter? Rising coordination demand at an interface is an early structural signal of mismatch—it indicates that design is being replaced by effort at the point of transfer.

SIGNAL CATEGORY DRILL-DOWN

When the monthly review requires deeper diagnosis, select the specific function × domain intersection and review it at signal category level using the Enterprise Signal Tables (Appendix 7). The signal categories for the relevant domain provide the diagnostic framework:

- **People + Alignment:** 6 signal categories (Leadership, Organizational Design, Communication Flow, Cultural, Incentive, Substitution and Cross-Domain)
- **Processes + Integration:** 5 signal categories (Structural Fit, Integration, Interface Conditions, Signals of Structural Mismatch, Process Governance)
- **Execution + Intelligence:** 7 signal categories (Execution Properties, Mode of Motion, Coordination, Intelligence,

Structural Conditions, Execution Capability, Performance Ritualization)

- **Customer + Interaction:** 5 signal categories (Relational, Customer Value Dimensions, Market Sensing, Customer Misalignment, Cross-Domain from C+I)
- **Economics + Metrics:** 5 signal categories (Cross-Domain Economic Received, Financial Strategy, Metrics, Economic Coherence, Cross-Domain Economic Sent)

The drill-down identifies which specific signals within the domain are driving the condition the weekly log surfaced. It answers the question the weekly log raises but cannot resolve: *What, specifically, is deficient or unstable at this intersection?*

Recording the Review

Record the interface reviewed, the diagnostic findings, and the structural assessment: Is this a domain condition or a function condition? That distinction determines whether renewal addresses the domain's architecture or the function's connections to the rest of the enterprise.

APPENDIX 4: QUARTERLY COHERENCE CONVERSATION

Once per quarter, the leadership team conducts a structured diagnostic conversation organized by domain. This is a diagnostic instrument, not a planning exercise or an alignment session. The conversation draws on three months of accumulated weekly observations and monthly interface reviews.

PREPARATION

Before the conversation, assemble the quarter's observation data:

- Thirteen weekly observation logs (Appendix 2)
- Three monthly interface reviews (Appendix 3)
- The pattern of current state across all function × domain intersections over the quarter: which intersections were consistently stable, which were deficient, which were unstable, and which improved

The "When Coherent" and "When Not Coherent" columns from the Enterprise Signal Tables (Appendix 7) provide the structural baseline for each domain's assessment.

THE CONVERSATION

Walk through each domain in sequence:

People + Alignment

Are shared interpretations of purpose and priority converging or diverging across the enterprise? Where is interpretive alignment strongest? Where has it weakened? What did the weekly logs reveal about leadership signals, communication flow, cultural patterns, and incentive alignment across business functions over the quarter?

Processes + Integration

Is structure carrying work, or has compensatory effort become the primary coordination mechanism? Which interfaces are under the most pressure? What did the monthly interface reviews surface about structural fit, integration, and recurrence patterns?

Execution + Intelligence

Is action the dominant mode of enterprise motion, or has intervention become routine? Is the enterprise learning from what execution produces, or is execution information dissipating before it reaches the decisions it should inform? Where did the weekly logs show velocity, load, or quality shifting across functions?

Customer + Interaction

Are customers experiencing coherence—consistency across interactions—or detecting variation between what the enterprise promises and what it produces? What did the relational signals, sensing cadence, and customer misalignment observations reveal over the quarter?

Economics + Metrics

Are financial signals reinforcing one another, or have contradictions appeared? Is the economic model still fitted to the operating conditions the enterprise currently faces? What did the cross-category reinforcement and margin behavior observations reveal?

THE DIAGNOSTIC OUTPUT

The conversation produces a shared reading of enterprise condition across all five domains simultaneously: the structural foundation for renewal decisions that address the system rather than its symptoms.

Three questions close the conversation:

1. Where is the enterprise's structural condition strongest, and what is sustaining it?
2. Where has structural condition shifted most significantly over the quarter, and what is driving that shift?
3. Where does renewal need to occur—and is the required renewal a domain condition, a function condition, or a system condition?

APPENDIX 5: COORDINATION AUDIT

Apply the coordination taxonomy from Chapter 8 to the enterprise's recurring coordination activities. Catalogue standing meetings, review forums, alignment discussions, and cross-functional checkpoints. For each activity, determine its structural classification:

- **Necessary coordination** resolves a real dependency that the work requires. Removing it changes outcomes.
- **Symbolic coordination** persists without producing change in how work moves. Removing it changes nothing except the calendar.
- **Compensatory coordination** exists because structure cannot carry the work it was built to carry. The meeting substitutes for the structural correspondence that is absent.

Symbolic coordination is eliminated or restructured.

Compensatory coordination is traced to its structural source: the specific deficit in correspondence between structure and work that the coordination is compensating for. That deficit is the renewal target, not the meeting itself.

The Weekly Signal Scan and Observation Log (Appendix 2) sharpens the audit. Intersections where coordination density showed as Deficient or Unstable over successive weeks frequently correspond to the same meetings and forums the audit catalogues. The audit identifies whether those coordination activities are necessary, symbolic, or compensatory. The weekly log identified them as structurally consequential. Together, the two instruments reveal where leadership attention has been absorbed by structural deficits rather than directed at resolving them.

APPENDIX 6: LEADERSHIP PATTERN AND ENTERPRISE VALUE CONSEQUENCE

These profiles describe recurring leadership patterns observed across more than forty enterprises over the course of nearly a decade of embedded, day-to-day fieldwork. They are not personality types, diagnostic categories, or fixed assessments. They describe the interaction between leadership behavior and enterprise structure—how specific patterns of leadership attention, judgment, and decision-making tend to shape the structural conditions that produce or consume enterprise value.

A leader may exhibit different patterns in different structural contexts. The same person who operates as a Ceiling Leader in one enterprise may operate as a Developer in another, where structural conditions support delegation and where the scale matches their capability. The profiles describe the pattern in context, not the person in isolation.

VALUE-COMPOUNDING PATTERNS

1. The Enterprise Value Builder

The leader who has built and sold enterprises before and understands enterprise value as something deliberately constructed, not a byproduct of revenue. Builds leadership teams with intention, delegates authority progressively, and maintains deep industry relationships that compound over time. Manages cash and capital with discipline, funds growth strategies in advance, and keeps financial architecture aligned with enterprise activity. Knows how to scale operations and delivery capability to support additional sales because they've done it before—often through M&A as well as organic growth. The enterprise under this leader compounds value across cycles because every function is built to reinforce the others.

2. The Connected Seller

The leader whose deep industry relationships and personal credibility generate sustained revenue growth. Knows how to evolve the sales approach as the enterprise moves through growth stages—what worked at USD 10 million doesn't work at USD 50 million, and this leader adjusts before the gap becomes a crisis. The enterprise grows because the leader's network opens doors that cold outreach never could. The limitation is that enterprise value creation remains concentrated in the leader's relationships. When the connected seller builds teams and systems behind the relationships, enterprise value compounds. When the relationships stay personal, the enterprise is one departure away from revenue contraction.

3. The Developer

The leader who invests deliberately in the people and capabilities beneath them. Hires for growth, not for the current cycle. Builds a leadership team that can carry the enterprise beyond what any single person could manage, and delegates progressively so that the enterprise's capacity expands as people develop. The limitation is pace—the developer builds durable capability, but without the connected seller's revenue engine or the enterprise value builder's full-system view, compounding is slower. Enterprise value accumulates through people, but the leader may underinvest in the commercial and financial architecture that turns capability into sustained results.

4. The Disciplined Operator

The leader who maintains financial control, funds strategies deliberately, and keeps the enterprise's resources matched to its activity. Cash is managed. Costs are understood. The enterprise doesn't outrun what it can support, and financial visibility is sufficient to present confidently to banks, investors, and regulators. The limitation is that discipline alone doesn't generate growth or compound enterprise value aggressively. The disciplined operator protects what exists and prevents destruction, but without the commercial instincts of the connected seller or the team-building capability of the developer, the enterprise sustains rather than expands. Enterprise value is preserved rather than created—a net positive that depends on other functions to convert protection into growth.

5. The Learner

The leader who integrates mistakes into the next cycle. When something fails, the failure is examined, and the approach changes. Each growth stage is navigated differently than the last because the leader absorbs what happened and adjusts. The limitation is that learning starts from correction, not from accumulated advantage. Enterprise value is created, but each cycle begins by recovering from the prior cycle's errors rather than building on its gains. The learner adapts, but the adaptation is incremental and slower than that of leaders who start from a stronger structural foundation. Net positive, but barely—the enterprise progresses without compounding.

VALUE-NEUTRAL TO VALUE-CONSUMING PATTERNS

6. The Mismatched Strategist

The leader who has the instinct to build enterprise value but applies the wrong tools. Typically has experience in larger enterprises and imports leadership techniques, organizational structures, or strategic frameworks that don't translate to the enterprise's current scale and context. The intent is present—this leader wants to professionalize, systematize, and scale. But the techniques create overhead, complexity, and misfit rather than performance. Resources are consumed by structure that doesn't match the work it's supposed to carry. Enterprise value is slightly net negative because the mismatch diverts energy and creates confusion, but the underlying foundation isn't being actively destroyed. With the right guidance, this leader can recalibrate—the instinct is an asset if the application is corrected.

7. The Ceiling Leader

The leader who builds the enterprise to a growth stage and cannot break through it. Often, the leader also controls everything, bottlenecking decisions and processes through their own bandwidth. The enterprise reaches a scale that matches the leader's personal capacity and then stops advancing. Revenue flatlines, capability stops expanding, and the leadership team beneath—if one exists—operates within boundaries the leader won't release. Enterprise value stops accumulating. It isn't destroyed suddenly, but the flatline means market position, competitive relevance, and talent retention quietly erode as the enterprise stands still while conditions around it change. Time becomes the destructive force—the longer the ceiling persists, the more enterprise value deteriorates.

8. The Technical Founder

The leader whose monetizable skill—technical or functional—created the enterprise but now constrains it. This leader can deliver the core product or service but cannot build teams, delegate to leadership, evolve the sales approach, or manage the financial and operational architecture that enterprise growth demands. The skill that launched the enterprise becomes its upper limit. The enterprise can generate revenue within the range of the leader's personal capability, but it cannot scale beyond that range. Enterprise value reaches a ceiling and begins to decline as the market, the customer base, and the competitive environment outgrow what one person's skill can carry. Talent turnover is typically high because capable people leave when they recognize the ceiling is the leader.

VALUE-DESTROYING PATTERNS

9. The Wheel-Spinner

The leader who doesn't learn from mistakes and can't implement advice from people with proven track records. Mistakes recirculate. The same problems appear in successive cycles with the same consequences. The enterprise has access to knowledge—from advisors, from board members, from its own experience—that never converts into changed behavior. Results stay average to below average because nothing compounds. What was built in one cycle is consumed by repeated errors in the next. Enterprise value erodes steadily because the enterprise is paying the cost of the same failures over and over without accumulating the benefit of correction. This leader is often hardworking and well-intentioned, which makes the pattern harder to interrupt—effort masks the absence of learning.

10. The Value Destroyer

The leader who actively destroys enterprise value through financial mismanagement, failed planning, and compounding miscalculation. Can't manage cash, can't control costs, overspends relative to revenue, and doesn't fund strategies in advance. Decisions are reactive, resource allocation is unplanned, and the enterprise earns but retains nothing. Enterprise value is consumed faster than it is created because every cycle produces less than it costs. Left uncorrected, this leader takes the enterprise into financial distress—not from market failure or competitive pressure, but from internal mismanagement that no amount of revenue can outrun. This is the fastest path to enterprise value destruction because the damage is self-inflicted and accelerating.

APPENDIX 7: ENTERPRISE SIGNAL TABLES

Signals are structural indicators—observable patterns that reveal whether the enterprise's architecture fits the work it carries. They are not metrics, KPIs, or diagnostic checklists. They are what the enterprise emits as it moves.

The tables that follow consolidate the enterprise signals described across the Five Enterprise Domain chapters (Chapters 6–10) into a structured reference organized by domain in the Natural Order sequence. The tables contain 120 signals across twenty-eight categories. Each signal is identified by where it is discussed in the text, what it reveals about system condition, and how it presents under coherent and incoherent conditions.

Each row presents one signal under two structural conditions. The "When Coherent" column describes what that signal looks like when the domain's architecture fits the work it carries. The "When Not Coherent" column describes what the same signal looks like when correspondence has weakened. The reader's task is to determine which column matches the condition observed at each business function × domain intersection.

The observation states recorded in the Weekly Signal Scan (Appendix 2) connect directly to these columns. A Stable reading corresponds to conditions described in "When Coherent": Structure is intact and work advances as designed. Deficient and Unstable readings correspond to conditions described in "When Not Coherent": The distinction between the two is the degree of structural insufficiency the leader observes at that intersection.

ENTERPRISE SIGNALS BY DOMAIN OVERVIEW

The 120 signals are organized across five domains in the Natural Order sequence. Within each domain, signals are grouped by category. Each category corresponds to structural content presented in the domain's chapter.

People + Alignment (Chapter 6): 27 signals across 6 categories

- Table A7.1: Leadership Signals
- Table A7.2: Organizational Design Signals
- Table A7.3: Communication Flow Signals
- Table A7.4: Cultural Signals
- Table A7.5: Incentive Signals
- Table A7.6: Substitution and Cross-Domain Signals

Processes + Integration (Chapter 7): 23 signals across 5 categories

- Table A7.7: Structural Fit Signals
- Table A7.8: Integration Signals
- Table A7.9: Interface Condition Signals
- Table A7.10: Structural Mismatch Signals
- Table A7.11: Process Governance Signals

Execution + Intelligence (Chapter 8): 26 signals across 7 categories

- Table A7.12: Execution Property Signals
- Table A7.13: Mode of Motion Signals
- Table A7.14: Coordination Signals
- Table A7.15: Intelligence Signals

- Table A7.16: Structural Condition Signals
- Table A7.17: Execution Capability Signals
- Table A7.18: Performance Ritualization Signals

Customer + Interaction (Chapter 9): 22 signals across 5 categories

- Table A7.19: Relational Signals
- Table A7.20: Customer Value Dimension Signals
- Table A7.21: Market Sensing Signals
- Table A7.22: Customer Misalignment Signals
- Table A7.23: Cross-Domain Signals

Economics + Metrics (Chapter 10): 22 signals across 5 categories

- Table A7.24: Cross-Domain Economic Influence Signals (Received)
- Table A7.25: Financial Strategy Signals
- Table A7.26: Metrics Signals
- Table A7.27: Economic Coherence Signals
- Table A7.28: Cross-Domain Economic Influence Signals (Sent)

Consult these tables when selecting which signal to observe in the Activity Blueprint (Appendix 1) and when interpreting what you see.

Enterprise Signal Architecture by Domain

Domain	Structural Role	What Its Signals Reveal	Signal Tables
People + Alignment (Chapter 6)	Interpretation—where shared meaning forms before work encounters structure	Whether the enterprise's interpretive conditions are stabilizing or fragmenting and whether variance is being contained or compounded through leadership, design, communication, culture, and incentives	Leadership; Organizational Design; Communication Flow; Cultural; Incentive; Substitution and Cross-Domain (27 signals)
Processes + Integration (Chapter 7)	Architecture—where work is sequenced, routed, and integrated across the enterprise	Whether the enterprise's process architecture still corresponds to the work it carries, and whether integration preserves context or loses it at every interface	Structural Fit; Integration; Interface Conditions; Signals of Structural Mismatch; Process Governance (23 signals)
Execution + Intelligence (Chapter 8)	Motion—where structure is tested through behavior and learning determines whether enterprise value is reinforced or diminished	Whether enterprise motion is carried by design or held together by effort, and whether learning returns to the domains where structural adjustment occurs	Execution Properties; Mode of Motion; Coordination; Intelligence; Structural Conditions; Execution Capability; Performance Ritualization (26 signals)
Customer + Interaction (Chapter 9)	Recognition—where enterprise behavior is interpreted as value and relational signals feed back into the system	Whether customers experience coherence across interactions, and whether relational intelligence reaches the domains where structural adjustment occurs	Relational; Customer Value Dimensions; Market Sensing; Customer Misalignment; Cross-Domain from C+I (22 signals)
Economics + Metrics (Chapter 10)	Viability—where motion is translated into economic meaning and enterprise value is protected across cycles	Whether the enterprise's economic architecture sustains what the other domains produce, and whether metrics reveal the system as a whole or fragment it into isolated indicators	Cross-Domain Economic; Financial Strategy; Metrics; Economic Coherence; Cross-Domain Economic Influences (22 signals)

Table A7.0

PEOPLE + ALIGNMENT SIGNALS (CHAPTER 6)

People + Alignment: Leadership Signals

Signal	What It Reveals	When Coherent	When Incoherent
Direction consistency	Whether leadership behavior stabilizes or fragments shared interpretation of purpose and priority	Direction remains stable under pressure; people infer priorities from behavior that reinforces stated intent	Emphasis shifts between interactions; teams receive incompatible signals about what matters and adjust locally
Decision timing	Whether decisions form at the pace the enterprise requires or accumulate unresolved	Decisions resolve when the work requires them; accountability is clear and authority is exercised without delay	Decisions linger, concentrate upward, or resolve inconsistently; dependency increases as teams wait for resolution
Strategic focus	Whether leadership attention remains concentrated or disperses across competing priorities	Priorities remain legible over time; tradeoffs resolve through consistent logic; attention reinforces structure	Focus shifts frequently; competing priorities produce locally rational action that is globally incompatible
Communi-cation structure	Whether leadership communication preserves shared meaning or introduces variance	Messages carry consistent meaning across contexts; communication reinforces coordination without additional effort	Messages contradict or fragment across channels; people reconstruct meaning independently at each interface
Adaptability	Whether leadership adjusts to changing conditions while maintaining interpretive stability	Adjustment preserves the enterprise's interpretive reference; change is absorbed without fragmenting shared meaning	Either rigidity (conditions change while interpretation remains fixed) or instability (every adjustment resets shared meaning)

Table A7.1

People + Alignment: Organizational Design Signals

Signal	What It Reveals	When Coherent	When Incoherent
Span of control	Whether the scope of responsibility matches the coordination demand placed on each role	Roles carry their coordination load without bottlenecking; decisions distribute appropriately	Roles are either overloaded (decisions concentrate) or underloaded (authority fragments without consequence)
Decision rights definition	Whether authority is defined and exercised where the work requires it	Decisions form at the point of highest structural information; escalation is rare	Authority is ambiguous; teams hesitate at boundaries or escalate routinely because ownership is undefined
Interface definition	Whether boundaries between teams preserve context and transfer work without loss	Handoffs transfer work with sufficient context; ownership passes cleanly	Handoffs require repeated explanation; context is lost at every transition; accountability dissolves at boundaries
Cross-team integration	Whether coordination across teams proceeds from structure or depends on effort	Teams coordinate through shared design rather than manual reconciliation	Coordination requires standing meetings, reconciliation forums, and personal relationships to sustain baseline motion
Scalability of design	Whether the organizational architecture carries increasing load without structural failure	Design absorbs growth, new roles, and increasing interdependence without losing coherence	Design that functioned at prior scale now produces bottlenecks, confusion, and compensatory workarounds

Table A7.2

People + Alignment: Communication Flow Signals

Signal	What It Reveals	When Coherent	When Incoherent
Vertical flow	Whether information moves between leadership and operations with sufficient context and fidelity	Leadership decisions are informed by operating reality; operating teams receive direction with meaning intact	Leadership decisions form without contact with operating conditions; direction loses meaning as it descends
Horizontal flow	Whether coordination between peer teams proceeds from shared context	Teams share a common reference that makes coordination implicit; lateral decisions remain compatible	Teams interpret the same conditions differently; coordination shifts to escalation and manual reconciliation
Relational flow	Whether information crossing the enterprise–customer boundary retains structural meaning	Customer signals reach the domains where structural adjustment occurs; execution reflects relational conditions	Customer signals remain isolated in customer-facing teams; internal behavior separates from external demand
Feedback loop integrity	Whether experience returns to the points where decisions are made, in time to inform adjustment	Learning circulates; corrections are proportional and timely; patterns are identified before consequences compound	Feedback is delayed, filtered, or ignored; decisions repeat without incorporating prior outcome; correction is always late

Table A7.3

People + Alignment: Cultural Signals

Signal	What It Reveals	When Coherent	When Incoherent
Behavioral norms	Whether shared expectations govern action or have softened into ambiguity	People operate from shared expectations without enforcement; accountability is embedded in interaction	Norms lose definition; behavior diverges from stated expectations; accountability disperses
Decision habits	Whether decisions follow consistent logic or have become locally optimized	Decisions form through compatible logic across contexts; tradeoffs resolve predictably	Decisions vary by team, leader, or context; resolution depends on who is in the room rather than on shared logic
Conflict patterns	Whether disagreement surfaces and resolves productively or is avoided and suppressed	Disagreement surfaces early and is resolved structurally; outcomes improve through challenge	Disagreement is avoided, personalized, or escalated; issues recirculate without closure
Openness under pressure	Whether truth circulates under stress or contracts into self-protection	Information surfaces without delay under pressure; reality is confronted directly	Communication contracts under stress; teams retreat into boundaries; coordination depends on escalation when convergence is most required
Cultural decay	Whether shared patterns are strengthening coherence or gradually losing definition	Patterns reinforce coordination and trust; the enterprise defaults to productive behavior under load	Norms soften; accountability disperses; hesitation replaces resolution; meetings shift from decision-making to performance; problems recur without closure

Table A7.4

People + Alignment: Incentive Signals

Signal	What It Reveals	When Coherent	When Incoherent
Reward alignment	Whether what is rewarded matches what the enterprise requires	Effort concentrates without compulsion; decisions reinforce enterprise direction; performance sustains across cycles	Teams pursue local success because incentive signals reward it; behavior diverges from stated priorities
Performance metric fit	Whether the measures applied to individuals and teams reinforce shared priorities	Metrics reinforce compatible behavior across roles and teams	Metrics contradict stated priorities; people optimize for what is measured rather than what is needed
Recognition patterns	Whether recognition reinforces enterprise-level contribution or local visibility	Recognition reinforces contribution to enterprise outcomes; trust builds through visible consistency	Recognition rewards individual effort (firefighting, workarounds) rather than structural contribution; compensatory behavior is celebrated
Career outcome logic	Whether advancement and opportunity reinforce coordination or competition	Career paths reinforce cross-domain contribution and structural capability	Advancement rewards functional depth or personal networks rather than enterprise-level impact
Decision rights as incentive	Whether authority structures reinforce shared ownership or territorial behavior	Authority is exercised to advance enterprise motion; ownership consolidates without enforcement	Authority becomes a resource to be defended; territorial behavior concentrates decisions for control rather than contribution

Table A7.5

People + Alignment: Substitution and Cross-Domain Signals

Signal	What It Reveals	When Coherent	When Incoherent
Substitution of effort for structure	Whether the enterprise sustains motion through design or through compensatory effort	Work advances through structural carry; coordination is embedded; oversight is proportional	Added effort, manual coordination, escalation, and oversight sustain motion at compounding cost; nothing appears broken because nothing has stopped
Cross-domain cost migration	Whether compensatory cost remains contained or propagates through the system	Domain interactions reinforce capability; cost is proportional to work	Process workarounds become execution constraints; execution instability becomes customer experience; customer inconsistency distorts financial signals
Diagnostic accuracy	Whether the enterprise identifies the origin of issues or treats symptoms at the domain where they surface	Issues are traced to their structural origin; correction addresses root condition	Process teams see process problems; execution leaders see execution problems; customer teams see market problems; each diagnosis is domain-accurate and system-insufficient

Table A7.6

PROCESSES + INTEGRATION SIGNALS (CHAPTER 7)

Processes + Integration: Structural Fit Signals

Signal	What It Reveals	When Coherent	When Incoherent
Friction at process boundaries	Whether work moves through structure cleanly or encounters resistance at transitions	Work advances through defined pathways without repeated reconciliation; effort converts directly into outcomes	Delay, confusion, and rework appear at handoffs; effort substitutes for structure at every transition
Volume sensitivity	Whether the process architecture carries increasing volume without proportional cost	Architecture scales without disproportionate coordination; throughput increases with manageable effort	Volume increases produce nonlinear coordination demand; the same work requires more effort at higher volume
Variability tolerance	Whether structure absorbs normal operating variation or breaks down under change	Structure accommodates variation within defined bounds; exceptions are absorbed without disruption	Minor variation produces cascading exceptions; processes that held under stable conditions fail when conditions shift
Decision routing	Whether decisions follow defined pathways or accumulate without resolution	Decisions resolve where the work requires them; authority is clear and routing is predictable	Decisions concentrate, wait for authority, or resolve inconsistently; routing depends on who is available rather than on structural design
Scalability of architecture	Whether structure carries increasing interdependence without losing fit	Architecture absorbs new roles, teams, and dependencies without requiring redesign	Architecture that functioned at prior scale now produces bottlenecks, workarounds, and increasing coordination cost

Table A7.7

Processes + Integration: Integration Signals

Signal	What It Reveals	When Coherent	When Incoherent
Context preservation across interfaces	Whether meaning survives transfer between roles, teams, and domains	Context transfers with the work; the receiving side operates from the same meaning as the sending side	Meaning is reconstructed at every interface; each team reinterprets what it receives; intent degrades with each handoff
Knowledge circulation	Whether learning from one part of the enterprise reaches the parts where it is structurally relevant	Experience circulates beyond its point of origin; patterns inform structural adjustment; exceptions produce redesign	Learning remains local; exceptions recur without producing correction; the distance between what the enterprise has learned and how it operates widens
Interface performance	Whether boundaries between domains carry work or absorb it	Interfaces transfer work predictably; ownership passes with definition; disagreement remains bounded	Handoffs become points of failure; coordination concentrates at boundaries; work stalls at transitions while teams negotiate responsibility
Technology amplification	Whether technology extends coherent structure or scales incoherent structure	Technology reinforces clear routing, visibility, and shared knowledge; modest tools perform well because they extend structural coherence	Technology inherits the misfit it encounters; implementation fails not because tools are deficient but because structure cannot carry what tools require

Table A7.8

Processes + Integration: Interface Condition Signals

Signal	What It Reveals	When Coherent	When Incoherent
Boundary accountability	Whether accountability passes with the work or dissolves at the point of transition	Ownership transfers with definition; the receiving side operates from clear accountability without renegotiation	Responsibility deflects at boundaries; handoffs require repeated clarification of who owns what; accountability dissolves at the point of transfer and must be reasserted through escalation
Exception absorption	Whether the interface structure contains disruption or propagates it	Exceptions are absorbed within the interface terms; disagreement remains bounded; disruption does not propagate beyond the boundary where it originated	Exceptions require escalation; disagreement expands into positional conflict; disruption at one interface propagates downstream because structure cannot contain it at the point of origin
Cross-functional flow continuity	Whether work advances across teams through structural carry or through improvisation	Coordination across teams proceeds from shared design; dependencies are anticipated; work advances without repeated interpretation at each boundary	Work depends on improvisation to cross boundaries; local priorities narrow; coordination shifts to escalation; information arrives late or requires reconstruction at every transition
Interface-specific coordination concentration	Whether coordination load is concentrating at particular boundaries, identifying which interfaces are under structural pressure	Coordination distributes across interfaces proportionally; no single boundary absorbs disproportionate reconciliation effort	Coordination concentrates at specific interfaces; particular boundaries between teams or domains absorb escalation, renegotiation, and manual handoff effort that surrounding interfaces do not require

Table A7.9

Processes + Integration: Structural Mismatch Signals

Signal	What It Reveals	When Coherent	When Incoherent
Rising coordination demand	Whether work requires increasing effort to sustain baseline motion	Coordination is proportional to work complexity; effort converts into outcomes	Coordination demand rises without corresponding increase in work complexity; more meetings, more handoffs, more reconciliation for the same output
Team interaction friction	Whether collaboration between teams proceeds from structure or depends on personal effort	Teams collaborate through shared design; working relationships are structurally supported	Collaboration depends on personal relationships; when individuals leave, coordination breaks down
Routine reliability	Whether standard processes produce consistent results	Standard work produces predictable outcomes; variation is within expected bounds	Routine work produces variable results; the same process produces different outcomes depending on who executes it or when
Learning circulation	Whether experience improves the system or remains isolated	Lessons are absorbed into process design; patterns are identified and addressed structurally	Lessons are discussed and forgotten; the same issues recur across cycles without producing structural change
Recurrence patterns	Whether the same issues reappear after apparently being resolved	Issues resolve structurally and do not recur; correction is durable	The same problems reappear in successive cycles; resolution addresses symptoms while leaving structural conditions intact
Customer and financial divergence	Whether process performance translates into customer experience and economic outcome	Operational performance produces corresponding customer satisfaction and financial stability	Operational metrics appear stable while customer experience degrades and financial signals weaken; process output is disconnected from downstream consequence

Table A7.10

Processes + Integration: Process Governance Signals

Signal	What It Reveals	When Coherent	When Incoherent
Architecture correspondence	Whether process design reflects current operating conditions or a prior configuration the enterprise has outgrown	Structure corresponds to the volume, variability, and interdependence the enterprise currently faces; architecture carries current work without persistent workarounds	Structure reflects a prior operating reality; workflows that once carried work reliably now require informal fixes, escalation, and manual coordination to sustain motion the architecture was not built for
Process renewal timing	Whether structural adjustment occurs before consequences compound or only after disruption forces correction	Renewal occurs as conditions change; fit is restored before coordination is displaced into effort; each cycle of adjustment is proportional and contained	Renewal is deferred until breakdown; each cycle of deferred renewal narrows the margin between operating conditions and structural limits; modest increases in demand produce disproportionate coordination cost
Fit visibility	Whether the enterprise can see its own operating conditions with sufficient accuracy and frequency to detect misfit early	The enterprise assesses fit across sequence, interface, routing, knowledge, and responsiveness dimensions; persistent misfit is recognized as an architectural condition rather than an execution problem	Operating conditions are misread or unexamined; structure is built to correspond to conditions that no longer exist; misfit is attributed to people or execution rather than to architectural correspondence
Structural interest interference	Whether positional interests obstruct the recognition or correction of architectural misfit	Information that surfaces the need for renewal reaches decision-makers without distortion; architectural adjustment proceeds on structural evidence rather than positional negotiation	Information that would surface renewal requirements is filtered or reinterpreted by the same decision pathways renewal would restructure; positions embedded in the current architecture resist changes that would redistribute authority or access

Table A7.11

EXECUTION + INTELLIGENCE SIGNALS (CHAPTER 8)

Execution + Intelligence: Execution Property Signals

Signal	What It Reveals	When Coherent	When Incoherent
Velocity	Whether work advances at the pace the enterprise requires	Work advances predictably; decisions form when needed; commitments are met without extraordinary effort	Work slows without identifiable cause; timelines extend; effort increases but pace does not
Variability	Whether execution produces consistent results or fluctuates unpredictably	Outcomes are predictable within expected bounds; quality remains stable across conditions	Results fluctuate between cycles; the same work produces different outcomes; predictability declines
Load	Whether demand is proportional to the enterprise's carrying capacity	Teams operate within capacity; pressure is distributed appropriately; recovery is built into the work cycle	Load concentrates unevenly; some areas overload while others remain underutilized; capacity is consumed without producing proportional output
Quality	Whether outputs meet the standard the work requires and customers expect	Quality remains stable under increasing volume and complexity; standards are maintained without individual effort	Quality fluctuates; rework increases; standards are maintained only through concentrated personal attention

Table A7.12

Execution + Intelligence: Mode of Motion Signals

Signal	What It Reveals	When Coherent	When Incoherent
Dominant mode of enterprise motion	Whether action, intervention, or propagation dominates execution	Action is the dominant mode; work advances as designed; progress depends primarily on structure rather than personal effort	Intervention becomes dominant; progress depends on corrective effort, overrides, escalation, and personal judgment substituting for structural support
Shift from independent to coordinated motion	Whether dependencies are carried by design or require explicit synchronization	Independent motion dominates; dependencies are resolved implicitly through structure	Coordinated motion intensifies; work cannot advance without active synchronization; explicit coordination substitutes for design
Propagation visibility	Whether ambient, system-sustained motion is recognized and governed	Propagation is recognized as enterprise motion; its consequences are monitored and accounted for	Propagation is invisible; automated processes, inherited commitments, and habitual activity carry more work and consequence than leaders realize

Table A7.13

Execution + Intelligence: Coordination Signals

Signal	What It Reveals	When Coherent	When Incoherent
Coordination density and persistence	Whether coordination accompanies action or has displaced it	Coordination is embedded in structure; it accompanies action without drawing attention	Coordination becomes continuous, explicit, and effortful; progress depends on synchronization rather than design
Coordination type distribution	Whether coordination is necessary, symbolic, or compensatory	Necessary coordination dominates; symbolic and compensatory forms are rare	Symbolic coordination persists without advancing work; compensatory coordination has become the enterprise's primary execution mechanism
Firefighting	Whether corrective intervention is occasional or has become the operating mode	Intervention is occasional and proportional; firefighting is rare	Firefighting is persistent; leaders are pulled into daily execution; exhaustion, dependency, and reactive decision-making characterize leadership behavior

Table A7.14

Execution + Intelligence: Intelligence Signals

Signal	What It Reveals	When Coherent	When Incoherent
Performance signals (execution-level)	Whether execution is generating interpretable information about structural fit	Signals are interpreted as information about structure; correction occurs before breakdown	Signals are treated as problems to suppress rather than conditions to interpret; the system escalates through greater pressure
Learning loop integrity	Whether insight returns from execution to the domains where structural adjustment occurs	Issues surface early; patterns are interpreted rather than isolated events; correction remains proportional; coherence persists through changing conditions	Issues remain isolated; recovery lengthens; defensiveness increases; decision quality deteriorates; the enterprise senses accurately but adjusts insufficiently
Execution–intelligence connection	Whether forward motion and returning insight remain coupled	Execution produces learning; learning produces adjustment; the loop sustains coherence through continuous correction	Execution repeats without correcting; intelligence produces interpretation that never encounters consequence; the loop is broken

Table A7.15

Execution + Intelligence: Structural Condition Signals

Signal	What It Reveals	When Coherent	When Incoherent
Responsible autonomy	Whether individuals and teams act decisively within scope without waiting for permission or compensating for missing structure	Decisions propagate without distortion; escalation declines; trust strengthens; adaptability increases	Leaders become bottlenecks; people hesitate at boundaries; teams wait for permission; execution slows to the speed of escalation
Cadence integrity	Whether leadership routines regulate flow, stabilize load, and connect execution to learning	Daily patterns synchronize near-term work; monthly learning converts experience into insight; quarterly renewal restores structural fit	Cadence hardens into ritualized activity; meetings repeat without producing adjustment; intelligence arrives too late or lacks a structural mechanism through which to act
Misalignment patterns	Whether upstream misfit is surfacing through execution	Execution advances without disproportionate effort; teams do not pull in opposing directions; workflows stable under load	Recurring delays in the same segments; questions resurface after appearing resolved; inconsistent decisions across teams; escalation becomes the default path for resolution
Technology amplification	Whether technology reinforces structural coherence or compounds structural misfit	Technology extends coherent workflows, strengthens routing, and reinforces learning loops	Technology inherits misfit; platforms underperform because structure cannot carry what they require; automation scales incoherence at machine speed

Table A7.16

Execution + Intelligence: Execution Capability Signals

Signal	What It Reveals	When Coherent	When Incoherent
Structure and tools amplification	Whether the architecture carrying work and the systems amplifying effort reinforce execution or compound distortion	Tools compundcoherent structure; the architecture carrying the work supports the tasks it encounters; the same tasks succeed regardless of who performs them	The same tasks fail regardless of performer; the constraint is structure or tools—the architecture does not support the work, or the systems amplifying effort compound the distortion rather than correcting it
Skills distribution	Whether capability is structurally distributed or concentrated in specific individuals	Capability is carried by the enterprise rather than by particular people; execution does not depend on the presence of specific individuals to sustain quality	Tasks fail only in the absence of specific individuals; the enterprise depends on capability that has not been structurally distributed; loss of key personnel exposes execution to immediate degradation
Capacity threshold	Whether the enterprise can execute at the scale its conditions demand or only at a lesser scale	Execution sustains quality and predictability under the volume the enterprise currently faces; capacity is proportional to demand	Tasks succeed individually but fail under volume; the enterprise can execute at one scale but not at the scale its conditions demand; capacity sets the threshold beyond which skills, tools, and structure lose effectiveness
Element interaction integrity	Whether the four Technical Capability elements reinforce one another or have decoupled despite individual adequacy	The four elements compound: tools extend and accelerate the motion structure channels; structure channels the skills capacity sustains; execution is reliable and scalable	The four Technical Capability elements are individually adequate but do not compound; the constraint is the interaction among them, not the strength of any element; investment in any single element does not resolve a coupling failure
Relational effectiveness	Whether the social dimension of execution is carrying Technical Capability into enterprise value, or Diluting and Eroding it across interfaces, teams, and relational fields	Work travels across interfaces without loss; signals reach the decisions they should inform; teams carry each other's execution needs without escalation; Technical Capability Creates and Amplifies enterprise value at full strength	Technical Capability is individually adequate but Diluted in transit; execution degrades at interfaces and handoffs; signals fail to travel; coordination requires repeated escalation; enterprise value Erodes as the relational channel deteriorates independent of skills, tools, structure, or capacity; the enterprise cannot out-perform the relational deficit with further technical investment

Table A7.17

Execution + Intelligence: Performance Ritualization Signals

Signal	What It Reveals	When Coherent	When Incoherent
Handoff standardization	Whether work transfers between roles and teams through defined patterns or through ad hoc negotiation	Handoffs follow consistent structure; the receiving side operates from sufficient context without renegotiating ownership or reconstructing intent at each transfer	Handoffs are improvised; each transfer requires direct negotiation; context is reconstructed from scratch; execution between leadership touchpoints depends on individual initiative rather than embedded practice
Triage and escalation structure	Whether exceptions route through defined paths or require improvisation to resolve	Exceptions enter a defined triage sequence; escalation paths are clear; resolution is proportional and contained; firefighting is occasional rather than persistent	Exceptions are handled ad hoc; escalation paths are unclear or bypassed; resolution depends on whoever is available; firefighting becomes the operating mode because no embedded practice absorbs exceptions structurally
Review and debrief integrity	Whether structured reflection produces adjustment or has degraded into ritual or absence	Review points and learning debriefs convert execution experience into structural adjustment; patterns are identified and correction reaches the domains where it applies	Reviews are absent, perfunctory, or disconnected from structural adjustment; experience accumulates without producing correction; the same issues recur because no embedded practice converts execution data into learning
Planning cycle synchronization	Whether planning across teams is synchronized through embedded practice or fragmented into isolated preparation	Planning cycles are synchronized; teams enter execution from shared preparation; dependencies are anticipated before work begins	Planning is isolated; teams prepare independently; dependencies surface only during execution; synchronization substitutes for preparation because no embedded practice synchronizes planning across boundaries

Table A7.18

CUSTOMER + INTERACTION SIGNALS (CHAPTER 9)

Customer + Interaction: Relational Signals

Signal	What It Reveals	When Coherent	When Incoherent
Direct customer signals	What customers communicate explicitly about their experience, needs, and perceptions	Feedback is specific, constructive, and reflects stable expectations; requests reinforce existing value logic	Feedback becomes vague, contradictory, or absent; customers stop communicating because engagement no longer seems productive
Behavioral signals	What customer actions reveal about enterprise coherence—independent of what customers say	Adoption patterns are stable; engagement deepens across cycles; renewal proceeds without renegotiation	Engagement patterns shift; adoption slows; renewal conversations change in tone; usage declines without explicit complaint
Market dynamics signals	How shifts in the broader relational field reshape the conditions under which enterprise coherence must be maintained	Market signals confirm position; the enterprise maintains relevance without defensive adjustment	Market signals expose misfit; competitive dynamics shift; customer expectations evolve faster than the enterprise adjusts
Competitive pattern signals	How customer expectations are reshaped by the alternatives available to them	The enterprise's value proposition is differentiated and sustained; competitive pressure is absorbed through structural strength	Customer expectations are reshaped by alternatives the enterprise has not accounted for; value comparisons undermine pricing and commitment logic
Platform and regulatory signals	How structural changes in the operating environment alter the enterprise's relational field	Platform and regulatory changes are absorbed through adaptive capacity; the enterprise maintains fit with evolving conditions	Platform dependency, regulatory shifts, or environmental changes create exposure the enterprise cannot absorb through existing architecture

Table A7.19

Customer + Interaction: Customer Value Dimension Signals

Signal	What It Reveals	When Coherent	When Incoherent
Functional value	Whether the enterprise reliably performs the work customers require	Delivery is reliable; capabilities match customer requirements; functional performance is consistent across interactions	Reliability degrades; capability gaps appear; functional performance varies depending on which part of the enterprise the customer encounters
Economic value	Whether pricing, cost, and commitment logic reflect what customers experience	Pricing aligns with perceived worth; cost logic is transparent and credible; economic commitment is sustainable for both parties	Pricing loses traction; discounting substitutes for recognized value; cost-to-serve misaligns with what customers are willing to sustain
Emotional value	Whether the enterprise sustains trust, confidence, and affinity through consistent behavior	Trust deepens across interactions; confidence in the enterprise's behavior is reinforced; customers advocate on the basis of lived experience	Trust erodes through inconsistency; confidence degrades; emotional investment withdraws as the gap between enterprise behavior and customer expectation widens
Social value	Whether the enterprise's identity and positioning reinforce the customer's own relational context	Association with the enterprise reinforces the customer's professional or social position; the relationship carries meaning beyond the transaction	Association becomes neutral or negative; the customer's context has shifted and the enterprise's positioning no longer aligns with it
Strategic value	Whether the enterprise contributes to the customer's capacity to advance their own priorities over time	The enterprise is embedded in the customer's strategic logic; the relationship compounds value across planning horizons	The enterprise is treated as interchangeable; strategic dependency shifts to alternatives; long-term commitment weakens

Table A7.20

Customer + Interaction: Market Sensing Signals

Signal	What It Reveals	When Coherent	When Incoherent
Sensing cadence integrity	Whether the enterprise maintains contact with relational reality across time horizons	Daily and weekly observation captures immediate shifts; monthly interpretation distinguishes signal from noise; quarterly recalibration keeps structure fitted to the relational field	Daily observation narrows; monthly interpretation becomes superficial; quarterly recalibration loses contact with actual conditions; sensing produces data without intelligence
Leadership attention to relational signals	Whether relational intelligence reaches the domains where structural adjustment occurs	Leadership treats relational signals as conditions requiring structural attention; response time is proportional; intelligence reaches upstream domains	Leadership filters, delays, or dismisses relational signals; response time lengthens; intelligence remains in customer-facing teams without reaching structural domains
Signal priority	Which relational signals reach leadership interpretation and which are filtered	Leadership attends to signals that reveal structural conditions; priority is determined by systemic consequence	Signals are prioritized by urgency, volume, or visibility rather than structural significance; consequential signals are missed while prominent ones consume attention

Table A7.21

Customer + Interaction: Customer Misalignment Signals

Signal	What It Reveals	When Coherent	When Incoherent
Mismatched expectations	Whether the enterprise's promises correspond to what it produces	Commitments correspond to capability; customers encounter consistency between promise and delivery	Expectations diverge from experience; customers encounter variation between what was promised and what is delivered
Emotional disconnect	Whether trust and confidence have separated from enterprise behavior	Emotional investment deepens through consistent experience; trust is reinforced across interactions	Trust has withdrawn; engagement continues out of necessity rather than confidence; emotional investment has been replaced by transactional calculation
Declining relevance	Whether enterprise output remains aligned with what customers value	The enterprise's offerings correspond to customer priorities; relevance is confirmed through sustained engagement	Customer priorities have shifted but enterprise output has not; adoption declines; alternatives gain traction
Interaction fatigue	Whether the customer's experience of engagement has become burdensome	Interactions reinforce the relationship; engagement requires proportional effort from both parties	Customers reduce engagement because interaction has become effortful, inconsistent, or unrewarding; silence replaces feedback
Value erosion	Whether the relationship is losing structural capacity to sustain commitment	Customer value compounds across cycles; the relationship strengthens through accumulated experience	The relationship draws down prior investment without renewing it; each cycle produces less value than the one before

Table A7.22

Customer + Interaction: Cross-Domain Signals

Signal	What It Reveals	When Coherent	When Incoherent
Signals to People + Alignment	Whether customer response reinforces or destabilizes shared interpretation within the enterprise	Customer adoption and recognition reinforce enterprise purpose; people interpret their work as meaningful	Customer resistance or disappointment fragments internal interpretation; people lose confidence in stated priorities
Signals to Processes + Integration	Whether customer experience reveals structural fit or misfit in the enterprise's process architecture	Customer experience confirms that structure carries work in a form customers recognize	Customer experience exposes where structure no longer corresponds to what customers encounter
Signals to Execution + Intelligence	Whether customer response reveals execution quality under real conditions	Customer behavior confirms execution consistency; outcomes track with what was intended	Customer behavior exposes where execution has become variable, delayed, or inconsistent
Signals to Economics + Metrics	Whether demand stability and pricing power reflect economic coherence	Demand is stable; pricing integrity is sustained; economic signals reinforce enterprise viability	Demand becomes volatile; pricing loses traction; economic signals reflect relational misfit

Table A7.23

ECONOMICS + METRICS SIGNALS (CHAPTER 10)

Economics + Metrics: Cross-Domain Economic Influence Signals

Signal Received	What It Reveals	When Coherent	When Incoherent
Priority and incentive consistency (from People + Alignment)	Whether effort is applied coherently and economic consequences reflect aligned human motion	Economic signals are stable because effort is coherent; capacity is applied to enterprise priorities	Wasted capacity, rising coordination burden, and inconsistent accountability register as economic cost of interpretive divergence
Cost-to-serve and scalability (from Processes + Integration)	Whether structure carries volume without disproportionate cost	Cost-to-serve is predictable; architecture scales without requiring proportional increase in expense	Rising cost-to-serve, limited scalability, and increasing expense to maintain the same output signal structural misfit
Execution variability and stability (from Execution + Intelligence)	Whether performance is strengthening, plateauing, or deteriorating	Economic signals reflect stable, improving performance; capacity pressure is manageable	Delay, overload, inconsistency, and recovery register economically; the enterprise is operating beyond what its architecture can sustain
Demand stability and pricing power (from Customer + Interaction)	Whether relational coherence translates into economic viability	Recognized and trusted value stabilizes demand and preserves pricing integrity	Weakening relevance surfaces as volatility, discounting, and reduced predictability

Table A7.24

Economics + Metrics: Financial Strategy Signals

Signal	What It Reveals	When Coherent	When Incoherent
Capital allocation coherence	Whether investment decisions reinforce enterprise architecture or fragment it	Investment reinforces priority, structural fit, and renewal requirements; allocation is disciplined and directional	Investment is fragmented, reactive, or disconnected from structural need; allocation signals competing priorities
Economic model fit	Whether the enterprise's economic logic matches its operating conditions	The model strengthens relevance, preserves pricing integrity, stabilizes margins, and keeps cost-to-serve predictable	Unsustainable cost structures, pricing that loses traction, compressing margins, weakening customer meaning, and faltering strategic commitments signal model misfit
Optionality	Whether the enterprise retains the capacity to redirect without destabilizing coherence	Economic flexibility is preserved; room to maneuver exists; overcommitment is avoided	Options have been consumed by prior commitments; redirection requires destabilizing existing structure
Adaptive capacity	Whether the enterprise can absorb change while preserving fit	The enterprise absorbs shifts in demand, competition, and conditions without compensatory effort or emergency intervention	Change produces crisis; adjustment requires disproportionate effort; the gap between conditions and architecture widens with each cycle
Risk accumulation	Whether exposure is recognized and bounded or compounding unobserved	Risk is visible, bounded, and proportional to capacity; exposure is monitored across domains	Risk accumulates structurally through misfit that persists without correction; each domain carries compounding exposure that isolated indicators obscure
Margin behavior	Whether margins reflect productive conversion or compensatory cost	Margins are stable or improving; cost-to-produce is proportional to output; pricing logic holds	Margins compress despite sustained effort; cost rises faster than value creation; the enterprise spends more energy to produce the same results

Table A7.25

Economics + Metrics: Metrics Signals

Signal	What It Reveals	When Coherent	When Incoherent
Cross-category reinforcement	Whether metrics across financial, operational, customer, organizational, and structural categories tell a consistent story	Signals across categories reinforce one another; patterns are legible; cause-and-effect relationships are traceable	Signals contradict across categories; operational gains fail to translate into economic outcome; customer metrics improve while financial metrics weaken
Metric fragmentation	Whether the enterprise interprets itself as a single system or through isolated indicators	Teams share a common interpretive frame; metrics produce shared meaning and compatible decisions	Teams rely on separate indicators; categories are isolated; leaders select measures that reinforce narratives rather than reflect reality
Risk visibility through metrics	Whether compounding exposure is detectable through integrated measurement	Risk is visible because metrics are systemic; no single category obscures the compounding exposure underneath	Isolated indicators each appear manageable; cost-to-serve rises while throughput looks stable; retention declines while revenue is sustained through acquisition
Forecast accuracy	Whether projections reflect enterprise conditions or outdated assumptions	Forecasts reflect operating reality; variance from projection is within manageable bounds	Forecasts lose accuracy; assumptions beneath projections are no longer grounded in shared interpretation; variance increases without identifiable cause

Table A7.26

Economics + Metrics: Economic Coherence Signals

Signal	What It Reveals	When Coherent	When Incoherent
Enterprise motion–economic model alignment	Whether the enterprise's behavior matches the economics required to sustain it	Motion matches how value is earned; capabilities reinforce customer meaning; cost-to-serve is predictable; the enterprise scales without disproportionate coordination cost	Architecture diverges from the economic model; financial instability appears as a downstream consequence of structural misfit
Effort-to-result ratio	Whether results are proportional to the effort applied	Results are proportional to effort; enterprise energy converts into enterprise value without compensatory overhead	People work harder; processes overload; execution becomes inconsistent; teams compensate manually for structural misfit—more effort produces the same or declining results
Cross-domain economic reinforcement	Whether economic outcomes reflect coordinated motion across all five domains or expose fragmentation that each domain's individual indicators obscure	Financial outcomes are traceable to structural conditions across domains; economic signals move in compatible patterns; no single domain's performance contradicts the whole	Economic outcomes diverge from what any single domain's indicators would predict; domains appear individually adequate while the system produces deteriorating economic results; the source of financial variance cannot be located within any single function or domain
Renewal timing and cost	Whether structural adjustment occurs proactively or only after consequences compound	Renewal occurs proactively; structure is updated before decay hardens into misfit; renewal cycles align with economic conditions	Renewal is reactive and costly; adjustment occurs only after consequences accumulate; structural decay compounds into structural misfit before correction begins

Table A7.27

Economics + Metrics: Cross-Domain Economic Influence Signals

Signal Sent	What It Reveals	When Coherent	When Incoherent
Economic signals to People + Alignment	Whether economic interpretation keeps human energy directed and expectations credible	Expectations are credible; commitments are realistic; incentives reinforce shared priorities; trust in effort-to-outcome conversion is maintained	Signals contradict; incentives pull in competing directions; shared meaning fragments because economic interpretation no longer grounds expectations
Economic signals to Processes + Integration	Whether economic stewardship sustains structural investment and interface integrity	Structural fit is preserved; investment in interfaces is reinforced; process decay is addressed before cost escalates	Processes overload; integration fractures; teams resort to workarounds; structural misfit becomes increasingly expensive to correct
Economic signals to Execution + Intelligence	Whether economic discipline keeps execution stable and learning loops productive	Execution is stable; work is predictable; teams operate below overload thresholds; learning loops produce structural adjustment	Rising variability; less reliable quality; slower responsiveness; teams compensate for structural gaps through effort rather than design
Economic signals to Customer + Interaction	Whether the value logic customers sense and respond to remains credible	Pricing aligns with perceived customer value; commitments remain credible; relevance strengthens; relationships stabilize	Pricing loses credibility; cost-to-serve misaligns with customer value; customer expectations diverge from enterprise capability

Table A7.28

APPENDIX 8: GLOSSARY OF TERMS AND DEFINITIONS

This glossary collects the governing terms and definitions used throughout *The Five Enterprise Domains*. Terms are organized in seven sections that reflect the book's architecture. The Enterprise System contains terms that describe how the enterprise operates as a whole, introduced across Chapters 1 through 5. The five domain sections that follow—People + Alignment through Economics + Metrics—contain terms specific to each domain, presented in the Natural Order sequence established in Chapter 3. Leadership and Stewardship contains terms that describe how leaders interpret and sustain the system, drawn primarily from Chapters 2 and 11.

Within each section, terms appear in the order they are introduced in the text. Chapter references are provided so readers can return to the full context in which each term operates.

THE ENTERPRISE SYSTEM

These terms describe the structural reality governing all enterprise behavior. They apply across domains rather than within any single one.

Enterprise System

Chapter 3

Enterprise System describes the enterprise operating as a unified whole—the totality of its domain interaction, relational field participation, and structural behavior governed by the Natural Order. References to "the system" mean this: the enterprise as an integrated, continuous pattern of motion across its five domains and three relational fields, producing enterprise value through their interaction. The Enterprise System is the enterprise as it operates when its structural behavior is read as a whole rather than decomposed into parts.

Motion
Chapter 1
Motion is the observable movement of work, decisions, information, and responsibility initiated by the enterprise and propagated across its relational fields over time.

Enterprise Behavior
Chapter 1
Enterprise Behavior is the observable pattern of response produced by an enterprise as work, decisions, information, and commitments move through people, machines, systems, customers, and markets over time.

Coherence
Chapter 1
Coherence is the structural condition in which the enterprise's domains reinforce one another in motion, allowing effort, decisions, and information to compound rather than interfere. Coherence is verified through its observable consequences: declining coordination cost relative to output, quality that remains stable under increasing load, decisions that resolve without escalation, interfaces that carry work without repeated clarification, and enterprise value that accumulates across cycles rather than resetting with each one.

Correspondence
Chapter 7
Correspondence describes the structural fit between the enterprise's design and the work it carries. Where correspondence is present, work, decisions, and information move through structure without requiring compensatory effort. Where correspondence erodes, coor-

dination cost rises, execution becomes inconsistent, and enterprise value becomes harder to sustain. Correspondence is structurally distinct from both coherence and alignment: Coherence names the system-wide condition in which domains reinforce one another; alignment names the interpretive convergence among people that precedes execution; correspondence names whether structure matches demand at the point where work is performed.

Alignment
Chapter 1
Alignment is the condition of interpretation in which people share a common understanding of purpose, priorities, and direction at a given moment. It reflects whether meaning is aligned—whether intent is understood similarly across individuals and groups—before work encounters structure, load, and consequence.

Load
Chapter 1
Load is the total demand placed on an enterprise's structure, people, and decision pathways at a given moment, relative to the system's capacity to carry that demand without loss of coherence.

Flow
Chapter 1
Flow is the continuity of work as it moves through the enterprise—how decisions, tasks, information, and responsibility progress across roles, teams, and domains without unnecessary interruption, reinterpretation, or rework.

Natural Order
Chapter 1
Natural Order is the consistent structural pattern through which enterprises organize motion, coordinate activity, and produce enterprise value. It describes the architecture that governs enterprise behavior—not the behavior itself. Enterprises may operate with or

against this architecture, but they cannot alter the consequences. Enterprise motion that aligns with the Natural Order compounds enterprise value. Motion that does not produces rising coordination cost and declining performance that increase as misalignment persists.

The Five Enterprise Domains
Chapter 1
The Five Enterprise Domains are the five interdependent systems of activity through which enterprises organize motion, coordinate effort, and produce enterprise value. Together, they make the Natural Order visible in daily operation: how people align, how work is structured, how execution behaves under pressure, how customers interpret value, and how financial outcomes emerge.

Enterprise Energy
Chapter 2
Enterprise Energy is the total usable capacity of the enterprise to perform coherent, purposeful work—the combined human, structural, informational, financial, and technological resources operating in balance to create, amplify, and protect enterprise value.

Enterprise Value
Chapter 2
Enterprise Value is the capacity of an enterprise to produce, sustain, and renew meaningful outcomes over time. It emerges from the coherent interaction of people, structure, execution, customer experience, and financial discipline, and is preserved when the creation, amplification, and protection of enterprise value operate in balance. While enterprise value is not limited to financial outcomes, it is ultimately expressed through them. Over time, the enterprise's ability to create, amplify, and protect enterprise value shapes valuation, market capitalization, and the cash flows available to owners.

Enterprise Value Function Dualities

Chapter 2

Enterprise Value Function Dualities describe the paired constructive and destructive forces through which enterprise value is either compounded or depleted over time. For every constructive enterprise value function—Create, Amplify, and Protect—there is a corresponding counterforce—Destroy, Dilute, and Erode—that is simultaneously present within the enterprise system at the same time.

Create

Chapter 2

Create occurs when ideas, effort, and resources are converted into new enterprise value—new customers, new capabilities, new capacity, and new opportunity. Creation expands the range of outcomes the enterprise is capable of producing.

Amplify

Chapter 2

Amplify extends existing enterprise value by strengthening integration, coordination, and execution across the enterprise. It converts isolated success into sustained performance by reducing repetition, aligning pathways, and reinforcing what already functions. Amplification increases enterprise value by converting reuse, consistency, and scale into compounding performance rather than repeated reinvention.

Protect

Chapter 2

Protect preserves enterprise value already created by maintaining the conditions required for viability under pressure. It operates through economic discipline, governance, trust, and stability, ensuring that growth does not undermine the structures that support it. Protection operates as stewardship—preventing enterprise value from being diminished through overextension or neglect—rather than as restraint.

Destroy
Chapter 2
Destroy is the sudden collapse of enterprise value through acute structural failure. It appears when essential containment gives way and the enterprise can no longer carry the activity moving through it. Destroy consumes enterprise value at once and signals catastrophic loss that requires recovery rather than refinement.

Dilute
Chapter 2
Dilute is the most common destructive motion and the most frequently underestimated. It appears when enterprise value spreads too thin to reinforce itself. In dilution, enterprise value is not lost suddenly but consumed gradually through dispersion—redundant effort, repeated work, and secondary activity that prevents scale even when surface indicators appear stable.

Erode
Chapter 2
Erode is gradual decay—the slow reduction of capability, relevance, or performance over time. Unlike Destroy, which is sudden, or Dilute, which is diffuse, erosion accumulates quietly and often goes unnoticed. Erosion reflects sustained loss of renewal and maintenance. Left unaddressed, erosion compounds until it manifests as dilution or culminates in destruction.

Structural Resistance
Chapter 2
Structural Resistance describes the degree to which the enterprise's design impedes the movement of work, decisions, and information. It reflects the extra effort required to achieve the same outcome due to misfit, misalignment, or poorly configured interfaces.

Destructive Polarity
Chapter 2
Destructive Polarity describes a condition in which opposing forces cease reinforcing one another and instead cancel each other's effect. Energy is expended, but conversion weakens. The enterprise remains active, yet forward progress diminishes.

Structural Interests
Chapter 2
Structural Interests describe the condition in which individuals or groups within the enterprise benefit from the current arrangement of authority, information access, resource allocation, or decision rights in ways that resist structural renewal—even when that renewal would restore coherence across the system.

Structural Misfit
Chapter 2
Structural Misfit describes the condition in which enterprise design no longer aligns with current operational and relational demands. The enterprise continues functioning, but its structure no longer supports coherent motion. Work relies increasingly on compensatory effort rather than structural support. Structural Misfit is the fourth stage of the Coherence Breakdown Progression; when misfit persists without renewal, it compounds into Structural Decay.

Structural Decay
Chapter 2
Structural Decay describes the gradual loss of fit between the enterprise's structure and its current operating reality. As conditions change, the design that once supported coherent motion becomes increasingly misaligned. The system still functions, but it does so with rising resistance and diminishing ability to carry the work. Structural Decay is the fifth and final stage of the Coherence Breakdown Progression; it follows when Structural Misfit persists without

renewal, and the cost of restoration at this stage exceeds the cost of the original misfit.

Coherence Breakdown Progression
Chapter 2
The Coherence Breakdown Progression is the recognizable sequence through which enterprise coherence weakens when the enterprise does not structurally respond to what the five destructive forces produce. The sequence proceeds through rising Structural Resistance, Destructive Polarity, Structural Interests, Structural Misfit, and Structural Decay. Each stage produces observable signals that distinguish it from the others, and the form of renewal required escalates with each stage. At every stage prior to Structural Decay, renewal can arrest the progression, but the window for low-cost correction narrows as the progression advances.

Renewal
Chapter 2
Renewal is the enterprise's capacity to restore coherence by adapting structure, routines, and interfaces in response to misfit as conditions change. It sustains the enterprise's ability to Create, Amplify, and Protect enterprise value by ensuring that design continues to match scale, interdependence, and environment. Each domain chapter describes how renewal operates within that domain's specific architecture. Structural Renewal (Chapter 10) describes the ongoing recalibration activity through which this capacity is exercised—the specific work of restoring fit across processes, interfaces, roles, and economic architecture as conditions evolve.

Structural Simultaneity
Chapter 3
Structural Simultaneity is the system property by which all five Enterprise Domains are present and operative at the same time in every moment of enterprise activity. It explains why coherence or misalignment cannot originate in a single domain in isolation,

because the enterprise always exists as an integrated whole rather than as sequential parts.

Directional Dependence

Chapter 3

Directional Dependence is the predominant pattern by which the consequences of enterprise activity propagate across domains under sustained operating conditions. Interpretation conditions structure, structure conditions execution, execution conditions customer response, and customer response conditions economic signal. Directional dependence describes the primary causal pathway, not the only one. External events, discontinuities, and downstream shocks can simultaneously restructure conditions across domains.

Reverse Causation

Chapter 3

Reverse Causation describes how downstream events can directly restructure the interpretive conditions in People + Alignment, without passing through the forward directional dependence sequence. External events, internal shocks, and discontinuities can enter the system at any domain and simultaneously restructure conditions across multiple domains. When that occurs, the enterprise experiences a system-wide reconfiguration rather than a sequential cascade. Reverse Causation complements Directional Dependence: Directional Dependence describes how consequences propagate through the system under sustained conditions; Reverse Causation describes how discontinuities bypass that sequence entirely.

Performance Topology

Chapter 3

Performance Topology is the structural pattern that determines how enterprise value moves, interacts, and compounds across the Five Enterprise Domains. Mutual reinforcement across the domains produces a recognizable condition in which effort compounds, coordination remains embedded in structure, and enterprise value accumulates. As that reinforcement erodes, the enterprise compensates through rising coordination demand, expanding oversight, and increasing leadership intervention—responses that increase load rather than restoring coherence.

The Unwalled Enterprise
Chapter 4
The Unwalled Enterprise describes the structural condition in which the enterprise no longer depends on fixed physical, geographic, or structural separations to govern how work, decisions, and information move. It operates through interconnected systems rather than isolated functions, with partners, platforms, vendors, customers, and automated capabilities participating directly in enterprise motion.

Relational Field
Chapter 4
A Relational Field is described as a continuous, dynamic pattern of interaction through which people, teams, customers, partners, platforms, technologies, and market forces participate simultaneously in enterprise motion. The enterprise exists within three interdependent relational fields—the Enterprise Field, the Customer Field, and the Market Field—each of which shapes behavior differently and none of which operates in isolation.

The Enterprise Field
Chapter 4
The Enterprise Field describes the relational context in which the Five Enterprise Domains interact—people, processes, execution, customer interaction, and economics. It reflects how coherence is produced through their interaction: how shared meaning is established, how work is structured, how decisions propagate, and how enterprise value is created, amplified, and protected.

The Customer Field

Chapter 4

The Customer Field represents the expectations, interpretations, and behaviors of those the enterprise serves. Customers are not external observers. Their actions directly shape enterprise priorities, quality standards, timing expectations, capability requirements, and strategic viability.

The Market Field

Chapter 4

The Market Field encompasses all contextual forces beyond individual customer relationships: labor markets, suppliers, vendors, partners, service providers, platforms, investors, regulators, technologies, competitors, substitutes, and adjacent industries. This field shapes what is possible, acceptable, and sustainable, determining how differentiation emerges, how quickly the enterprise must adapt, and how enterprise value is interpreted.

Physical Asset Enterprise

Chapter 5

Physical Asset Enterprises are those that require physical assets to produce and deliver physical value. They depend on factories, machines, facilities, inventory, and physical workflows. They move matter through space, and their operation is governed by capacity, throughput, load, sequencing, and physical constraint.

Intangible Asset Enterprise

Chapter 5

Intangible Asset Enterprises are those that require intangible assets to produce and deliver intangible value. Knowledge, expertise, relationships, data, software, and intellectual property constitute their primary assets. They coordinate meaning, judgment, and information—governed by interpretation, learning, decision timing, and relational coordination.

PEOPLE + ALIGNMENT

People + Alignment
Chapter 6
People + Alignment is the enterprise domain through which interpretation, trust, and shared meaning form wherever the enterprise comes into contact with people, establishing the conditions for coherent human motion.

Substitution
Chapter 6
Substitution is the enterprise's compensatory response to degraded interpretive conditions within People + Alignment. It appears when shared meaning, common reference, and compatible interpretation have eroded to the point where work proceeds without them. The enterprise does not halt; it replaces structural fit with added effort, workarounds, and localized solutions that sustain motion at rising cost. Substitution operates as the system's response to absent conditions, and its presence indicates where interpretive renewal is required.

Variance Amplification
Chapter 6
Variance Amplification describes the structural mechanism through which small differences in leadership emphasis, timing, or resolution expand across multiple interpretive surfaces simultaneously. Because leadership interaction operates as a high-gain signal source within People + Alignment, local inconsistencies—different priorities communicated to different teams, timing mismatches between decisions, unresolved tensions left to propagate—produce enterprise-wide interpretive divergence. Variance Amplification is distinct from the Amplify enterprise value function: Amplify extends existing enterprise value through integration and coordination; Variance

Amplification describes interpretive divergence expanding through enterprise structure.

PROCESSES + INTEGRATION

Processes + Integration
Chapter 7
Processes + Integration is the enterprise domain through which work, decisions, and information are sequenced, connected, and carried wherever the enterprise must coordinate their movement, translating shared alignment into repeatable and predictable motion.

Fit
Chapter 7
Fit is the governing condition of the Processes + Integration domain. It describes the relationship between what the enterprise is attempting to do and how it is built to operate—specifically, the relationship between the nature of the work being performed, the scale at which it operates, the complexity it must carry, the capability available, the information required, the technology in use, and the decision patterns that coordinate activity. Fit is not static. It changes as any of these conditions change. Present fit reinforces motion through structure. Where it does not exist, the system absorbs the deficit through delay, duplication, and coordination cost that compound as demand increases.

Interface
Chapters 4, 7
Interface is the structural boundary where work, decisions, or information transfer between roles, teams, or Domains. Because interfaces carry the highest coordination load, they are the first locations where incoherence becomes visible. In an unwalled enterprise, interfaces also exist between the enterprise and its relational fields—between the enterprise and customers, between the enterprise and partners,

and across systems, platforms, and workflows. Well-designed interfaces sustain coordinated enterprise movement. Weakened interfaces produce friction in execution and interpretation.

Friction

Chapter 7

Friction is the first mechanical evidence that structural correspondence has been lost within Processes + Integration. It appears when enterprise conditions evolve while process architecture remains fixed, and it surfaces consistently and early—before performance outcomes register change. Friction is distinct from Structural Resistance: Structural Resistance describes rising effort required to achieve outcomes across the enterprise system as coherence weakens; Friction describes resistance specifically at the points where work, decisions, or information must transfer across enterprise domain boundaries. Friction requires structural redesign, not additional effort.

Knowledge Integration

Chapter 7

Knowledge Integration is the structural mechanism within Processes + Integration through which experience circulates across the enterprise rather than remaining isolated within roles or teams. It governs how execution insight returns to structure, how customer signals reshape process design, how lessons become updated routines, and how exceptions produce redesign rather than repetition. Knowledge Integration operates through four structural mechanisms: After-action integration converts execution results into structural adjustments before the next cycle begins; cross-functional knowledge transfer carries insight generated in one domain to the domains whose structure it must alter; structured exception analysis treats recurring exceptions as architectural evidence rather than operational incidents; interface feedback circulation routes learning through the same interfaces that carry work. Where these mechanisms are absent, the enterprise generates learning it cannot structurally absorb.

System Integration
Chapter 7
System Integration describes the structural role technology performs within Processes + Integration. Technology does not substitute for integration; it amplifies the structural condition that already exists, extending coherent structure further and faster, or scaling incoherent structure at the speed of automation. Technology can also introduce structural conditions that did not previously exist. In both cases, coherence must be present in the design that technology implements. System Integration functions as designed only when workflow logic is sound, roles and handoffs are defined, decision authority is established, required information is available, and business rules remain stable.

EXECUTION + INTELLIGENCE

Execution + Intelligence
Chapter 8
Execution + Intelligence is the enterprise domain through which enterprise design is carried into action across all processes and converted into learning, insight, and adaptive response wherever that action encounters consequence. It governs how work advances under load and how feedback returns to sustain renewal.

Modes of Enterprise Motion
Chapter 8
Modes of Enterprise Motion are the distinct, active ways enterprise motion advances and encounters consequence—through propagation, action, or intervention—regardless of whether that motion is human-initiated, system-generated, or automated.

Propagation
Chapter 8
Propagation is the ambient motion of the enterprise. It is the execution that continues regardless of current intent, attention, or intervention, sustained by prior decisions, established structure, routines, incentives, and automation. Once released into the system, this motion persists on its own, advancing work, consuming capacity, and producing consequence without requiring anyone to actively do anything in the moment.

Action
Chapter 8
Action is deliberate, forward-moving execution that advances work within coherent structure. It is the mode of enterprise motion enterprises exist to sustain. In action, people and systems perform expected work, decisions are acted on as intended, and tasks progress without requiring repeated clarification, escalation, or manual intervention.

Intervention
Chapter 8
Intervention is deliberate execution applied to correct, override, or compensate for structural or interpretive misfit. It exists because the enterprise cannot carry work through design alone. In intervention, motion advances not because structure carries the work, but because people step in to carry it temporarily.

Coordination
Chapter 8
Coordination is the deliberate synchronization of motion across two or more people, teams, or systems. It is not a mode of enterprise motion itself, but a mechanism that operates within and around those modes. Coordination shapes how motion proceeds, not whether motion exists.

Necessary Coordination

Chapter 8

Necessary Coordination exists when work itself requires shared timing, shared interpretation, and concurrent action—and when enterprise structure is built to carry those dependencies. It may be continuous or sustained, embedded in routines or formal forums, but it remains proportional to the work it resolves. Necessary coordination resolves real dependencies and advances execution without requiring compensatory effort to sustain coherent execution.

Symbolic Coordination

Chapter 8

Symbolic Coordination appears when synchronization persists even though it no longer resolves dependencies or advances execution. Standing meetings continue, alignment forums remain in place, and coordination rituals multiply despite producing little change in outcomes. Participation becomes a proxy for governance rather than a mechanism for progress. Symbolic coordination replaces structural design with discussion and accountability with presence, and capacity erodes while work appears to be governed.

Compensatory Coordination

Chapter 8

Compensatory Coordination appears when work no longer advances unless people step in directly to reconcile conflict, resolve ambiguity, or override constraints in real time. Coordination is no longer a mechanism within execution; it is the execution. Motion advances through intervention rather than design, consuming capacity faster than it can be restored, and binding execution to specific individuals rather than to enterprise structure.

Execution Capability

Chapter 8

Execution Capability is the enterprise's structural capacity to carry work into action under real conditions. It is not individual talent, effort, or intent. It is the combined effect of Technical Capability and Relational Effectiveness operating together as a system—expressed only in motion and visible only through behavior.

Technical Capability

Chapter 8

Technical Capability encompasses the four structural elements of Execution Capability that determine what the enterprise can do. *Skills* are the functional and technical abilities people bring to work—combining knowledge, judgment, experience, and interpretation. *Tools* are the workflow systems, communication platforms, automation, and analytics that extend and accelerate their effort. *Structure* is the architecture that channels their motion, governing where work begins, where decisions land, how information travels, and how exceptions are handled. *Capacity* is the system's ability to carry operational load without losing coherence. When these four elements reinforce one another, execution makes possible what the enterprise is built to do.

Relational Effectiveness

Chapter 8

Relational Effectiveness is the social dimension of Execution Capability—the enterprise's capacity to carry work through human interaction. It governs whether Technical Capability Creates and Amplifies enterprise value or Dilutes and Erodes it in transit. Relational Effectiveness operates at two levels simultaneously. At the individual level, each person's contribution to enterprise value is contingent on their own Relational Effectiveness—the degree to which they communicate clearly, collaborate across boundaries, and sense and respond to signals from those they work with and serve. At the enterprise level, the aggregate Relational Effectiveness of all people operating across teams, interfaces, and relational fields determines whether the enterprise's collective Technical Capability Creates and Amplifies enterprise value or Dilutes and Erodes it in transit. Relational Effectiveness is not a secondary condition of execution; it is the delivery mechanism through which Technical Capability either Creates and Amplifies enterprise value or Dilutes and Erodes it.

The Execution Multiplier

Chapter 8

The Execution Multiplier describes the relationship between Technical Capability and Relational Effectiveness in producing enterprise value motion: Technical Capability × Relational Effectiveness = (+/–) Enterprise Value. The relationship is multiplicative rather than additive because weakness in either element scales the entire product down. The multiplier operates at two levels simultaneously—at the individual level, where each person's contribution to enterprise value is contingent on the product of their own Technical Capability and Relational Effectiveness; and at the enterprise level, where the aggregate Relational Effectiveness of all people determines whether the enterprise's collective Technical Capability Creates and Amplifies enterprise value or Dilutes and Erodes it in transit. The enterprise cannot out-perform a relational deficit with technical excellence.

Responsible Autonomy

Chapter 8

Responsible Autonomy is the observable capacity of individuals and teams to act decisively and consistently within their scope without waiting for permission or compensating for missing structure. It is not a delegation preference or a management philosophy; it is a condition of enterprise execution that emerges from clear role definition, defined decision pathways, reliable information, stable interfaces, and learning mechanisms that close quickly enough to sustain judgment.

CUSTOMER + INTERACTION

Customer + Interaction
Chapter 9
Customer + Interaction is the enterprise domain through which execution is interpreted as value, converting enterprise behavior into perception, perception into demand, and demand into relational signals that feed back into the enterprise and guide renewal wherever enterprise behavior is encountered.

Perceived Customer Value Gap
Chapter 9
The Perceived Customer Value Gap is the distance between what the enterprise believes it is delivering and what customers perceive. This gap reveals coherence or incoherence faster than formal measurement because it registers through customer behavior before it registers through enterprise reporting. Enterprise motion that reinforces customer priorities strengthens value perception; motion that separates from those priorities weakens it. The gap becomes visible as declining functional reliability, weakening economic integrity, loss of emotional resonance, erosion of social identity, or loss of strategic relevance.

ECONOMICS + METRICS

Economics + Metrics
Chapter 10
Economics + Metrics is the enterprise domain through which motion is translated into economic meaning wherever enterprise motion encounters consequence, enterprise value is protected across cycles, and decisions are grounded in the enterprise's actual capacity to create, sustain, and renew value.

Optionality
Chapter 10
Optionality is the enterprise's preserved capacity to redirect resources, commitments, or structure without destabilizing coherence. It is not flexibility in general; it is the specific economic condition in which redirection remains affordable and structurally sound.

Adaptive Capacity
Chapter 10
Adaptive Capacity is the enterprise's structural ability to absorb change, reallocate resources, and maintain coherence without requiring compensatory effort or emergency intervention. It is not general preparedness; it is the specific economic and structural condition in which the enterprise can respond to shifting demands while preserving fit.

Structural Renewal
Chapter 10
Structural Renewal is the ongoing recalibration of processes, interfaces, roles, and economic architecture required to restore fit as scale and relational conditions evolve. It is not an initiative; it is a necessary response to the natural decay of fit in living systems. Structural Renewal names the operational activity of the general Renewal capacity defined in Chapter 2. It is positioned within Economics + Metrics because Financial Strategy determines whether renewal is affordable, sustainable, and appropriately paced.

Economic Coherence
Chapter 10
Economic Coherence describes the systemic condition in which enterprise motion, structural design, customer meaning, and economic logic reinforce one another, sustaining enterprise value without compensatory effort. It reflects whether the enterprise's architecture can reliably convert energy into durable enterprise value over time.

LEADERSHIP AND STEWARDSHIP

Stewardship

Chapter 2

Stewardship is the ongoing responsibility of keeping the enterprise aligned with its Natural Order as conditions change. It is visible in how leaders notice, interpret, and respond to the signals the system produces, and in their willingness to adjust structure, refresh interfaces, and sustain renewal so that information, intent, and learning continue to move reliably across the enterprise.

Leadership Pattern and Enterprise Value Consequence

Chapter 2

Leadership Pattern and Enterprise Value Consequence is the relative capability of a leader to create or destroy enterprise value over time. It reflects where a leadership pattern sits on the continuum between compounding and consuming enterprise value—estimating the probability of the leader's impact on enterprise value under a known or demonstrated pattern.

Enterprise Signal

Chapter 11

Enterprise Signal describes an observable pattern in motion, load, interaction, or response that indicates a change in systemic coherence before performance metrics register its effects. Enterprise Signals are not measurements; they are early indicators of how the enterprise is behaving as a system. They show whether reinforcement continues or whether misfit is forming.

ACKNOWLEDGMENTS

This work reflects the sustained engagement of many professional contributors whose discipline shaped its development.

The structural and technical editorial work for this manuscript was conducted internally at Enterprise Science. I am grateful to Kevin Anderson & Associates for their copy editing support in the final stages of production.

The observations in this book were drawn from multi-year enterprise engagements conducted through Teel & Company. I acknowledge the team at Teel & Company and the enterprise clients served through that work. Their operating demands formed the context in which these structural observations were refined. Although this manuscript was developed independently of those engagements, the structural insights presented here were shaped by that operating experience.

The cover design was developed by Resound Creative. I am grateful for their imagination, creativity, and resourcefulness in translating the structural character of this work into a visual form.

Any errors or omissions remain my responsibility alone.

To those whose professional work informed the observations presented here: thank you.

ABOUT THE AUTHOR

Chuck Teel CPA is a corporate strategist and the founder of Teel & Company Strategists & CPAs, a corporate-focused firm serving midmarket enterprises on matters of strategy, structure, execution, and building enterprise value.

Over more than two decades, he has worked inside midmarket enterprises—first as a corporate officer in CFO and senior financial leadership roles with direct institutional accountability for financial performance and execution, then as a practitioner embedded inside client organizations with direct day-to-day responsibility for finance, human resources, operations, and administration.

His work has centered on understanding how enterprises behave in practice—how day-to-day decisions, coordination, and structure interact over time to shape performance. Across nearly a decade of embedded client work inside more than forty midmarket enterprises, a consistent structural pattern emerged. How strategy, structure, and execution reinforced one another under real operating conditions determined which enterprises compounded enterprise value and which consumed it.

In the practitioner role, Chuck partnered with CEOs, founders, and investment-backed leadership teams to examine enterprise behavior at the system level—identifying where enterprise value was being created, sustained, or lost through design rather than through isolated decisions.

This work forms part of Chuck's broader body of work in Enterprise Science, which traces enterprise value from financial outcomes back to the daily operational decisions, processes, and execution that produce them—making visible the structural conditions under which enterprise value is formed. It reflects a practitioner's perspective shaped by recurring patterns observed across more than forty midmarket enterprises, rather than a prescribed methodology or abstract theory.

Chuck holds an MBA in Strategic Management from the University of Chicago Booth School of Business, a Post-Baccalaureate Certificate in Accounting from Indiana University, and a Bachelor of Science in Business with a Concentration in Financial Information Systems from Indiana University. He is a licensed certified public accountant, a recipient of the Illinois CPA Society Distinguished Service Award, and has served as an executive lecturer at Loyola University Chicago's Quinlan School of Business and as an instructor for Becker CPA Exam Review.

www.ingramcontent.com/pod-product-compliance
Ingram Content Group UK Ltd.
Pitfield, Milton Keynes, MK11 3LW, UK
UKHW020838290926
15470UKWH00004B/1415

9 781971 628004